POLICY CONTROVERSIES IN HIGHER EDUCATION

Recent Titles in
Contributions to the Study of Education

POLICY CONTROVERSIES IN HIGHER EDUCATION

Edited by
Samuel K. Gove
and Thomas M. Stauffer

*Prepared under the auspices
of the Policy Studies Organization*

Contributions to the Study of Education, Number 19

GREENWOOD PRESS
New York · Westport, Connecticut · London

Library of Congress Cataloging-in-Publication Data

Policy controversies in higher education.

(Contributions to the study of education
ISSN 0196–707X ; no. 19)
  Bibliography: p.
  Includes index.
  1. Higher education and state—United States.
2. Politics and education—United States.
3. Educational equalization—United States.   I. Gove,
Samuel Kimball.   II. Stauffer, Thomas M.   III. Policy
Studies Organization.   IV. Series.
LC173.P65   1986   379.1'54   86–4646
ISBN 0–313–25381–1 (lib. bdg. : alk. paper)

Library of Congress Catalog Card Number: 86–4646
ISBN: 0–313–25381–1
ISSN: 0196–707X

First published in 1986

Greenwood Press, Inc.
88 Post Road West, Westport, Connecticut 06881

Printed in the United States of America

The paper used in this book complies with the
Permanent Paper Standard issued by the National
Information Standards Organization (Z39.48–1984).

10 9 8 7 6 5 4 3 2 1

Contents

Tables

Introduction

As we enter the mid-eighties, higher education is being confronted by many issues, and many serious problems. This is true in the United States as well as elsewhere in the world. Quite a few of the problems are financial, but there are also many others. In this country declining enrollments are of great concern. A companion problem—some would say a resulting problem—is the need to make curricular changes to adjust to our changing times.

To discuss these issues, both present and emerging, we asked several scholars from different disciplines to write policy issue papers. This project was undertaken under the aegis of the Policy Studies Organization. An earlier product of the effort appeared in that organization's journal from a symposium entitled *Higher Education Policy* (Policy Studies Journal, September 1981).

In the symposium issue we offered an agenda for higher education policy research. The essays in the present volume react to some of the issues raised at that time. In our earlier introduction, which we will not repeat here, we commented on the politics of higher education literature and some of its shortcomings. Politics once again plays a prominent role in this collection. In fact, the reader of these essays will note that if there is one common theme here, it is that "politics" in the broadest sense of the term permeates all of higher education. Keeping that theme in mind, we would like to use this introduction to highlight some of the higher education controversies raised by our collaborators in the following chapters.

An almost universal problem facing higher education today is funding. In this country the federal government is increasingly withdrawing its financial support. This has raised concerns about future developments in the areas of quality and equality. Whether individual states can take up the slack is questionable, as they too are facing financial problems. Economic problems exacerbated by demographic changes are causing higher education institutions to cut enrollments, which in turn will mean reductions in tuition incomes in many places. Such cutbacks may in fact be in order, but their effect on other aspects of higher education should not be overlooked. For example, the fact that numerous institutions have a very high percentage of older tenured faculty means that younger faculty will have to be let go. One solution that has been offered calls for university managers to develop a more systematic approach to planning and resource allocation.

Another issue our contributors raise has to do with coordination among higher education institutions. One author thinks the wave of the future is regional coordination rather than statewide coordination, which is the approach usually taken today. Another author, taking one specific example where such a coordination effort was undertaken, describes the difficulties of creating a statewide consortium on energy resource development. Efforts of this kind will be more common as the pressures for inter-university cooperation increase.

The middle and longest section of our collection focuses on the complex issues we refer to as accountability and equal opportunity. The thorny issue of accreditation is discussed from several angles. Higher education has accepted this relatively new process with mixed degrees of enthusiasm. The process itself is quite political, again using that term in its broadest sense. It is also becoming increasingly embroiled in more narrowly defined political concerns. Those related to the federal government have raised some very serious questions. So, too, has the issue of accreditation procedures for black colleges and universities. Underlying the problem here is whether there should be separate standards for black institutions, and more importantly, if black schools should even continue to exist in these days of desegregation.

Government involvement goes beyond the issue of accreditation. A significant example is recent federal legislation extending the general retirement age to seventy. This will sharply affect younger faculty, which in reality means women and minorities. One entire chapter deals with the special problem of female administrators and their attempt to crack a male-dominated profession.

Public service is usually the third listed role of universities behind teaching and research. The term is difficult to define. It is even more difficult to encourage a statewide system to expand its public service programs. The question in most institutions is: Does public service fit? Assuming that this question is answered in the affirmative, then we need to ask: How do we determine an acceptable reward system for public service contributions? Related to the broad issue of public service is the somewhat more specific question of whether we are training the right mix of students for future scientific manpower needs. Our contributors on that subject think we are not.

Finally, our volume considers some comparative higher education issues from around the world. One contributor tells us about the planning process for higher education in Africa, a chapter that has broad implications for other developing countries. The process, again highly political, is not orderly. It also carries some messages for those of us in the more developed part of the world. The final contribution considers the private-public finance conflict throughout the world. We usually think of such private-public competition as being peculiar to this country, but we are told it is found in many other countries as well.

These, very briefly, are the higher education controversies raised in this book. We believe they are the major ones facing us today—and for the next decade. The authors use different approaches and arrive at different conclusions, but all are current and real, and deserve our attention.

In seeking solutions to the problems raised here we should keep in mind the characteristics of the highly complex higher education policymaking system as described by our lead contributors. In other words, we should remember that

- There are several levels at which political and policymaking activities occur in higher education.
- Various forms of political relationships occur within and across institutional and governmental levels.
- Relationships between higher education and public authority are characterized by interdependence, with numerous points of interpenetration.

The editors are indebted to many persons, particularly the contributors who have stuck with us through untold administrative and procedural problems. The Policy Studies Organization, represented by Stuart Nagel, continued to be supportive throughout the long process of putting the manuscript together. Anna J. Merritt has done yeoperson staff and editorial work beyond the call of duty. And Shirley Burnette, a whiz at the word processor, has handled the manuscript most expeditiously.

PART I

POLITICS AND HIGHER EDUCATION

1

Politics and Policy in Higher Education: Reflections on the Status of the Field

Leif S. Hartmark and Edward R. Hines

The dramatic growth in the size, scope, and complexity of higher education during the postwar period has been accompanied by a growing concern for and involvement in higher education by public policy structures at the local, state, and national levels. As this public involvement in higher education became more extensive, higher education itself also became more public in character. The programs and policies of higher educational institutions and systems are increasingly subject to review by agencies external to the campus; and a growing sphere of educational activity is dependent upon some form of public support or affected by governmental regulation. The long-cherished myth of the separation of education from politics has lost its claim to reality.

Despite this growing interaction between higher education and public policy structures, most of the serious scholarship on the politics of higher education has been relatively recent, with much of it appearing within the past decade. As a result, the politics of higher education as a field of study is in a formative stage of development. An extensive review of the literature, published earlier, suggests several major patterns within this broad area of concern and the status of this area as a field of study.[1] Many of the impressions summarized here are consistent with both previous and subsequent literature reviews.[2]

The study of higher education politics and policy is by its very nature an interdisciplinary field of inquiry, exhibiting tremendous diversity in theoretical perspectives and topical coverage, with a generally underdeveloped methodological base and a lack of consensus on the meaning of basic concepts. According to Paul Dressel and Lewis Mayhew, the defining characteristics of a discipline include "a general body of knowledge . . . a specialized vocabulary and a generally accepted basic literature . . . some generally accepted body of theory and some generally understood techniques for theory testing and revision . . . a generally agreed upon methodology . . . and recognized techniques for replication and revalidation of research and scholarship."[3] According to several observers, the study of higher education politics and policy is lacking in all of these respects. While it may not be necessary for this field to advance to the status of a discipline, according to Cameron Fincher the field will not mature until it begins to develop at least some of these characteristics of a discipline.[4]

Patricia Crosson and Charles Adams assessed the status of the literature on higher education politics at the state level, and since the literature on the state level appears to be the most extensive and advanced, their findings may apply even more forcefully to the field as a whole. There is little explanatory, disciplinary research, and researchers do not attempt to develop or test theory in their studies. Much of the research is descriptive, relying on very broad ill-defined concepts as a means of organizing data rather than using theoretical frameworks. Where such frameworks are used, they are borrowed from a number of social science disciplines including sociology, economics, and political science. While much of the research at the state level qualifies as policy research, there is little explicit discussion of theories and methods for policy analysis. In terms of methodology, case studies predominate, although there are a growing number of studies concerned with more generalizable or comparative data; and finally there is limited but growing use of quantitative research methods.[5] These problems are not unique to higher education research. Frederick Wirt and Douglas Mitchell have similarly characterized the more generic field of educational politics as having a weak theoretical foundation which leads to contradictory findings.[6]

The politics of education as a field of study also lacks consensus on the boundaries of the field. According to Paul Peterson, "The range of topics that is quite properly considered part of the educational politics field cuts across virtually the entire political science discipline." Peterson further suggests that the politics of education lacks a conceptual or theoretical focus and that its only defining characteristic is the common interest in the substantive policy area of education: "Even viewed as a field of policy analysis the politics of education is no more a separate field of study than, say, the politics of agriculture, the politics of housing, or the study of political activity in any other substantive policy area."[7]

Research on the politics of higher education exhibits this same limitation of sharing at best only a common substantive focus on higher education, but not a cohesive theory or conceptual orientation, or a consensus on basic concepts and terms. This is partly a function of the difficulty in defining politics, and distinguishing it from policy. Moreover, it may also be a function of the topical diversity evident in educational research in general.

Many of these concerns can be summarized in terms of the characteristics of the field. First, the field exhibits a broad diversity of theoretical perspectives and topical foci. On the one hand, this merely parallels the rich, multifaceted character of higher education and its numerous points of contact with the political process. On the other hand, this diverse menu of subject areas presents a panoply of possibilities. Such disparate concerns as higher education finance, institutional governance, statewide coordination, faculty unionism, institutional planning, student financial aid policy, and state budgeting, can all be properly considered within the purview of the politics of higher education.

Second, as Crosson and Adams's analysis of the literature aptly demonstrates, there is wide variation in the extent to which theory is used in higher education politics research, the character of that theory, and its uses as explanation, as a principle of data selection, as description, or as prescription. Crosson and Adams also identify one major category of literature that cannot be classified as research or related to any but the broadest conception of theory, but which provides commentary on important issues by individuals with extensive research and personal experience in higher education policy. While not research in the traditional meaning of that term, this largely prescriptive literature contributes in important ways to the research agenda in this area.[8]

In summary, there are varying purposes or agendas within higher education policy research. That research can be oriented to description, explanation, criticism or evaluation, or some combination. Second, it may emphasize educational policy or politics. Third, policy research exhibits the basic tension between the purposes of the scholar for basic research or advancing understanding and the needs of the policy participant for applied research directed to immediate action.

This paper addresses these concerns in several ways. A taxonomy of higher education politics and policy is offered as a heuristic device for mapping the field, suggesting both the range of topical diversity and its boundaries and outlining some of the relationships between higher education systems and public policy structures. Second, this framework is applied in a discussion of the concerns surrounding accountability of higher education to public policy structures. Third, the various research agendas noted earlier are examined by use of an analytical paradigm for political and policy research. The divergent perspectives of the researcher and policymaker are discussed in terms of three levels of analysis: descriptive, explanation, and evaluation. The implications of this paradigm for research on higher educational politics and policy are suggested, as are some of the potential relationships between the discipline of political science and the more applied policy research.

MAPPING THE FIELD

Politics is a protean term, and its meaning varies with the context in which it is used. More formal definitions of politics are familiar, such as Harold Lasswell's "Who Gets What, When, How," politics as "the authoritative allocation of values," or the acquisition and uses of power and influence.[9] As Heinz Eulau notes, a universal definition of politics may be an illusive goal: "Political seems to be a residual rather than a generic term. This makes it futile to search for characteristic features of political behavior apart from an institutional or situational environment that shapes and patterns certain types of interpersonal relations."[10]

Even when politics is limited to the realm of higher education, the term can be used in numerous ways to refer to a variety of activities. The enactment of federal legislation for higher education and the dynamics of the faculty meeting bear little resemblance to one another, but they both can be viewed as forms of politics. However, to what extent should we be concerned with the latter at the expense of the former? By adopting a broad definition, we risk trivializing politics. One of the strengths of David Easton's definition of politics as the authoritative allocation of values is that it underscores the idea that for a set of behaviors to be political, they must involve some authoritative action. Further, lest we become engrossed in the politics of the PTA, this authoritative action should involve something of a public purpose or, in the case of higher education, it should be concerned with educational policy in some form. Thus, educational policy and politics are related in important respects.

At the same time, it is equally important to distinguish between them. Public policy is set within a context of societal expectations, demands, and constraints, and it involves purposive collective action directed toward the solution of a societal problem or the resolution of a common issue. Policy does not just happen; policy is "made" through a complex, more or less deliberative process, which can be characterized as having various stages.[11] Politics in contrast, can be described as the interaction of competing interests, individuals, or groups over the preferred formulation or outcome of a given policy issue. Political activity may occur at each stage of the policy-making process. Put simply, policy is the "what" of the process; politics deals with the "how" and "whom."

Politics can affect any aspect of the policy process; indeed it is a driving force behind the process. Further, to the extent that policymaking involves the exercise of power, then all policy can be seen to be political in character. However, the converse does not hold. The policy process does not subsume all of politics. There are many forms of political activity (e.g., machine politics, party politics, group conflict) that may be only tangentially related to formal public policy. Consequently, we also need to be wary of definitions that confine politics to the realm of public policy. This is particularly true for higher education where educational policy has become increasingly a matter of public concern, thereby blurring the traditional distinctions between public policy and educational policy.

The implications of all of this are that we need a conception of politics that is sufficiently discriminating to differentiate politics from random conflict, and yet flexible enough to accommodate the varied contexts in which higher education interacts with the political system. For present purposes, we suggest a working definition of politics that is predicated on the assumption that politics occurs at various levels within higher education or between the academy and the broader political system. In this sense, politics is concerned with patterns of interaction and conflict over values, interests, and goals relating to the perceived needs of higher education and public authority.

A Taxonomy of Higher Education Policy

Politics and policy both relate to a process. Policy is viewed in terms of the content or substantive purpose of decision making, while politics is viewed in terms of the process itself, including the antecedents and results of a policy decision, relationships among the various actors in the process, and their underlying interests and purposes. In this respect the institutional context of policy becomes important. For example, political conflict within an academic department is quite different from the politics of federal financing of postsecondary education. Each can have far-reaching but radically different effects upon the outcome of a given policy process.

Politics has two dimensions: 1) it occurs at various institutional levels or *loci*, and 2) it is focused on a variety of substantive areas or *policy domains*. These two constructs, the locus of politics and the policy domain, can be viewed as two dimensions of a matrix, which can be extrapolated to produce a logical taxonomy of the politics of higher education (see Table 1.1).

Three loci of politics are identified: institutional, extramural, and govern-

Table 1.1
A Taxonomy of Higher Education Policy

POLICY DOMAIN	LOCUS OF POLITICS		
	INSTITUTIONAL	EXTRAMURAL	GOVERNMENTAL
PURPOSES	Missions Broad academic policy	Master planning Accreditation	State policy on scope and quality of H.E.; Public/Private balance; Land grant tradition; Federal higher ed. amendments
VALUES & NORMS	Academic freedom Institutional autonomy	Professional standards and norms	Policies on access and choice Philosophies on who benefits and who pays
PROGRAMS	Academic standards Program planning	Professional licensing Program review	Program budgeting Categorical aid
MANAGEMENT	Personnel policy Campus management	Collective bargaining Multicampus coordination	Administration regulation Court rulings Audits
RESOURCES	Budgeting Resource acquisition	Resource allocation competition	Educational finance

mental. The *institutional* column indicates political activity within a single institution or issues largely oriented to institutions. Institutional governance would be one example. By *extramural* we mean activity beyond a single institution. This includes both interinstitutional relationships (e.g., the development of institutional consortia) and the relationships between institutions and quasi-governmental educational agencies, such as statewide coordinating agencies and multicampus governing boards. The *governmental* column indicates the numerous points of contact with as well as the mutual influence of higher educational institutions and their intermediaries on the broader political system.

The policy domain is conceptualized in terms of five levels in a hierarchy from the most broad and abstract to the specific and concrete.

Purposes. The first level deals with the fundamental purposes and goals of higher education. Political conflict over issues of purpose and mission occurs within and among the institutional, extramural, and governmental levels.

Within an institutional locus this is manifested in general academic policy, institutional charters or mission statements, and the basic identity, purpose, and constituency from which the institution draws its legitimacy.

At the extramural level, comparable issues of purpose are articulated through such activities as master planning, statewide coordination, and reviews by accrediting agencies. Examples of interface between institutional and extramural concerns are the tensions between institutional aspirations and the constraints of a statewide master plan; or interinstitutional competition for status, clientele, resources, or political influence within a state.

Government influences the institutional missions and purposes for higher education in at least three respects: 1) in the design and legitimation of the structure of higher education through constitutional or statutory provisions such as the establishment of institutions, their governing boards and statutory powers, establishing state boards, coordinating agencies, or 1202 commissions; 2) in reacting, reviewing, and responding to policy initiatives for higher education such as approving state master plans; and 3) in more proactive policy initiatives directed toward higher education through study commissions, task forces, and legislative investigations.

Values and Norms. Higher education is by its very nature value-oriented, for several reasons. Colleges and universities are custodians and purveyors of society's values, traditions, and norms. At the same time, higher education is dedicated to the criticism of society and the rearticulation of society's values, consistent with its mission to discover new knowledge. Second, colleges and universities themselves require adherence to certain values of academic freedom, peer review, and institutional autonomy which differentiate them from most other kinds of institutions. Third, higher education attempts to serve multiple values, many of which are in conflict. The tension between the loyalty of faculty to the professional discipline beyond a single institution and the demands of that institution is one case in point. The inherent tension between meritocratic and egalitarian values reflected in the policies of colleges and universities is another source of intra-institutional dynamics and conflict.

At the extramural level one can identify tensions between academic and societal values toward research, and the relative ambivalence of some institutions toward public service, perhaps due to fears of becoming a captive of the constituencies or interests they attempt to serve. There is also an inherent tension between the role of colleges and universities as active participants with responsibilities for involvement and leadership in the community and the responsibility of higher education to serve as disinterested social critic.

In the governmental locus basic values are manifested in major policies, which are indications of the level of public confidence in higher education or the public commitment to such goals as quality, access, and choice. This nation's long-standing leadership in science and technology, the nearly universal access it provides its citizens to postsecondary education, and the significant public and private investment in higher education testify to the value this nation has historically placed on education. There is also another sense in which higher education is used as an instrument of social policy. Federal and state policies directed to affirmative action, accessibility for the disabled, health and safety regulations, federally aided training programs, etc., all exhibit this tendency by government to enlist the participation of higher education in activities deemed to advance public, governmentally sanctioned social policy goals.

Programs. Academic program planning and administration are among the most significant policy functions at the institutional level. Analogous functions at the extramural level include program review, regulation, and professional licensing. Program budgeting and categorical grants by state and federal government are parallel functions of the governmental locus.

Management. The management area is concerned with the development and administration of personnel policy as well as other administrative activities necessary for the effective functioning of an institution. As illustrated in Table 1.1, these are reflected in activities like multicampus coordination and collective bargaining at the extramural level, and administrative regulation, judicial review, and financial auditing at the governmental level.

Resources. Institutions require the careful budgeting and management of several types of resources, including human, financial, and physical. They must also seek financial support from government, private philanthropy, or through student recruitment. Interinstitutional activities include multicampus resource allocation and intercampus competition for resources. Educational finance, including institutional support at the state level, and student financial aid programs from state and federal governments are also illustrative.

Implications

The taxonomy discussed above outlines some areas of interaction between education policy and politics as well as the forms that interaction can take. As such, its use is primarily analytical. In the real world many of the activities cut across categories. To cite one illustration, faculty governance within an institution could be concerned with all five of the policy domains. Other activities, such as strategic planning, not only transcend many of these categories on a vertical dimension (e.g., purposes, programs, resources), but also deal with several loci of the horizontal dimension (i.e., the relationship of an institution with its external environment). Despite these limitations, the taxonomy serves a heuristic function by identifying the range and diversity of phenomena that can be considered within higher education politics. To that extent it could be a useful device for mapping the boundaries of the field, and for beginning to describe the interrelationships among various facets of this diverse area of inquiry.

The taxonomy may also serve a heuristic function by identifying areas where further research is needed. For example, research is needed in the area of the interface between state and federal policy for higher education, or such phenomena as interinstitutional competition for enrollment and resources, and the relationships of educational institutions to the local community, to name a few.

One conclusion to be drawn from the taxonomy is that there are numerous points of interface among higher educational institutions, the political system, and their intervening structures. Second, within each policy domain there are parallels between institutional policy and public policy. This underscores the point that the traditional belief in the separation of education from politics no longer describes this complex system of relationships. Rather, as the taxonomy illustrates:

- There are several levels at which political and policymaking activities occur in higher education.
- Various forms of political relationships occur within and across institutional and governmental levels.
- Relationships between higher education and public authority are characterized by interdependence, with numerous points of interpenetration.

THE ACCOUNTABILITY PROBLEM

One of the classic issues in the higher education literature involves the tension between independence or autonomy of higher education and the countervailing pressures for greater public accountability. This accountability issue has often been viewed in absolute terms. One of the implications of the present analysis is that government and higher education interact on a variety of dimensions, and the effects of this tension on higher education will vary with the form and context of the interaction.

A great deal of popular and scholarly literature has dealt with the growing role of government in the governance of public higher education. State governments and state coordinating boards are exercising more control and introducing more levels of review over universities and colleges. Governors and executive budget agencies are having a growing impact on the financial independence of public universities.[12] The accumulation of additional layers of review and coordination in higher education, the imposition of new forms of control over individual campuses, and the rise of multicampus systems and statewide coordinating boards are related concerns.[13] The Carnegie Commission and others have recommended institutional arrangements that will enhance university autonomy, particularly in the areas of intellectual conduct, academic affairs, and administrative arrangements. This could be accomplished by encouraging the states to use broad instruments of coordination, by preserving independent boards of trustees and by continuing to vest the faculty with power over academic matters.[14]

A number of factors have contributed to the perceived erosion of institutional autonomy. Chief among these has been the growth in the scope and magnitude of public higher education, which has not only heightened political attention but also extended bureaucratic control. These in turn have increased the demands for more specific and detailed information. In addition to the increasing size and complexity of higher education, several other developments have also affected higher education's situation: increased competition for public funds; problems with inflation, productivity, and enrollment; a perceived decline in the value of the college degree; and the recurrent imbalances in the supply of and demand for trained manpower.[15]

The issue of accountability is generally posed in zero-sum terms: Increases in external demands for information and additional measures of coordination and control result in a direct loss of institutional autonomy. To cite the Carnegie Commission on Higher Education, "External authorities are exercising more and more authority over higher education, and institutional independence has been declining. The greatest shift of power in recent years has taken place not inside the campus, but in the transfer of authority from the campus to outside agencies."[16]

Ironically, the persistence of this view may have hindered research on the relationship between higher education and government because of the failure to recognize this problem as simply one special case of a much broader trend. Higher education may not be unique in the extent to which it has become subject to governmental regulation. In fact, this overregulation may be symptomatic of the decline in power and legitimacy of institutions throughout society.[17] Moreover, a fixation on the intrusiveness of government can lead to a "victim perspective," which fails to recognize the extent to which the subjects of governmental regulation can influence that regulation. According to Richard Halverson, "By overemphasis on the regulatory powers of governmental agencies, it is easy to slip into a perspective on the politics of higher education in which colleges and universities are seen as the victims of politics, as disadvantaged contenders in the endless struggle for money and autonomy."[18] Finally, we need to be more discriminating in our discussion of governmental involvement in higher education. Robert Berdahl suggests a useful distinction between substantive autonomy, which deals with issues of policy and programs, and procedural autonomy, which is essentially a concern for administrative flexibility. According to Berdahl, although procedural controls may have some nuisance value, they do not affect the more fundamental concerns of substantive autonomy.[19]

We would argue that the accountability issue needs to be viewed in political rather than moral terms. The meaningful question for analysis is not which sector has what authority, but rather what decisions are made, by whose authority, at what level of detail, and with what effect on the perquisites of either the university or the state.

Forms of Accountability

Drawing upon our taxonomy, several forms of accountability can be identified. Each may be viewed in terms of its effects on higher education. We suggest five distinct forms of accountability, each corresponding to one of the five policy domains of the taxonomy (see Table 1.2).

Systemic Accountability. The fundamental purposes of higher education are inextricably linked with and dependent upon societal goals as reflected in public policy. While public policy should never dictate or impose a mission upon higher education, government does influence higher education in at least three respects: 1) in designing the structure of higher education within a state or by determining its role in the pursuit of national objectives; 2) in responding to policy initiatives by higher education (e.g., approving master plans, establishing new programs, appointing members of governing boards); and 3) through policy initiatives directed to higher education (e.g., study commissions, legislative hearings, landmark legislation). This order of activ-

Table 1.2
The Accountability Paradigm

POLICY DOMAIN	FORM OF ACCOUNTABILITY
Purposes	Systemic
Values/Norms	Substantive
Programs	Programmatic
Management	Procedural
Resources	Fiduciary

ity is concerned with establishing and maintaining the basic system of higher education.

Substantive Accountability. Higher education, like other institutions, is subject to a growing volume of incentives, mandates, and regulations intended to serve some broader social policy objective. They range from civil rights to civil defense. As an educational enterprise, higher education can be seen as carrying a special responsibility to set an example in the community. To the extent that our institutions live up to that standard, external inducements may not be necessary. In other words, higher education responds to substantive accountability through its involvement in specific substantive public policy goals.

Programmatic Accountability. This represents a type of contractual obligation to achieve certain stated objectives in exchange for financial support. One example on the state level is the politics of the budgetary process, particularly where appropriations are based on some form of program budgeting or funding explicitly concerned with the achievement of programmatic objectives. These objectives may vary in sophistication or comprehensiveness, including statewide planning systems, performance budgeting, or enrollment planning. This can also refer to the proverbial strings attached to federal categorical grants. The important point is that the educational system can be held accountable for the achievement of stated program objectives.

Procedural Accountability. Educational institutions are subject to a myriad of administrative requirements and controls such as laws, judicial rulings, administrative regulations, contractual obligations, collective bargaining agreements, etc. While compliance with these requirements can be costly and divert energy from the primary missions of teaching and research, the thrust of this form of accountability is largely procedural in nature.

Fiduciary Accountability. This refers to the extensive system of financial control, pre-audit, and related safeguards that have developed over the past several decades of public sector accounting. Beyond the purely technical ramifications it can have, fiduciary accountability is often used as a vehicle for affecting substantive policy. For example, the budgetary process can open major policy disputes under the guise of efficiency or budgetary propriety. Fiduciary accountability also frequently leads to extensive reporting requirements which may also have far-reaching ramifications.

To summarize, higher education politics and policy are complex and multifaceted, operating in a variety of institutional contexts and substantive domains. A major implication is that any analysis of these relationships should attempt to discern among these various forms of accountability, and should treat separately the impact of each upon higher educational institutions and systems.

POLITICAL ANALYSIS AND POLICY RESEARCH

Earlier it was noted that the field of higher education politics and policy tends to be dominated by descriptive research lacking in theoretical rigor. Even among the examples of research that do display a fairly high level of rigor, a plethora of theoretical frameworks and approaches is apparent.[20] One possible explanation for this is the number of agendas or purposes that higher education research is being called upon to serve.

In their insightful analysis of the literature Crosson and Adams employ James S. Coleman's distinction between disciplinary research and policy research: "According to Coleman, disciplinary research is intended primarily for the accumulation of knowledge and theory about a certain group of phenomena and thus for further development of the discipline. In contrast, policy research is intended to provide guidance for action and for policy development."[21] Since the policy sciences are relatively new and undeveloped, some overlap or blurring between policy research and the host disciplines of sociology, economics, political science, and others is probably unavoidable. When dealing in the realm of policy, there are additional research agendas that need to be considered. Wirt and Mitchell suggest four types of research relevant to policy: descriptive, explanatory, critical, and forecasting.[22] Descriptive research deals with the collection of basic information on the policy area and some comparisons among different cases. Explanatory research deals with the antecedents of a given policy, and it also deals with its effects. In this respect it is similar to disciplinary research. Critical research is concerned with an assessment of the results or effectiveness of a given policy, or the effectiveness of a policy process in producing a satisfactory outcome. Forecasting involves the analysis of policy variables and their interrelationships for the purpose of projecting or extrapolating potential policies and their future consequences.

Of these, forecasting could be viewed as a special case of explanatory research in that the understanding of a past event is epistemologically related to projecting that understanding forward in time to forecast potential future outcomes of known relationships among variables. For this reason we will be concerned only with the three activities of description, explanation, and evaluation.

Since this field is concerned with the politics of higher education, it may suffer from some of the same difficulties facing political science in general. Specifically, there is some ambiguity in separating politics from policy. Second, there is a historic tension between the study of politics as a discipline concerned with basic knowledge and as a more applied policy science.

Robert Spadaro identifies two long-standing dimensions of this issue: normative prescription versus a positivistic commitment to value-free description. More recently, this has been manifested in the tension between social scientists committed to applied research on societal problems and advocates of a more analytical, predictive, and theory-dependent social science.[23] Within political science some eschew the current trend to reorient the discipline toward public policy, while others argue that failure to embrace public policy analysis will leave the field moribund. One advocate of the public policy position has even argued that "policy research is political science."[24]

Policy research means different things to different analysts. Those who are primarily concerned with policy tend to view policy research as an applied activity directed to the analysis and solution of specific public policy problems. The more disciplinary-oriented social scientists are concerned with research on the nature of the policy process. This latter form of policy research begins to overlap, if not supersede, traditional political science which similarly has been more concerned with the policy process than the content or impact of policy.

This debate between the policy sciences and the social sciences produces competing conceptions of politics. There is a clear risk in defining politics solely in policy terms. While policy is important as an area of research concentration, it is only one concern in the field of politics. What is needed are conceptualizations of policy and political analysis which allow for different forms of policy research. At the same time, this should be sufficiently differentiated from politics so as not to limit political science to a sole and potentially mundane concern with policy issues.

An Analytical Paradigm

Given these competing agendas for research and practice, it is understandable that the term "policy research" can refer to a number of analytically distinct activities. For the sake of analysis, it may be helpful to differentiate these various activities in terms of two dimensions: the primary focus of the research and the level of analysis, as shown in Table 1.3.

Let us first look briefly at the focus research. Policy research may exhibit a substantive focus on policy as such; or it may focus more on the policy process, including but not limited to its political dimension. Several scholars have cautioned that research on the politics of education must move beyond a focus on inputs to the policy process and deal more directly with the substance of policy, policy implementation, and its impact upon the policy environment. According to Grant Harmon, the field of higher education research needs to deal with both process and product: "Unless policy studies link formulation and output processes with implementation and impacts, their practical value, as well as their contribution to theory, will be severely limited."[25]

Next, we need to look at the levels of analysis. Policy research and political analysis both operate on at least three levels: a primary level, that of the policy practitioner involved in applied research; a secondary level where academic scholarship is concerned with disciplinary research; and a third level, dealing with meta-analysis or evaluation.

Primary research is conducted by applied researchers who are close to the policy process through their formal role, experience, or recognized expertise (e.g., professional staff, advisors, consultants, etc.). Such research is largely descriptive and is concerned with identifying policy issues and recommending alternatives. In contrast to more scholarly research it is problem-focused, and its goal is to participate in or influence the decision-making process.

Disciplinary research, by comparison, operates at a level once removed from this primary activity. Rather than engaging in policy, the intent of disciplinary research is to explain and ultimately to predict policy processes and outcomes. It has a more nomothetic orientation, seeking general patterns of behavior rather than an idiosyncratic focus on a specific policy problem within a given setting. The object of this research is developing and testing theory, rather than participating in the policy process or influencing policy formation.

The third level corresponds in logical structure to the relationship of the philosopher of science to the scientist. It represents the activity of explicating and reflecting on the conduct of policy and policy research. In this sense it also has a strong evaluative orientation. It deals either with an evaluation of policy and its impact upon the policy environment, or an evaluation of the policy process itself.

A more detailed look at these three levels might be useful at this point. Using Table 1.3 as a guide, we will describe the levels of analysis in terms of the six variants of policy research.

Table 1.3
Research in Politics and Policy: An Analytical Paradigm

LEVEL OF ANALYSIS

    · Mode of Analysis
      ·· Objective
       ··· Actors

FOCUS OF RESEARCH

	Substantive Policy or Impact	Policy Context or Process
I) Applied · Descriptive, problem focused, idiosyncratic ·· Participation or influence ··· Practitioner, professional staff, consultants	Policy Analysis	Political Feasibility Analysis
II) Disciplinary · Objective, explanatory, nomothetic ·· Understanding, hypothesis testing, theory building ··· Scholar	Policy Research	Process Research
III) Evaluative · Critical, Meta-analytic ·· Improvement ··· Evaluator	Evaluation Research	Meta-Policy Analysis

Applied Analysis. Applied social science research directed to a particular policy problem or issue is what we generally refer to as *policy analysis.* This is what Carol Weiss and others are concerned about when they discuss the utilization of social research by policymakers.[26] An illustration from higher education would be an analysis by legislative staff of the costs and benefits of alternative student financial aid programs.

Political Feasibility Analysis. This is applied research directed to the policy process, and perhaps the least developed of any of the research foci displayed in the paradigm. In one sense this is less a formal analysis than an informal, intuitive activity generally performed by practitioners, their immediate advisors, and, to a lesser extent, policy analysts. The term is borrowed from Arnold Meltsner, who argues that in order for analysts to have an impact on policy, their policy formulation must be preceded by a political feasibility analysis which identifies the relevant actors, motivations, beliefs, resources, and the opportunities and constraints of the given policy site.[27] This almost parallels policy analysis, except that the focus of applied research is on political variables rather than policy variables. To illustrate, political feasibility analysis would involve an assessment of the political environment, the influential policy actors, their political dispositions toward policy alternatives, and the identification of strategies to influence key decision makers toward a preferred policy alternative.

Disciplinary Research. Two forms of disciplinary research are suggested: policy research and process research. *Policy research* is the study of policy for the purpose of explaining the policy system. This is comparable to Thomas Dye's definition of policy analysis: "the systematic identification of the causes and consequences of government activity, the use of scientific standards of inference, and the search for reliability and generality of knowledge in the form of systematic theory."[28] Dye goes on to describe the concern with the causes of public policy as "policy determination research" and the study of consequences as "policy impact research." Using an illustration from educational finance, policy research in Dye's sense could be an analysis of determinants of public expenditures for higher education, or more specifically, an analysis of the characteristics of low tuition states versus high tuition states.

Process Research. This is analogous to policy research, except that the focus is on the decision-making process—the "how" of policy rather than the "what." This distinction can be illustrated by Spadaro's plea that we pay attention to policy as well as process:

If we are trying to explain a specific welfare policy, it is important to know why policy makers decided the way they did on that policy, how it was implemented, and how resources were allocated; but it is equally important to know or try to know also the impact and success of the policy, the symbolic or intangible results of that policy in perceptions and expectations, and the function of feedback for new welfare policy, which means not only new specific welfare policies but also the general policy environment.[29]

Lawrence Gladieux and Thomas Wolanin's research on the passage of the Education Amendments of 1972 is a good example; it exhibits a balance between policy research and process research.[30] With respect to policy research, the study explains the specific provisions of the federal legislation and how it shifted federal financing priorities toward student-based aid and away from direct institutional aid. They also analyze the impact on higher education during the first three years of implementation of the amendments.

Their discussion of the relationships at each stage of the policy process is an equally important contribution. They conclude, for example, that the policy outcomes were shaped by circumstantial factors, that the emergence of issues was a complex, social-political process, that there were diverse sources of alternatives for policymakers which tended to be narrowed to a small number of viable options, and that new policy tended to represent incremental adjustments to previous policy decisions.

Evaluative Analysis. The evaluative level includes the two activities of evaluation research and meta-policy analysis. *Evaluation research* is related to policy analysis and policy research in that they all share a focus on policy per se. Evaluation research attempts to apply the methodology and relevant theory of social research to an analysis of the extent to which the implementation of policy achieved its objectives. It is often more rigorous and systematic than the policy analysis which supported the program's initial implementation. To the extent that program revision or improvement is a by-product of evaluation research, this research may serve a similar function to that of policy analysis.

Meta-Policy Analysis. Primarily concerned with evaluating policy analysis through an examination of the policy process, meta-policy analysis is specifically concerned with the nature and extent of the utilization of policy analysis in decision making, its impact on policy and, ultimately, upon the policy system. It relies extensively on process research but takes it one step further by examining the influence of the policy process on the character of decisions made.

Linda Ingeson provides a description of policy research that reflects several elements in our matrix. She notes that relatively little is known about "(a) the linkages among the organizational structures involved in the policy-making process and their functions in respect to one another; (b) the relationships between these structures and processes and the implementation, evaluation and review of policies; and (c) the role of research in informing both sets of processes."[31] Points (a) and (b) fall within our conception of process research. A concern with the role of research in informing those processes (point c) is an apt description of what we mean by meta-policy analysis. According to Weiss, the key research questions regarding the utilization of research in policymaking all focus on the policy process: "How do policies get made?" and "What information do decision making groups seek to pay attention to?"[32]

There is a growing body of literature on the influence (or lack of it) of policy analysis in the policy process. Robert Andringa found that policy research and studies ranked ninth out of ten among factors influencing federal education legislation, according to an informal survey of congressional staff.[33] G. E. Sroufe suggests that evaluation research is itself a political act: "What to evaluate, how, when and by whom, and who decides the criteria are all tied to outcomes which are political resources in the allocation of stakes."[34] David Florio indicates that different types of analysis and information are useful at different stages in the policymaking process, and the need for specific information targeted on the issues increases as the process moves from issue identification to deliberation and decision.[35] Wirt and Mitchell describe a multifaceted dynamic process of interaction between policy and research: "Knowledge alternatively describes, explains, criticizes and forecasts a world where policy maintenance and change interact constantly."[36]

Meta-policy analysis can be useful in giving as a broader understanding of the nature of the policy process and the broader societal and historical forces which give rise to policy concerns. Jerome Murphy speaks of a "paradox of state educational reform," meaning that each set of solutions to an existing problem brings with it the seeds of a new set of problems. He argues that many of the efforts of the 1960s to broaden participation, strengthen decision-making structures, and to introduce analysis have resulted in overloaded communication channels, increasingly complex decision processes, and in the mobilization of narrow constituency groups which have fragmented the social consensus needed to support educational policy.[37] Elizabeth Hansot and David Tyack point to the cyclical pattern of fundamental educational reforms, suggesting that if we can find patterns in the historical issue-attention cycle this may help policymakers discover the underlying causes of educational reform.[38]

In summary, a better understanding of the policy process and its relationships to broader societal conditions and trends is relevant to our understanding of public policy and the role of analysis in influencing that policy. Thus meta-policy analysis should become a very important part of the research agenda for social scientists concerned with educational policy and public policy.

The Question of Complementarity

According to Spadaro there is a certain ambivalence within the political science community regarding a fuller immersion in the public policy area for fear that "public policy could swallow all of political science."[39] One implication of the analytical paradigm discussed above is that process research is a necessary complement to policy research. Furthermore, since process research calls for many of the same skills and perspectives associated with political science, this discipline can make a needed contribution to policy research without becoming absorbed into an undifferentiated policy science.

Second, findings from studies in the area of higher education politics can be brought to bear on more general questions of policy research. To cite a specific example: A dissertation on the appropriations process for higher education in Minnesota identified many legislative strategies and behaviors that are highly consistent with Aaron Wildavsky's findings on the congressional appropriations process.[40] Thus research on the policy process for higher education can contribute to our understanding of policy processes in general.

Third, research across subject matter areas can be complementary and synergistic. Owen Porter's study of the determinants of influence in the Michigan legislature suggest that legislators take their cues from legislator colleagues who are viewed as "experts" in a policy area. Actors outside the legislature exert their influence through a two-step information flow in which the legislative expert becomes the target in the effort to influence the legislature as a whole. This finding could be relevant to questions of legislative influence for higher education as well. According to Porter, "Our knowledge of how the process of deciding differs among different fields within the same legislative body is still quite limited."[41]

This complementarity of political analysis and policy research goes both ways; higher education policy research also strengthens the field of higher education politics. For example, as noted earlier, much of the literature on higher education policy is largely commentary. However, even this literature focuses attention on relevant issues for more systematic research on the policy process. Finally, attention to meta-policy analysis—or the study of how research influences policymaking—contributes to our understanding of both the policy environment in which this research must be carried out, and also the character of the policies themselves and their impact upon the higher education system.

CONCLUSIONS

The diversity of theoretical frameworks and perspectives—indeed the notable lack of a coherent theory of higher education politics—may be largely explained by the numerous agendas in the rather eclectic field called the politics of higher education. On one level, this is directly attributable to the diversity of topical foci. Our taxonomy of politics and policy in higher education helps illustrate the range and boundaries of the field: It defines three institutional loci of politics and five substantive policy domains. In addition, there are five forms of accountability; in other words, five general areas in which higher education systems are influenced by public authority.

A second explanation for the current state of the literature on higher education politics is due to its multiple research agendas. Research may legitimately focus on any of six distinct realms: policy analysis, political feasibility analysis, policy research, process research, evaluation research, and meta-policy analysis. This analytical paradigm suggests that politics and policy, while integrally related, are in reality quite distinct. At the same time, applied, disciplinary, and evaluative research in each area can be complementary and synergistic.

The implications of this discussion for the broader field of policy research may be that a focus on policy processes (which has been the traditional domain of political science) is a necessary and complementary adjunct to the policy sciences. For the field of higher education research this may mean that a consensus on the concepts and theoretical perspectives is unlikely in the near future. Such a paradigmatic closure may not, however, be necessary. In fact, it should not be expected in light of the broad domain which this field currently addresses and the multiplicity of functions which the politics of higher education literature can be expected to serve.

Areas for Further Research

It is to be hoped that this discussion, along with the earlier reviews by Crosson and Adams, Samuel Gove and Barbara Solomon, Samuel Gove and Carol Floyd, and others,[42] will demonstrate the need for a more extensive and stronger "second-order" literature on higher education politics and policy. Such a literature would be concerned principally with articulating and advancing the status of this field of inquiry and could serve at least four functions.

First, we believe the field would be enhanced by more reflective research and commentary on the status of the field as an area of inquiry, the role of theory in research, gaps in existing coverage, and the identification of new directions in the field. This reflective literature would be concerned with such questions as the nature of the field of higher education politics, its relationship to other disciplines, and its potential contributions to scholarship and practice.

Second, there is a need for more synthetic research. The literature base contains a growing body of research findings, many of which are limited to case studies. Many more are buried in doctoral dissertations, which could be generalized and tested to form a richer and more useful knowledge base on the politics of higher education.

A third need is to develop better theory by which to structure the field, to organize research findings, and to guide future research. This theory should never be monolithic. Rather it should take the form of multiple theoretical frameworks and perspectives addressed to the specific purposes at hand (i.e., policy research vs. disciplinary research; description vs. explanation or evaluation, etc.).

Finally, this second-order literature would be concerned with defining the boundaries of the field, and dealing further with such conceptual problems as the nature of politics and policy in higher education as well as their interrelationships.

This chapter suggests a taxonomy of higher education politics and policy as one means for beginning to map the field. It also provides a paradigm of political research and policy analysis to help identify some of the distinct and often competing agendas and perspectives from which to approach higher education. These two constructs are offered in the hope that they will stimulate further discussion and make some small contribution toward the development of a more reflective literature on higher education politics and policy.

NOTES

1. Edward R. Hines and Leif S. Hartmark, *The Politics of Higher Education*, AAHE-ERIC, Higher Education Research Report No. 7, 1980, Washington, D.C.

2. Samuel K. Gove and Barbara W. Solomon, "The Politics of Higher Education: A Bibliographic Essay," *Journal of Higher Education* 39 (April 1968):181–95; W. C. Hobbs and J. D. Francis, "On the Scholarly Activity of Higher Educationists," *Journal of Higher Education* 44 (1973):51–60; Paul L. Dressel and Lewis B. Mayhew, *Higher Education as a Field of Study* (San Francisco: Jossey-Bass, 1974); Patricia H. Crosson and Charles S. Adams, "Map of the Field—Higher Education Research at the State Level" (Paper presented at the Annual Forum of the Association for Institutional Research, Denver, Colorado, May 1982, ERIC, ED 220 023).

3. Dressel and Mayhew, *Higher Education*, pp. 3–4.

4. Cameron Fincher, "Higher Education," in *The International Encyclopedia of Higher Education*, vol. 5, ed. A. Knowles (San Francisco: Jossey-Bass, 1977), pp. 1998–2000.

5. Crosson and Adams, "Map of the Field."

6. Frederick M. Wirt and Douglas E. Mitchell, "Social Science and Educational Reform: The Political Uses of Social Research," *Educational Administration Quarterly* 18 (Fall 1982):1–16.

7. Paul E. Peterson, "The Politics of American Education," in *Review of Research*

in Education, ed. Fred Kerlinger and John Carrol (Itasca, Illinois: Peacock, 1974), p. 349, cited in Grant Harmon, "Reassessing Research in the Politics of Education" (Paper presented at the Annual Meeting of the American Political Science Association, Washington, D.C., August 1980).

8. Crosson and Adams, "Map of the Field," pp. 6–7.

9. Harold D. Lasswell, *Politics: Who Gets What, When, How* (New York: McGraw-Hill, 1936); David Easton, *A Systems Analysis of Political Life* (New York: John Wiley, 1965); Robert Dahl, "The Concept of Power," *Behavioral Science* 2 (July 1957):201–218.

10. Heinz Eulau, *The Behavioral Persuasion in Politics* (New York: Random House, 1963), p. 1.

11. Frederick M. Wirt, "Is the Prince Listening? Politics of Education and the Policy Maker" (Paper delivered at the 1980 Annual Meeting of the American Political Science Association, Washington, D.C., August 1980); Carol Weiss, *Using Social Research in Public Policy Making* (Lexington, Mass.: Lexington Books, 1977).

12. Malcolm Moos and Francis Bourke, *The Campus and the State* (Baltimore: Johns Hopkins University Press, 1958).

13. Robert O. Berdahl, *Statewide Coordination of Higher Education* (Washington, D.C.: American Council on Higher Education, 1971); Lyman A. Glenny, Robert O. Berdahl, Ernest G. Palola, and James G. Paltridge, *Coordinating Higher Education for the 1970s: Multicampus and Statewide Guidelines for Practice* (Berkeley: University of California, Center for Research and Development in Higher Education, 1971); James G. Paltridge, *Conflict and Coordination in Higher Education: The Wisconsin Experience* (Berkeley: University of California, Center for Research and Development in Higher Education, 1968); and Frank Newman, "Autonomy, Authority and Accountability," *Liberal Education* 59 (March 1973):13–26.

14. Carnegie Commission on Higher Education, *Governance of Higher Education: Six Priority Problems* (New York: McGraw-Hill, 1973); and *Priorities for Action: Final Report of the Carnegie Commission on Higher Education* (New York: McGraw-Hill, 1973).

15. Frederick E. Balderston, *Managing Today's University* (San Francisco: Jossey-Bass, 1974).

16. Carnegie Commission, *Governance of Higher Education,* p. 1.

17. Robert H. Bork, "The Limits of Governmental Regulation," in *The University and the State: What Role for Government in Higher Education,* ed. Sidney Hook, Paul Kurtz, and Miro Todorvich (Buffalo, N.Y.: Prometheus Books, 1978).

18. Richard P. Halverson, "Interest Group Liberalism in State Politics of Higher Education" (Paper presented at the Annual Meeting of the American Educational Research Association, Washington, D.C., April 1975).

19. Berdahl, *Statewide Coordination of Higher Education,* pp. 10–12.

20. Crosson and Adams, "Map of the Field"; Hines and Hartmark, *Politics of Higher Education.*

21. Crosson and Adams, "Map of the Field," p. 6.

22. Wirt and Mitchell, "Social Science and Educational Reform," p. 8.

23. Robert N. Spadaro et al., *The Policy Vacuum: Toward a More Professional Political Science* (Lexington, Mass.: Lexington Books, 1975), p. 4.

24. Thomas Dye, "Political Science and Public Policy: Challenge to a Discipline," in *The Policy Vacuum*, ed. Spadaro et al., p. 53.

25. Grant Harmon, "Reassessing Research in the Politics of Education" (Paper presented at the Annual Meeting of the American Political Science Association, Washington, D.C., August 1980), p. 15.

26. Carol Weiss, *Using Social Research in Public Policy Making* (Lexington, Mass.: Lexington Books, 1977).

27. Arnold Meltsner, "Political Feasibility and Policy Analysis," *Public Administration Review* 30 (November/December 1972):859–67.

28. Dye, "Political Science and Public Policy," p. 32.

29. Spadaro et al., *Policy Vacuum*, p. 7.

30. Lawrence E. Gladieux and Thomas R. Wolanin, *Congress and the Colleges* (Lexington, Mass.: D. C. Heath, 1976).

31. Linda Ingeson, "Center for Educational Research and Policy Studies, Three-Year Plan" (Unpublished paper, State University of New York at Albany, January 1981), p. 2.

32. Weiss, *Using Social Research*, p. 10.

33. Robert C. Andringa, "Eleven Factors Influencing Federal Education Legislation," in *Federalism at the Crossroads*, ed. Samuel Halperin and George R. Kaplan (Washington, D.C.: Institute for Educational Leadership, 1976), cited in David H. Florio, "What Do Policy Makers Think of Educational Research and Evaluation?" *Educational Evaluation and Policy Analysis* 1 (1979):61–87.

34. G. E. Sroufe, "Evaluation and Politics," in *The Politics of Education*, ed. J. D. Scribner, National Society for the Study of Education, 76th Yearbook, Part 2 (Chicago: University of Chicago Press, 1977), pp. 287–318.

35. Florio, "What Do Policy Makers Think?"

36. Wirt and Mitchell, "Social Science and Educational Reform," p. 14.

37. Jerome T. Murphy, "Progress and Problems: The Paradox of State Reform," in *Policy Making in Education*, ed. Ann Lieberman and Milbrey W. McLaughlin, National Society for the Study of Education, 81st Yearbook, Part 1 (Chicago: University of Chicago Press, 1982), pp. 195–214.

38. Elizabeth Hansot and David Tyack, "A Usable Past: Using History in Educational Policy," in *Policy Making in Education*, ed. Lieberman and McLaughlin, pp. 1–22.

39. Spadaro et al., *Policy Vacuum*, pp. 26–27.

40. James T. Borgestad, "The Politics of Higher Education: A Case Study of the Communications Between the University of Minnesota and the 1975 Minnesota Legislature" (Ph.D. dissertation, University of Minnesota, 1976); Aaron Wildavsky, *The Politics of the Budgetary Process*, 2d ed. (Boston: Little, Brown, 1974).

41. H. Owen Porter, "Legislative Experts and the Outsiders: The Two-Step Flow of Communication," *Journal of Politics* 36 (August 1974):730.

42. Samuel K. Gove and Carol E. Floyd, "Research on Higher Education Administration and Policy: An Uneven Report," *Public Administration Review* 35 (January/February 1975):111–18; Gove and Solomon, "Politics of Higher Education."

2

Politics and Higher Education: The Strategy of State-Level Coordination and Policy Implementation

Darryl G. Greer

> One is tempted to think that policy is made through a sequence of steps (or a set of interlocked moves). . . . This way of looking at policymaking is useful for some purposes, but it tends to view policymaking as though it were the product of one governing mind, which is clearly not the case. It fails to evoke or suggest the distinctively political aspects of policymaking, its apparent disorder, and the consequent strikingly different ways in which policies emerge . . . sometimes the outcome of a political compromise among policymakers, none of whom had in mind quite the problem to which the agreed policy is the solution. Sometimes policies spring from new opportunities, not from "problems" at all.[1]

Higher education coordinating boards are a typical form of higher education supervisory agency in the United States; in fact, roughly one-half of the states have such agencies. Each of these boards faces a constant political dilemma: It is viewed by the executive and legislative branches of state government as a state agency whose purpose is to regulate the operation of institutions of higher education; it is viewed by institutions of higher education as an agency whose purpose is to advocate the needs and aspirations of the institutions to state government and to assist them in obtaining state resources to meet their perceived needs. How a state higher education coordinating board deals with this dilemma ensures that higher education policymaking is a dynamic process, one shaped by interaction between political and higher education actors, and one more likely to follow a conflictual pattern than not.

Somewhat surprisingly, much of the research on state-level higher education coordinating boards has not focused squarely on the policymaking and implementation processes and the way these agencies go about the job of "coordinating." Historically, observers tend to focus minimally on the variety of interactions between educational and political actors and instead focus narrowly on the formal structure and functions of coordinating agencies. Accordingly, these agencies have been viewed by some observers as "middlemen" and "intermediaries" whose involvement in the policymaking process is discontinuous rather than constant.[2]

Yet, state higher education coordinating boards are a specific policy response to a relatively recent social and political problem. (Approximately one-half of state higher education coordinating and governing boards were created between 1960 and 1972.) The confluence of two historical factors facilitated the creation of these agencies in the 1950s and 1960s: First, the post–World War II baby boom produced an unprecedented number of young people who reached college age in the 1980s. Second, through the political process society made a commitment to provide substantial public financial support to higher education to meet this demand. However, the fundamental reason for the creation of coordinating boards—to plan for the growth of higher education within a state—no longer exists; different imperatives now drive higher education planning, and centrifugal rather than centripetal forces will shape higher education planning in the 1980s.

A decline in public confidence in education, a projected precipitous decline in the traditional college-age population,[3] and demand from government for greater accountability by higher education indicate that the role of the coordinating board may be changing. The Education Commission of the States suggests that whereas the question in many states during the decade of the 1960s was whether or not coordinating boards were necessary to plan for the expansion of higher education, state governments are now asking whether or not these agencies have enough authority to perform in a different planning climate.[4] During a time of growth, coordinating boards, which by definition lack the formal authority to mandate changes in institutional behavior, have been fairly successful in mobilizing policy resources—by resorting to a form of political entrepreneurship—to influence change in state higher education policy and institutional behavior. The future role of these agencies, however, is changing rapidly. Even though they have played a central role in higher education policymaking, their viability depends ultimately on how responsive they are to exogenous social forces and the political process that fostered their creation.

SOME INITIAL ASSUMPTIONS

The purpose of this chapter is to present some general propositions about the role of a state higher education coordinating board, its policy resources, some of the determinants of state higher education coordination, the role of conflict in state higher education policymaking, and conditions under which coordination of institutions of higher education and policy implementation may be successful. It is hoped that these propositions are applicable in both practice and theory concerning state higher education policymaking and that they assist the reader in understanding how a coordinating board undertakes coordination and policy implementation in a political setting.

Conclusions and generalizations contained herein are drawn from my 1979 case study of coordination and policy implementation by the Ohio Board of Regents, Ohio's higher education coordinating board.[5]

The case study focuses on interactions between the board of regents and fourteen senior state-assisted and private universities and political actors during 1976–1977 to create an inter-university energy research consortium to address state energy resource development problems.[6] The case scenario, which will not be reviewed in detail here, deals with formulation of policy goals by the regents for utilization of university research potential by the state, coordination with university actors on defining a cooperative energy research program, creation of a permanent Ohio Inter-University Energy Research Council (IUERC) to carry out such a program, and board of regents and institutional interaction with the federal government and Ohio General Assembly to obtain formal recognition and financial support for the council.

Even though the case itself is somewhat dated, it is still relevant to understanding the role and behavior of a coordinating board. The case is not a deviant one; rather it is one that serves as a typical illustration of a coordinating board's approach to coordination and implementation. The particular case of university energy research coordination was chosen for a number of reasons. First, it was chosen specifically because it reflects higher education's interaction with political actors on an issue not directly related to the state appropriations process—a process that has been widely studied by researchers and practitioners. Additionally, the case represents a "pure" coordination issue, one directly related to a coordinating board's "master planning" function, which is one of its primary responsibilities. Finally, it was selected because it contains each of the four major actors who effect state higher education policy as identified in previous studies: the legislature, the governor, the coordinating board, and universities. This case, however, is significant beyond the substantive issue of state-university research cooperation. A coordinating board's attempt to "coordinate" does not necessarily bring about coordination. Coordination, like implementation, cannot be separated from the broader policymaking process.

In this regard, the case study and this summary of its major findings benefit especially from the theoretical contributions of Aaron Wildavsky and Jeffrey Pressman who view policymaking as a process that depends upon complex sets of interrelated decisions.[7] Setting policy and carrying it out necessarily involve bargaining, negotiation, and adjustment. Implementation of policy goals where the authority to mandate a given outcome is absent requires coordination, cooperation, and conflict resolution. Wildavsky and Pressman's study of the Economic Development Administration's employment program in Oakland indicates that coordination requires complex reciprocal interaction, the goal of which is to produce compatibility of goals and action. However, coordination also requires some initial agreement on goal definition; accordingly, strategies designed to achieve a certain goal (implementation) cannot be separated entirely from the definition of that goal (policy formulation).

According to Wildavsky and Pressman, "Implementation may be viewed as a process of interaction between setting of goals and actions geared to achieving them." Therefore, the authors state, the study of that process "requires understanding that apparently simple sequences of events depend on complex chains of reciprocal interaction."[8] The actors involved, their individual goals, resources available, and the length of time it takes to move from one decision point to another all affect the process of implementation.

The process of coordination is not any simpler, these authors maintain. Coordination should produce, but also requires, harmony of goals. Coordination does not come about simply because an actor desires to coordinate with other actors; it involves bargaining, compromise, and consent. Wildavsky and Pressman contend that coordination means getting done what must be done without specifying what to do.[9] Coordination, then, may be defined as the process of achieving harmonious action and compatibility of goals; as such it is an important part of the implementation process.

Among higher education policymakers and policy science researchers, little has been written about the patterns of behavior of state coordinating boards. Legalistic studies of what they coordinate do not tell us how they choose to coordinate or how coordination ties into state-level policymaking. My purpose, then, is to formulate some generalizations about how a coordinating board behaves in the coordination and implementation process.

CREATING AN ENERGY RESEARCH CONSORTIUM

Conflicting Policy Goals

Four specific policy objectives that flow from the Ohio Board of Regents' 1976 *Master Plan* guided the board's efforts to create a cooperative university energy research consortium.[10]

1. Basic and applied research make a significant contribution to the state of Ohio. Accordingly, special research efforts by Ohio's universities to address state problems should be undertaken. Those research activities that address and provide solutions to special state problems should be recognized and promoted by the state. The board of regents, then, should seek a special state appropriation recognizing this research activity.

2. Research is also important to the academic and financial vitality of state-supported institutions of higher education. It is an integral part of the educational process, especially at the graduate level, and is supported primarily from sources other

than state government. Therefore, externally funded research should be promoted by the regents.

3. Because the majority of research funds are separately budgeted and flow from federal and private sources, higher education and not the state should exercise control over use of funds.

4. Research efforts directed toward special state problems should be cooperative in nature, utilizing the combined resources of each of Ohio's institutions. A consortium approach should be promoted by the board of regents.

The board's efforts to create a research consortium to accomplish these objectives illustrate that central actors can agree on a general policy goal (promotion of university research) without ever obtaining specific prior agreement of means or particular goals. Conflict was generated not only because of disagreement over goals, but also because the goals of some actors were means to an end for other actors. For example, while obtaining state research funds was a goal for Ohio's senior universities, funding from the state was a means by which it could direct university resources. Conflicting goals can be identified among universities, between universities and the Ohio Board of Regents, between the board and the political system, and between universities and the political system.

Within Ohio's higher education system each university is an autonomous actor governed by its own independent board of trustees, yet each institution is also highly dependent upon its sister institutions. Given that no public policy support (such as financial support for academic programs or research) exists in infinite supply, any independent decision by one institution to attract that support affects other institutions' ability to attract the same support. In the energy research case, institutions were anxious to obtain a new source of state funding only as long as new "rules of the game" were not imposed that upset each institution's independence to compete for the new monies. Put another way, some universities decided to risk obtaining new funding sources rather than to risk upsetting their relative position within the status quo. For example, Ohio State University's belief that it should play a special role in the research consortium reflected that institution's perception of its "favored" position as the state's leading research university. The university's desire to obtain a special portion of potential new funds created significant tension with other universities throughout the implementation process, especially during the Ohio General Assembly's consideration of legislation that established a cabinet-level energy agency, provided funds for university energy research, and created the IUERC. Conversely, it was in the interest of smaller universities to ensure that any new funds be shared in an equal fashion, thereby giving them a larger marginal return on their investment in a research consortium.

Another conflict over goals existed between the universities and the Ohio Board of Regents. Whereas the universities and the board both hoped to attract new state and federal research dollars, the board's additional goal was to build a mechanism under which cooperative research efforts could develop. The regents justified this cooperative approach in two ways: First, no single research university within the state ranked above twenty-third in federally sponsored research. Only Ohio State, Case Western Reserve University, and the University of Cincinnati ranked among the top one hundred universities in the nation in this category.[11] Because the board's chancellor felt strongly that these institutions were not competing successfully for many federally sponsored research programs, he believed that cooperation would both reduce significant intra-state competition for federal research funds and strengthen Ohio universities' chances of attracting research grants by offering research contractors unique shared facilities and faculty resources. In addition to the chancellor's desire to build a stronger reputation for Ohio's universities—thus allowing them to attract more federal monies—he hoped to use the energy research consortium as a means of demonstrating higher education's importance to state government. These goals obviously conflicted with the universities' fundamental interest in retaining the principles of institutional autonomy and academic freedom, since some universities viewed state involvement in university research as an infringement on their freedom to establish research priorities independently. Accordingly, universities agreed to participate in the IUERC only if participation remained voluntary and institutions retained full control over submission and selection of research proposals as well as control of research funds.

In the political arena the board of regents saw cooperative research as an opportunity to attract funds for universities that it had not been able to secure during the state appropriations process and to demonstrate Ohio universities' importance as a state resource. At the same time, political actors viewed the board as a mechanism that could harness untapped resources to help solve a pressing public policy problem (energy resource development) not directly related to higher education. This conflict between actors on goals and means was caused by the actors' different perceptions of the problem. The conflict generated by these discordant perceptions over goals and means became readily apparent during the legislature's consideration of a regents' proposal to recognize the IUERC in law.

Similarly, whereas universities sought state funds to support energy research, political actors desired a university commitment to respond to state needs without prior commitment of state funds to support institutional research efforts. On another level, individual institutions, such as Ohio State University and Ohio University, sought to obtain from the legislature and the governor special "lead institution" recognition and financial support which caused serious conflict between institutions and the legislature.

A Strategy for Coordination

The energy research case indicates that the Ohio Board of Regents followed an identifiable strategy (as opposed to not developing a strategy) in its attempt to coordinate university actors and implement its Inter-University Energy Research Council proposal. One prominent aspect of the board's operating strategy was its attempt to mobilize external resources to influence higher education and political actors. From the beginning of the board's coordinating activities, it sought to win university support for its policy recommendations by offering universities "the carrot" of state and federal financial rewards. Without the incentive of external financial support the regents could not obtain the universities' agreement to cooperate in a research consortium. The institutions were not willing to risk their internal resources on a cooperative project until new state or federal financial support was available. Accordingly, instead of trying to influence universities to first establish a working consortium that could attract state and federal dollars, the regents sought to obtain external support prior to establishment of a working research consortium.

The regents developed an interdependent state and federal strategy in order to leverage political support for external funding. At the state level the regents emphasized to the Ohio General Assembly and universities the possibility of acquiring substantial federal funds to support the research consortium. At the same time, the regents sought federal financial support by telling federal officials that state funding for the IUERC would become available with the enactment of legislation that formally recognized the council in law. Without firm commitments from either the state or the federal government, then, the regents sought to influence each actor to commit research funds based on an unrealized commitment from the other actor. Even though the board did not initially gain the financial support it sought, this strategy was successful in sustaining university and legislative interest and participation in the project.

Another identifiable strategy practiced by the board was to establish responsibility for routine decision making below the top institutional policy-making levels. Even though the chancellor did originally seek agreement from the university presidents to create an energy research consortium, structural and process decisions concerning creation of the IUERC were handled in large part by subordinate actors. Once a general consensus was reached that allowed the chancellor to move ahead with implementation of a coordinated university research program, the program was implemented by regents' and legislative staff and university faculty representatives. The chancellor used a National Science Foundation grant early in the project's development to identify institutional actors who would carry out a coordinated research program long before substantive agreement on the means of implementing such a program was reached with the presidents.

The university presidents' insensitivity to a state-level problem identified by the regents, their lack of expert knowledge in the field of energy research, lack of time to deal with any single problem for an extended period, and personal hidden agendas stemming from their roles as organizational leaders, forced the regents to involve lower level university actors in the implementation process. The latter were not inhibited by the negative characteristics of the university presidents. In fact, throughout the implementation process, the major shared decisions that had to be made concerning the establishment of the IUERC were made by subordinate university actors. Thus the presidents were absolved of the responsibility for both setting policy and implementing policy objectives. This separation of responsibilities helped greatly to sustain the board's momentum in implementing its program.

Another important strategy employed by the board was to provide enough flexibility in the implementation process to adjust to changing goals among competing actors. The board wisely did not try to change institutional goals to fit its own goals. Instead, the board recognized the existence of conflicting goals and sought to adapt the IUERC mechanism to provide for assimilation of conflicting goals. For example, the board of regents recognized that any cooperative research program that did not include Ohio State University's participation would not be a viable program. That institution's size and ability to mobilize resources from within and outside Ohio made its cooperation a necessary condition for creation of a statewide research consortium. In other words, if Ohio State agreed to work with the regents, other institutions would follow. Accordingly, rather than lose Ohio State's participation, the chancellor managed to identify a special role for Ohio State regarding certain features of the research program without jeopardizing support from other universities or totally compromising the regents' commitment to an interinstitutional research consortium.

Legislative debate about the role of universities in assisting a new Ohio Department of Energy required that the board of regents be flexible enough to include the competing goals of the universities in its proposal for formal recognition for the IUERC. The board managed to integrate successfully into a single piece of legislation institutional aspirations and its IUERC proposal in a manner that served university interests, while at the same time strengthening the board's authority to oversee coordination of university energy research activities through a university consortium.

Problems of Coordination and Implementation

Wildavsky and Pressman state that the failure to implement is too often attributed to the absence of agreement among policy actors on a given end or goal. They suggest that failure to implement may also stem from problems created by the implementation process itself once an end has already been agreed upon.[12] Accordingly, participants may agree on the substantive end of a proposal but still oppose the means for carrying out the proposal. Wildavsky and Pressman give several reasons for why this may be so: direct incompatibility with other commitments; a preference for other programs; simultaneous commitments to other projects; dependence on actors who lack a sense of urgency; differences of opinion among leaders on organizational roles and procedures; and insufficient resources.[13]

The energy research coordination case illustrates each of these roadblocks to the implementation of goals. Ohio State University's insistence on special recognition as the "lead institution" among the consortium of universities was incompatible with the smaller institutions' goals of guaranteeing equal participation among all institutions. To obtain the participation of each of the fourteen universities, the regents faced the dilemma of assuring equity for each institution and at the same time establishing a unique role for Ohio State. A similar incompatibility of goals that hindered coordination was competition between Ohio University and Ohio State for special designation as a federal coal research laboratory. Even though the regents viewed designation of a federal coal laboratory as an issue separate from creation of a research consortium, the universities' commitment to the project and their legislative lobbying forced the regents to integrate the two proposals.

The disposition of individuals responsible for coordination and differences of opinion over organizational roles and procedures were also impediments to implementation. For example, the chancellor's dependence on Ohio State's dean of the College of Engineering early in the development of a program for research coordination hindered development of the program, because the dean did not share the chancellor's sense of urgency about starting such a program. Also, the regents' efforts to use a National Science Foundation grant to create a voluntary research consortium without prior commitment of state or federal funding failed to engender enough excitement among the faculty or state government leaders to move beyond discussion of procedural problems to identification of substantive issues. Similarly, university presidents showed a low sense of urgency in assisting the regents to resolve the conflict among the board, the universities, and the legislature on designating a federal coal laboratory through the IUERC.

An important aspect of activities that led to creation of the IUERC involved establishing a consensus on the proper organizational role of the Ohio Board of Regents and outlining specific procedural steps for creating the council. Differences over how university research projects would be funded, and who would decide how projects would be selected, overshadowed consideration of substantive areas of university research interests.

Coordination by the Ohio Board of Regents was hindered not only by differences and shifts in particular goals, but also by problems associated with communicating with other actors and the timing of decisions. One of the board's fundamental challenges was to identify contacts in Ohio universities who could help accomplish policy objectives. For example, at Ohio State University alone, the president, his assistant, the graduate dean, the dean of the College of Engineering, the vice president for public affairs, the legislative liaison, and the internal energy programs director all played important roles in communicating Ohio State's interest to the board. Each of these actors had a different perspective on the regents' goals based on their particular institutional role. Because no single actor exercised continuous responsibility for communicating the university's interest, communications often became confused.

The regents found communicating effectively with the General Assembly and the governor equally frustrating at times. Several legislators who served on the energy committees in both the House and Senate confessed that they never fully comprehended the board's goals. While the regents assured the legislature that each of the fourteen universities was supportive of the board's proposal for a state-recognized university research consortium, individual institutions continued to lobby legislators independently of the regents, resulting in confusion in the legislature over whose proposal to support. Because of pressures and counterpressures, legislators whose districts encompassed one institution or another found it difficult to commit votes to an institution or to the board. Additionally, the board never identified a means of establishing effective communications with the governor's office. Even though special attempts to enlist the governor's support were made through individual regents and staff members who had close working or personal ties to the governor, the board was not successful in capturing the governor's attention, much less his support. On the other hand, easy access to the Speaker of the House through the regents' chairman facilitated communications with the General Assembly.

Finally, the timing of certain decisions had a significant effect on implementation. For example, the Speaker's personal request that the regents conduct a study of university energy research potential and establish a research council gave an important boost to the legitimacy of the board's proposal. The confluence of this request and the introduction of legislation to create a state Department of Energy came at a time far enough along in the board's coordinating activity to allow the board to integrate into the legislation its IUERC proposal with substantial prior agreement between the board and universities on some basic procedural ground rules for the research consortium. Similarly, the enactment of federal legislation requiring designation of a coal research laboratory permitted the board the means of communicating to the Ohio General Assembly how state support for university energy research could leverage federal monies into Ohio. Introduction of the federal coal laboratory designation also had the important effect of introducing a new unanticipated substantive issue into the legislative process that had to be resolved.

A COORDINATING BOARD'S POLICY RESOURCES

At least four general policy resource variables can be identified that either assist or hinder a coordinating board's ability to implement policy: time, information-expertise, constituency support, and authority.

The resource of time means the amount of time that the coordinating board is willing and able to commit to a given policy problem. Obviously, this factor ultimately affects the allocation of other resources, the implementation process, and the policy outcome. The amount of time the organization spends on a program is also indicative of the importance attached to that program and its legitimacy as defined internally by the organization. Therefore, the time that a coordinating board's staff commits to implementing its major planning recommendations reflects the amount of internal cohesiveness on the issue. A consensus on policy objectives by board members and the absence of internal conflict over the commitment of staff time and other resources to a project enhances greatly the executive officer's freedom to pursue implementation without delaying decisions for board discussion and approval.

Another important policy resource variable that affects the implementation process is information and expertise. The ability of the coordinating board to collect, assimilate, and disseminate data that support its policy position and help to influence decisions of other policy actors plays an important role in implementing policy. A coordinating board clearly benefits if it is the primary provider of information concerning higher education to state government. For example, in the Ohio energy research case study, even though another state agency, not the Ohio Board of Regents, had primary responsibility for energy policy development, the board rather than the energy agency was viewed by the General Assembly as the more legitimate supplier of information concerning university energy research potential. The board of regents, not the new Ohio Department of Energy, was given the authority to coordinate Inter-University Energy Research Council activities and the federal coal laboratory designation largely because the board could amass large amounts of relevant data that were not readily available to the other policy actors.

Constituency support is another resource variable that affects the implementation process. Other observers have suggested that higher education has a relatively weak and noncohesive constituency on which to build. One former state higher education executive officer has asserted that a coordinating board, because of its unique role, can depend on only two sources of support—the governor and the legislature.[14] The Ohio Board of Regents and its chancellor clearly spent a substantial amount of time attempting to develop executive and legislative interest in the research consortium proposal. However, the strained relationship between Ohio's governor (who advocated abolishing the board of regents) and the board (many of whose members had been appointed by a previous governor of a different party affiliation) seriously hurt the board's ability to obtain legislative support for its recommendation of state funding for university energy research. Similarly, even though the board obtained strong backing from the Speaker of the House for its proposal, the absence of broader-based support within the

House limited the Speaker's ability to commit the chamber to accept the board's recommendations.

The Education Commission of the States, in its *Challenge: Coordination and Governance in the '80s,* indicates that the politics of higher education in the 1980s will require even greater coordinating board reliance on the governor and legislature if such boards are to assume a stronger role as state supervisory agencies.[15]

A coordinating board's lack of formal authority to require inter-institutional cooperation, however, does not mean that it is unable to manipulate resources in order to gain compliance. For example, the Ohio Board of Regents mobilized coercive, remunerative, and normative means of obtaining other actors' compliance with its goals.[16] The board obviously gained an important source of coercive power (the threat of punitive action) when the Speaker of the House issued a directive to create a research council that would report to the legislature on university energy research activities. In effect, the Speaker's request not only added legitimacy to the regents' proposal for a research consortium, but it also gave the board authority to enlist university cooperation that it might otherwise not have acquired. The potential negative reaction of the legislature to university noncompliance with the board's request for information was enough to ensure university compliance.

The board was also able to acquire important remunerative power (control over allocation of material resources) when it was given the authority to choose an Ohio university as a federal coal laboratory designate. Because the board obtained the authority to determine how a coal laboratory would be established, it gained considerable control over material resources important to universities.

Finally, the board applied normative resources (symbolic rewards and sanctions) as a means of enhancing its authority. The chancellor's agreement to promote Ohio State as the "lead institution" in the energy research consortium served as a significant symbolic reward. It was also a potential remunerative reward to the university that had assisted the regents in gaining continued support from Ohio State. At the same time, the chancellor presented information to the legislature that indicated a relatively poor ranking among Ohio universities for federally sponsored research dollars. The data also showed that other states had made a greater commitment of financial support for energy research programs as a means of applying negative normative pressures on both universities and the legislature.

In summary, a coordinating board's ability to use its existing resources and to extract new resources from the external environment substantially influences its ability to acquire compliance from other policy actors to implement its policy recommendations. Because these resources do not remain constant over time, policy actors tend to use policy resources strategically to get the maximum return on the investment of their limited resources. Thus the coordinating board's resource base and special function in the policymaking process suggest that it too adopts an identifiable strategy for coordination and policy implementation.

DETERMINANTS OF HIGHER EDUCATION POLICY AND COORDINATION STRATEGIES

I have defined implementation as the process of interaction between goal setting and actions undertaken to achieve them. Coordination—which is part of the implementation process—is defined as the process of achieving compatible goals and harmonious action. At least four major factors can be identified that influence significantly state-level higher education policy coordination and implementation. These coincide with recent contributions from scholars studying the implementation process: the external socioeconomic environment, external political conditions, the structure of the higher education system, and idiosyncratic dispositions of policymakers.[17]

Perhaps the most fundamental observation that can be made is that higher education's future is inexorably linked to changing external social and economic demands. Dramatic changes in higher education policy are more likely to be triggered by environmental demands than solely by internal system requirements. Clearly, the international energy crisis of the mid–1970s, more than internal system demands, prompted the Ohio energy resource consortium activity. The rapidly changing external environment requires that a coordinating board find ways to bring higher educational services in line with societal demands and available resources.[18] The dramatic growth in state financial support for higher education in the past two decades flowed primarily from social and political decisions concerning the need for an expanded higher education system and the presence of a national economy able to sustain that expansion. The changing demographics of the nation's population are expected to result in a sharp decline in younger traditional-age full-time students, creating more competition among higher education, business, and the military for a smaller pool of young men and women. These new external forces will significantly affect program planning and financial resource management in American higher education. Furthermore, Robert Wood suggests that in addition to an economic and demographic downturn, other exogenous forces in the form of legal decisions to remedy social injustices, unionization of the educational profession, consumerism, and special interest groups have worked to erode confidence in American education. Wood argues that these forces have led to a palpable loss of sense of purpose in education, which to be restored requires a transformation in the structure of the educational system.[19] Recent reports expressing growing national concern about educational quality issued by the College Board, the Education Commission of the States, the Twentieth Century Fund, and the U.S. Department of Education indicate clearly that such a transformation has begun.[20]

A second important determinant of state-level higher education policy is a state's political environment. Heinz Eulau has suggested that past legislative norms concerning the importance of higher education's role in society, its independence from government regulation, and the special authority of individual legislators in higher education policymaking have significant influence on higher education policy formation and outcomes.[21] If Wood's analysis is correct, however, it appears that the traditional political norms regarding support of education have been rapidly deteriorating. Accordingly, legislators may be more willing to sacrifice higher education policy demands even when they do not compete directly with demands from other sectors of government, unless such demands have a demonstrable economic or employment payoff to the state.

Additionally, the professionalization and ascendancy of state legislative bodies as policy-initiating agencies have an important effect on policy formation and implementation. The Education Commission of the States' study suggests that state legislatures are more likely than not to take an increasingly active role in regulating higher education, especially on budget-related issues, a development which may lead to the increased politicization of higher education decision making in the 1980s. Recent survey research by Alan Rosenthal and Susan Fuhrman indicates not only that more professional state legislatures are likely to scrutinize higher education more closely, but also that there may soon be a high turnover in the number of older legislators who are "educational specialists" and leaders.[22] This too portends a major shift in the manner in which legislatures approach educational policymaking.

The structure of a state's higher education system is a third determinant of policy implementation and coordination. The number of actors within the system surely influences the formulation of strategies for coordination. Wildavsky and Pressman point out that as the number of actors that have to be coordinated increases, the more difficult it becomes to achieve coordination; and as the number of actors with potentially divergent goals increases, so too do the number of decisions and length of decision-making time increase.[23] For example, coordination of the fourteen Ohio universities involved in the energy research consortium was hampered by structural factors such as tensions between public and private universities and among state-assisted universities with different missions receiving different amounts of sponsored research support. The changing external environment will probably exacerbate rather than ease such structural tensions among levels and sectors of higher education in the immediate future.

Finally, personal factors play an important role in the higher education policymaking process. The attitudes, experiences, and actions of individual policymakers importantly affect policymaking. For example, in the Ohio energy research case, the governor's negative attitude toward the board of regents, which he believed no longer served any useful purpose, virtually assured that the executive branch would not endorse the board's proposal for a state-supported, university research consortium. On the other hand, the board chairman's personal commitment to carry out a consortium approach to energy research and his close personal relationship with state Democratic leaders assisted the regents' program substantially. Thus, individual policymakers' attitudes and perceptions about higher education significantly influence policy outcomes. For these busy people perception is reality.

The interaction of forces within and between each of these four factors plays an important role in determining how policy goals are defined, resources are allocated, implementation strategies are developed, and conflict is resolved. Because each major policy actor (the universities, the coordinating board, the governor, and the legislature) is influenced differently by these policy determinants, each actor defines the policy problem differently. As Charles Lindblom points out, the definition of a problem as a public policy problem does not flow from a single governing mind; each policy actor will formulate his own definition of the problem.[24]

The Role of a Coordinating Board

Because each policy actor identifies different policy problems and establishes different policy goals, the nature of inter-organizational policymaking is likely to be conflictual. According to Eugene Litwak and Lydia Hylton, the fundamental difference between *intra-organizational* and *inter-organizational* conflict is the absence in the latter process of a well-defined authority structure that has the power to mandate and enforce resolution of conflict between autonomous units.[25] Whereas the authority structure *within* an organization does not usually require external resolution of conflict, resolution of conflict *between* organizations does require external coordination. In other words, inter-organizational conflict requires coordination. Thus, the higher education coordinating board has a special role to play in the policy-making process.

As discussed earlier, higher education policy is not created solely by the demands of state-level political actors or by higher educational institutions. Rather, the policymaking process is intensely creative and interactive and requires mutual adjustment to conflicting goals. A coordinating board for higher education has the important functions of communicating demands between the higher education and political systems and the environment, and converting these demands into policy supports. Accordingly, a board's political functions as contrasted to its formal legal functions include interest aggregation, interest articulation, and resource mobilization.

Historically, institutions of higher education have criticized moderately strong coordinating boards similar to the Ohio Board of Regents for failing to mobilize effectively political support for higher education programs. At the same time, state government actors often attack a coordinating board for failing to eliminate inefficient institutional management practices. The formal legal structure of a board, giving it limited regulatory and virtually no formal enforcement power, suggests that the coordinating board was not created primarily to fulfill either of these roles. Some observers have also suggested that the coordinating board's role is to serve as an "intermediary" or "buffer" between state government and higher education in order to eliminate conflict within higher education and between higher education and state government. Even though these boards often play an adjudicatory role, it is doubtful that their primary political function is to eliminate conflict, given an individual institution's ability to intervene directly in the political decision-making and policymaking processes.

It has been proposed here that conflict creates a need for coordination, and that when coordinating boards such as the Ohio Board of Regents were created, they were not given the authority to exercise power in a way that would substantially rearrange an institution's relations with its individual constituencies or with state government. In other words, the traditional manner in which inter-institutional conflict had been resolved—through the political process—was not changed by the creation of such boards. If the coordinating board's role is not to eliminate conflict, then, it seems plausible to assume that its role is to provide for the orderly resolution of conflict and, more importantly, to rationalize and legitimize state-level policy decisions that affect higher education.

Seen in this light, a coordinating board's master plan serves to bring together the information and concerns from the larger social environment, state government, and higher education and to put the collected data on an orderly agenda that will serve the broad interest of the state rather than the relatively parochial interests of individual institutions. Accordingly, the co-ordinating board serves an important maintenance role for the entire system. Through it policy inputs are communicated between higher education and the external environment, thereby providing for continuity and change in higher education policy.

The energy research case shows that a board plays an innovative and active role rather than a passive one in the higher education policymaking process. The Ohio Board of Regents viewed itself as having responsibility for implementing its master plan recommendations concerning university research coordination, and acted throughout the energy research case to influence both university and political actors. As an active policymaker, the board acted clearly to manage its policy resources and to develop a strategy for influencing other policy actors to implement policy.

SUMMARY AND CONCLUSIONS

This chapter's purpose has been to present some generalizations about the process by which a higher education coordinating board approaches coordination of institutions and implementation of state-level policy for higher education based on a case study of the Ohio Board of Regents. It has been argued here that it is not a coordinating board's function to remove higher education institutions from politics nor to eliminate conflict among higher education institutions. Instead, I have suggested, the conflict within higher education and higher education's competition for scarce state re- sources are the important, necessary conditions which helped create boards like the Ohio Board of Regents in the first place and which sustain their present function. Additionally, the expansion of state systems of higher ed- ucation, and the increasing dependence of institutions within those systems on state government for allocation of financial support, increase rather than decrease the likelihood of conflicting goals among institutions and between institutions and state government.

Coordinating boards have become an important state-level actor in chan- neling higher education's demands into the political arena and translating state government's demands into rational public policies for higher educa- tion. As such, these boards face institutions with little formal authority to mandate changes in their behavior and face state government with little constituency support from higher education for the board's policy recom- mendations. Given this dilemma, such agencies are highly dependent on their ability to mobilize external resources to influence institutions and to foster political support for their policy recommendations. Accordingly, im- plementation of policy objectives by a higher education coordinating board cannot be studied independently from the political environment in which the board must work. The Ohio Board of Regents' ability to create a uni- versity research consortium depended as much on its interaction with po- litical actors as on its ability to influence actors within higher education. The conflictual nature of the higher education coordination process suggests that no rigid "best solution" to policy implementation can be identified at the beginning of the implementation process; an implementation strategy that allows a coordinating board to adjust its goals and means of implementation to accommodate the introduction of changing goals of political and higher education actors offers a greater chance for successful coordination and policy implementation.[26]

Furthermore, I have suggested that successful coordination of colleges and universities on a given policy issue depends on especially two variables: the extent of conflicting goals among the actors to be coordinated and support from the political system for the coordination activity. Since one of the objectives of coordination is to bring about changes in institutional behavior, the ability of a coordinating board to effect policy change within a coordinated state system of higher education depends on the relationship between these variables. Table 2.1 suggests that different types of policy outcomes might be expected based on the relationship between high or low conflicting goals within higher education and between higher education and the state, and

Table 2.1
Projected Higher Education Policy Outcomes in a Coordinated System of Higher Education

		Political Support for a Coordinating Board's Policy Recommendations	

Intensity of Goal Conflict Level:
  Inter-Institutional
    Institutional/State
		High	Low

	High High	Coordinated 1 Change	Incremental 2 Change
	High Low	Coordinated/ 3 Imposed Change	Incremental 4 Change/Status Quo
	Low High	Imposed 5 Change	Status Quo 6
	Low Low	Policy 7 Consensus	Abortive 8 Policy

high or low political support for a coordinating board's policy goals. Because the study upon which these projected outcomes are based focuses primarily on coordination of goals between higher education institutions and the state (the Ohio Board of Regents and political actors), rather than inter-institutional conflict resolution, they are somewhat speculative. Even so, these projected outcomes represent propositions that can be tested by other practitioners and researchers.

Box 1 in Table 2.1 suggests that the highest likelihood for coordination of actors occurs when there is relatively high conflict among higher educational institutions and between them and the state, and high political support for a policy recommendation from the coordinating board. Under these conditions a coordinating board will be called upon to bring about a compatibility of goals between institutions and the state. This generalization, however, should not suggest that political actors need agree totally with the specific objectives to be served by a given policy recommendation. Goal conflict and differences of opinion over the means and ends of policy lead to an environment in which changes in institutional behavior and coordination of institutional and state goals are likely to occur. Even under these conditions full policy implementation will probably be difficult to achieve.

A second expected outcome is that where high goal conflict exists within higher education and where high institutional-state conflict exists, together with low political support for change, incremental rather than dramatic changes in policy and institutional behavior are more likely to occur.

High political support for a policy when there is high conflict among institutions, and low conflict between them and the state, as suggested by the third box, may lead to a politically imposed change in higher education which requires some coordination of institutions. An example here might be a legislature's acceptance of a coordinating board's recommendations for changes in a state-administered program, such as student financial aid, with relatively little institutional consultation.

Where high inter-institutional conflict exists with low institutional-state conflict, and where there is low political support for the coordinating board, a mixed policy outcome of incremental change or maintenance of the status quo is projected, as illustrated by box number four. These conditions probably lead a coordinating board to attempt to "coordinate" institutions, yet provide the board with a low chance for success. Without external political support and the ability to influence institutions directly, the coordinating board is unlikely to bring about significant change under these conditions.

As a fifth outcome, imposed change seems likely to occur where there is high support for the coordinating board and low inter-institutional conflict, and high institutional-state goal conflict. State-level decisions about institutional management may illustrate this conclusion. Typically, there is low conflict among institutions concerning how each one manages its own affairs. However, the state does take an active interest in institutional management of state resources. Accordingly, by requiring that a coordinating board undertake special efforts to study and improve institutional management practices, state government attempts to impose certain changes in institutional behavior.

Under the conditions of low inter-institutional conflict, high institutional-state goal conflict, and low political support for a coordinating board's policy recommendation, maintenance of the status quo is predicted (box 6). These conditions lead to a situation where there is conflict between state and institutional goals, but not enough political consensus for coordination. For example, an instructional program that a coordinating board believes would have high value to the state may not be offered because the institutions view it as having limited value to themselves. The coordinating board, without the authority to intrude on institutional and faculty academic prerogatives, and facing no strong inter-institutional competition for such program authority, would probably have limited ability to bring about change.

A seventh suggested outcome is that a policy consensus and high chance for policy implementation exists where there is low conflict among actors and high political support for a policy recommendation. Under these conditions coordination of institutions is required, and there is a high chance for successful policy implementation.

Finally, where there are both low political support for change and low conflict among colleges and universities, and between them and the state, a coordinating board would not be able to promote coordination and change. The absence of conflict and lack of political support, in effect, would require the board to seek different means for influencing change.

In addition to the conclusion that several conditions exist under which coordination may occur, one final point concerning a coordinating board's ability to implement policy relates to the developmental nature of the policymaking process. It should not be assumed that policymaking and implementation always flow in logical sequence through the four stages of problem identification, policy formulation, policy legitimization, and policy application. The stages of legitimization and formulation for a coordinating body may be reversed or carried out simultaneously.[27] For example, a coordinating board's master plan serves to legitimize its goals as well as to establish a substantive base for formal policy action. The special role of a coordinating board discussed earlier suggests that it is more likely that the stage of legitimization precedes the final formulation of policy ends.

Suggestions for Future Examination

State-level higher education policy is especially dependent on a rapidly changing external environment and the political system. Changes in societal demands on higher education will cause concomitant changes in public policymakers' demands and expectations about higher education's role in society. Emerging contemporary demands to improve educational quality will surely create new pressures on institutions of higher education and coordinating boards, as well as secondary schools, to be responsive. It should not be assumed that policymakers' attitudes toward higher education need remain constant. Several years ago, Heinz Eulau and Harold Quinley's report on state officials' attitudes toward higher education suggested the existence of certain legislative norms in higher education policymaking.[28] Since this report, important changes in state legislatures have taken place (as recently documented by Rosenthal and Fuhrman), including increasing professionalization of legislatures and their greater policy independence from the executive branch. Because higher education faces a new planning period—one marked by declining enrollment, economic base, and public confidence rather than growth—it would be helpful to revisit prior research to find out which norms are still operative and which new ones have developed. Public policymakers' renewed interest in educational quality and education's role in economic development suggest places to begin. Negative attitudes toward education may be turning around.

While most coordinating boards were created to help states plan for the expansion of state-supported systems of higher education, the period of rapid growth in traditional higher education seems to have come to an end. As legislatures demand greater accountability from institutions, will coordinating boards' power to influence institutional behavior increase or diminish? In an era of financial instability and exciting new service opportunities in higher education, will political actors view coordinating boards as viable structures through which political demands can be channeled, or will new structures be created? Future research on state-level coordinating boards should focus on these questions and how the formal and informal roles of such boards change in response to new demands.

NOTES

1. Charles E. Lindblom, *The Policy Making Process* (Englewood Cliffs, N.J.: Prentice-Hall, 1968), p. 4.

2. For excellent discussions of state-level coordination and governance, refer to the now classic study by Lyman A. Glenny, *Autonomy of Public Colleges* (New York: McGraw-Hill, 1959); also by Glenny, *Coordinating Higher Education for the '70s* (Berkeley, Calif.: Center for Research and Development in Higher Education, 1971); Robert O. Berdahl, *Statewide Coordination of Higher Education* (Washington, D.C.: American Council on Education, 1971); and more recently John D. Millett, *Conflict in Higher Education* (San Francisco: Jossey-Bass, 1984).

3. A recent cogent summary analysis of the widely researched enrollment decline in higher education has been prepared by David W. Breneman, *The Coming Enrollment Crisis: What Every Trustee Must Know* (Washington, D.C.: Association of Governing Boards, 1982).

4. Education Commission of the States, *Challenge: Coordination and Governance in the '80s*, ECS Report No. 134, Denver, 1980.

5. Much of the discussion that follows is adapted from my longer study, "Politics and Higher Education: A Case Analysis of Coordination and Policy Implementation by the Ohio Board of Regents" (Ph.D. Dissertation, Stanford University, 1979). A briefer presentation of major findings of this study appeared as "State-Level Coordination and Policy Implementation," *Policy Studies Journal* 10 (1981):32–47. The Ohio Board of Regents was created in 1963 and is responsible for planning for postsecondary education in Ohio. Its major duties include coordination of the state's biennial budget for higher education, master planning for higher education, academic program review and approval, and authorization of new campuses and academic centers in the state. The board consists of nine public members appointed by the governor (and two legislators as ex officio members); however, the board selects the chancellor, who serves as chief executive officer. I served as assistant to the chancellor of the Ohio Board of Regents during 1976–1979.

6. The fourteen universities that make up the Ohio Inter-University Energy Research Council are University of Akron, Bowling Green State University, Case Western Reserve University, Central State University, University of Cincinnati, Cleveland State University, University of Dayton, Kent State University, Miami University, Ohio State University, Ohio University, University of Toledo, Wright State University, and Youngstown State University. The council is formally established by Ohio law (*Ohio Revised Code*, Sections 3333.04, 1551.11, and 1551.16) and its major responsibilities include advising the Ohio Department of Energy on

energy research and resource development and carrying out energy research projects. The council may accept state and federal monies to accomplish these purposes.

7. Aaron B. Wildavsky and Jeffrey L. Pressman, *Implementation* (Berkeley: University of California Press, 1973).

8. Ibid., pp. xv, xvii.

9. Ibid., pp. 133–35.

10. Ohio Board of Regents, *Higher Education in Ohio Master Plan: 1976* (Columbus, 1976); see especially pp. 38, 41, 48, 58–59, 77–82, 88. See also Greer, "Politics and Higher Education," pp. 103–109.

11. National Science Foundation, "Federal Support to Universities, Colleges and Selected Non-Profit Institutions, Fiscal Year 1974," NSF 76–305, Washington, 1976.

12. Wildavsky and Pressman, *Implementation*, p. 98.

13. Ibid., pp. 99–102.

14. John D. Millett, *Politics and Higher Education* (University: University of Alabama Press, 1974), p. 132.

15. Education Commission of the States, *Challenge*, p. 12.

16. These forms of organizational power resources are recognized by Amitai Etzioni in his "A Basis for Comparative Analysis of Complex Organization," in *A Sociological Reader on Complex Organizations*, 2d ed., ed. Amitai Etzioni (New York: Holt, Rinehart and Winston, 1969), pp. 59–76.

17. See the contribution of Carl E. Van Horn and Donald S. Van Meter, "The Implementation of Inter-governmental Policy," in *Policy Studies Review Annual 1977*, vol. 1, ed. Stuart S. Nagel (Beverly Hills: Sage Publications, 1977), pp. 97–120.

18. Anthony Downs suggests that rapid changes in the external environment produce concomitant innovations in organizational search strategies. See especially his discussion in Anthony Downs, *Inside Bureaucracy* (Boston: Little, Brown, 1967), pp. 191–210.

19. Robert Wood, "The Disassembling of American Education," *Daedalus* 109 (Summer 1980):99–113.

20. College Board, *Academic Preparation for College* (New York, 1983); National Commission on Excellence in Education, *A Nation at Risk* (Washington, D.C.: U.S. Department of Education, 1983); Task Force on Education for Economic Growth, *Action for Excellence* (Education Commission of the States, 1983); Twentieth Century Fund Task Force Report, *Making The Grade* (New York, 1983).

21. Heinz Eulau, *Technology and Civility* (Stanford, Calif.: Hoover Institution Press, 1977), pp. 43–56.

22. Alan Rosenthal and Susan Fuhrman, "Shaping State Education Policy," Education Commission of the States, *Compact* 15 (Fall 1980):22–27; see also Fuhrman and Rosenthal, *Shaping Education Policy in the States* (Washington, D.C.: Institute for Educational Leadership, 1981); and Rosenthal, *Legislative Life* (New York: Harper and Row, 1981).

23. Wildavsky and Pressman, *Implementation*, pp. 102ff.

24. Lindblom, *Policy Making Process*, p. 13.

25. Eugene Litwak and Lydia Hylton, "Interorganizational Analysis: A Hypothesis on Coordinating Agencies," in *A Sociological Reader on Complex Organizations*, ed. Etzioni, pp. 339–56.

26. For lengthy discussions of the flexibility of the policymaking process, see

especially Raymond A. Bauer and Kenneth J. Gergen, *The Study of Policy Formation* (New York: Free Press, 1968), and David Braybrooke and Charles E. Lindblom, *A Strategy of Decision* (London: Free Press of Glencoe, 1963). These authors suggest that it is the disjointed nature of policymaking that allows conflicting goals to be accommodated. Accordingly, the strategy of "disjointed incrementalism" promotes rather than inhibits policy implementation.

27. See, for example, Charles O. Jones' study, *Clean Air: The Policies and Politics of Pollution Control* (Pittsburgh: University of Pittsburgh Press, 1975).

28. Heinz Eulau and Harold Quinley, *State Officials and Higher Education* (New York: McGraw-Hill, 1970).

3

Regionalism and Institutional Proximity in Statewide Planning: Coordination Concepts and Principles to Counter Chaos

S. V. Martorana and L. A. Nespoli

Interest and action in statewide planning to guide the development of post-secondary education date back at least four decades to studies made by some states to establish policy needs after the disruptive years of the Great Depression and World War II. Since that beginning, statewide planning has grown steadily more important, and it seems that for the foreseeable future it will continue to grow, although for different reasons. Some evidence for this is found in the annual survey of major issues facing state higher education agencies; a review of the surveys since 1979 reported by the State Higher Education Executive Officers (SHEEO) shows "master planning" to have risen early during the five-year period from fourth to second place among the concerns reported and to be among the highest ranked year after year.[1]

Despite this substantial and demonstrable record of importance attached to statewide planning and coordination in the field of postsecondary education, relatively few results of analytical inquiry are reported in the literature. Major interest has been focused on the issue of balance between institutional autonomy and state interest in higher education via the planning process and, more recently, on the development of base measures or indices by which the productivity of institutions[2] or the relative performance of states can be judged.[3]

The central thesis of this chapter is that the study of statewide planning and coordination of higher education can and should proceed to a more theoretical level in order to derive stronger principles on which to base higher education policies and practices. The authors submit that regionalism and the related concept of proximity of institutional identities are already operative, albeit in subtle and relatively unrecognized form, in the policies and operating decisions that govern statewide higher education planning and coordination. It now merits further attention and refinement as the state of the art of statewide planning and coordination continues to be advanced.

CHANGING CLIMATE AND NEW DESIGN PRINCIPLES FOR AMERICAN POSTSECONDARY EDUCATION

A historic change took place in the United States in the mid-seventies: The class entering the first grade of the nation's elementary schools was smaller by some 600,000 than that of the year before. These "missing" first graders will soon be absent from the high school graduating classes and then from college freshman enrollments. In describing these conditions, some have referred to a "steady state" situation for American postsecondary education in the 1980s and beyond.[4] But current and anticipated enrollment declines, along with new fiscal conservatism evidenced at the federal as well as state levels of government nationwide (California's enactment of Proposition 13 was followed by a spate of similar developments in other states), seem to indicate that the situation will be far from "steady."

Educational policymakers at all levels of leadership are wrestling with and attempting to respond to the new pressures and conditions. They are searching for ways to maintain the dynamism and quality of higher education in a period when resources have stabilized or, even worse, in many cases are diminishing.[5] As this occurs, several broad policy trends can be noted. One is an increasing acceptance and use nationwide of comprehensive statewide planning and coordination.

Some of the issues addressed within the framework of statewide planning are matters primarily internal to the postsecondary education community— academic program planning and review, for example. Others touch upon questions broad enough to elicit general public policy attention. Inter-institutional relations, actions, and planning are one such area of concern. It is drawing attention at the national,[6] state,[7] and institutional levels.[8] Although there are many reasons for this increasing attention to inter-institutional cooperation, perhaps most significant is the potential for substantial cost savings and benefits through different types of cooperative arrangements.[9] In any case, whether the issues generated by statewide planning are major public policy concerns or mainly of interest to professional educators, it seems clear that most states are moving toward a more aggressive statewide planning posture as they brace for the adjustments that will be required by postsecondary education in the 1980s and beyond.

Several recent works have attested to this more active role by state-level agencies in the affairs of postsecondary institutions and organizations.[10] It is not our purpose here to trace the history of this change in attitude toward acceptance of a higher level of statewide planning and coordination. Suffice it to say that comprehensive statewide planning for the future of postsecondary education is here on a widespread scale, and it is probably here to stay.

At the same time it must be admitted that the activity of planning has proceeded with little evidence of being either an art or a science. There indeed has been considerable attention in the literature of postsecondary education to the extension of the statewide planning function to all segments of the enterprise as well as to all aspects of operations—personnel, programming, and so on. But little concern has been shown for the qualitative aspects of state-level planning.

There have, of course, been some notable exceptions to this generalization. One is the space utilization manuals produced by John Russell and James Doi in the 1950s.[11] Another is the important work by D. K. Halstead on state indices related to planning.[12] Despite these worthy efforts, more attention needs to be given to the planning process itself so that it will be improved qualitatively as well as extended quantitatively.

Warren W. Willingham has suggested that we will soon see the development of "second generation" state models of planning and coordination—models that will have a lasting impact on American postsecondary education.[13] One purpose of this chapter is to present evidence showing that increased state-level attention to regional interinstitutional cooperation—referred to here as regionalism—could become just that kind of new design principle in the statewide planning process. Long recognized as important in preserving the identity of particular localities in the planning structure and process, regionalism is now increasingly viewed by public policymakers as providing a deeper focus for planning, one that builds on more than simple factors of institutional location.

Regionalism and Regionalization: Definition and Status

One of the major challenges of comprehensive statewide planning is to achieve appropriate accountability of all postsecondary educational institutions while at the same time protecting the degree of independence that is essential for their continued vitality as academic organizations. Neither proponents of extreme institutional autonomy, what might be called a "market model," nor those of complete centralization of operation controls, can present convincing evidence that their design is the likely model for general adoption throughout the United States. Efforts to find a middle ground by adopting some form of interinstitutional cooperation or regional perspective are appearing in a growing number of states.

Regionalism is defined here as that view of a geographic subsection of a state (or of several adjoining states) that considers all (or a number) of the postsecondary educational components within the region collectively and seeks to establish a coordinated relationship among their goals, programs, and/or resources; furthermore, only regional policies and actions that are officially recognized by one or more agencies with legal authority to act on postsecondary educational matters in a state are included as manifestations of regionalism.[14] This last criterion serves to separate regionalism from other types of interinstitutional activities such as voluntary consortia. It also provides a basis for associating the concept of regionalism more closely with the duties and practices of state policymakers, particularly their exercise of planning and coordinating functions at the state level.

The concept of regionalism is, of course, not unique to the postsecondary educational enterprise. In fact, regional planning efforts are emerging on many different fronts—in elementary and secondary education, in non-education-related state governmental functions such as health care, economic development, transportation, and others, and in numerous federal activities that either implicitly or explicitly encourage regional governmental planning in the states. In many cases these efforts are considerably more advanced than those within postsecondary education. However, recent data suggest that the impact of this varied activity on postsecondary regionalism developments has so far been minimal.[15] In short, a direct dialogue and exchange of ideas between noneducation governmental authorities and state-level postsecondary interests on approaches to regional planning has not yet occurred to any significant degree.

Nevertheless, when interest in regional inter-institutional cooperation has been initiated and pursued at substate levels, postsecondary institutions and noneducational organizations of all types have successfully joined forces to share resources so that learning opportunities could be extended to surrounding communities. A national survey recently completed by the American Association of Community and Junior Colleges identifies more than 10,000 cooperative working relationships between local colleges and community-based groups.[16] In all, these regional arrangements serve over 1.5 million people.

Regionalism involving strictly postsecondary institutions is also attracting considerable notice across the nation,[17] although developments are occurring more rapidly in some states than in others.[18] In 1978 thirty-six of the fifty-four states and territories reported that they were giving serious attention to regionalism as an aspect of long-range planning and coordination of postsecondary educational resources. Within the thirty-six states, a total of ninety-eight regionalization actions had been implemented or were under study, a regionalization action being defined as a specific program or structure for implementing the regionalism concept and policy.

Others have described postsecondary regionalism in more general terms as a mechanism for accomplishing a refinement of institutional responsibility—that is, an effective division of labor through interinstitutional cooperation on a regional scale.[19] This is consistent with established guidelines for statewide planning—Halstead's "principle of differential functions," for example.[20] It is also consistent with what other observers of the American postsecondary scene have described as a need for a new way of thinking about excellence in higher education—specifically, a point of view that encourages each type of postsecondary institution to achieve excellence in terms of its own declared purpose and within the framework of what is in practical terms possible.[21]

Burton Clark draws a similar conclusion based on cross-national comparative analyses. He states that differentiation is a prime requirement for the viability of higher education systems, and that this can best be accomplished by separating and anchoring institutional roles through the statewide planning and coordinating processes. In his words, "Institutional differentiation is the name of the game in the coordination of mass higher education . . . [and] the name of differentiation is legitimation of institutional roles."[22]

Legitimation of institutional roles in ways that are consistent with the notions of regionalism and regional planning, however, can be a difficult (some may say even impossible) task. In their final report for a field project dealing with planning and coordination of postsecondary education in regions cutting across state borders, S. V. Martorana and Eileen Kuhns offer these relevant conclusions:

Institutions and organizations actually engaged in, or for other reasons having a legitimate interest in the quality (effectiveness and efficiency) of post-secondary education in the region, will respond positively to initiatives calling on them to enter into a cooperative regionwide effort to enhance that quality.

Such institutions and organizations will participate in regional cooperative programs even though their primary responsibility, and source of authority for functioning, is a state system which has only a partial interest in the region.

A major requirement in establishing and expanding use of the concept of regionalism as a basic approach to regional planning and coordination of post-secondary education is acquiring for it a greater legitimacy in both public policy and institutional policy arenas.[23]

The concepts of differential functions and institutional differentiation pose a number of questions for theorists as well as practitioners concerned with statewide planning and coordination: By what processes are (or should) institutional functions be determined? To what extent do (or should) forces external to the institutions enter the process? And, however determined, how can acceptance and legitimacy of the functions decided upon and assigned to institutions or sectors of institutions be developed for statewide planning and coordination purposes? The discussion that follows is pertinent to these questions.

INSTITUTIONAL PROXIMITIES

Very much related to this discussion of differentiation and the definition of institutional roles is what one of the present authors has elsewhere called "institutional proximities."[24] As institutions interact through various processes to establish appropriate roles, groupings or clusters of institutions begin to emerge. More precisely, a certain affinity develops among institutions that share some common value orientation. The term "proximity" is used, therefore, to indicate this sense of "belongingness with" which exists between and among institutions.

Richard Johnson has found institutional proximities to be rather well-defined among postsecondary educational institutions throughout the country.[25] And he discovered certain patterns to those proximities. Specifically, institutions report that the major sources of influence on their educational programs (i.e., organizations with which they have "proximity") are institutions sensed to be "close to home" and typically come from others within the same category of institutions as classified by the Carnegie Commission on Higher Education.

There are several different kinds of institutional proximity. That is to say, the sense of "belongingness with" among institutions can be based on any number of factors. And, in fact, institutions do seek out a multiplicity of institutional proximities. They naturally want to develop as many camps of support as possible. An excellent illustration of this is the long-standing voluntary interinstitutional effort to compile financial and related management information by the University of Chicago and the state universities in the "Big 10" Conference.

The regionalism concept incorporates primarily the element of spatial or geographic proximity, but three other kinds of institutional proximity are also considered here because they are so often found operating openly or subtly when policy decisions encouraging a regional approach to statewide planning and coordination are made; these are: 1) sector (public or private); 2) segment (institutional type); and 3) program (level of degree offered).

Interest and intent to capitalize to the fullest on these institutional proximities lie at the heart of efforts to develop and then implement comprehensive statewide planning for postsecondary education. The problem, of course, lies in guiding their application to a state's needs in ways that put the proximities in maximum use while simultaneously diminishing possibilities of confusion, wasteful duplication, or purposeless competition.

Considerations of Proximities in the Planning Process

What can be said about the relationship between proximities shared by postsecondary educational institutions and their interest in developing cooperative activities with one another? Speaking about general organizational behavior, Clark suggests that markedly different organizations can live side by side in a "symbiotic relation." Organizations that are similar, on the other hand, with heavily overlapping functions, are very likely to conflict.[26]

Others have expressed this same notion but in somewhat different terms. For example, Kenneth Andrews sets forth the concept of "distinctive competence," suggesting that organizational change will be either abetted or resisted depending on whether the proposed changes are seen to build on or threaten the distinctive competencies of an organization.[27] Similarly, the idea of "domain consensus" suggests that organizations will act in a coordinated manner if there is strong agreement about their respective domains and little, or controlled, effort to expand domains.[28]

Does this principle—whether it is called symbiosis, distinctive competence, or domain consensus—hold for postsecondary educational institutions? If so, what are the implications for the statewide planning process and more specifically, for state efforts, regional or otherwise, aimed at encouraging interinstitutional cooperation through this process? In the authors' earlier national study of regionalism in American postsecondary education, several principal elements were used to differentiate the types of regionalization actions found throughout the country: 1) geographic areas included in the actions; 2) types of institutions included; and 3) levels of academic programs involved. As mentioned earlier, ninety-eight actions were identified in the states and were described according to their goals, organizational structure, finances, outcomes, and other pertinent characteristics. The question of interest now is: Do these regionalization actions bring together institutions with shared proximities, or is the converse true? Do the actions tend instead to encourage cooperation among institutions that do not share proximities?

Regionalization actions, by definition, bring together in a cooperative effort institutions within the same geographic region, however that region is defined. Thus, the institutions involved in regionalization actions minimally share spatial or geographic proximity. But what about sector, segmental, and program proximity? Are these positive or negative considerations for regional interinstitutional cooperation? What do the data on the regionalization actions show?

Sector proximity is based on the consideration of public versus private educational interests. That is, institutions from the same sector can be said to share proximity. The data in Table 3.1 show that forty-five regionalization actions include only institutions from one sector. In other words, fewer than one-half of the actions are based on a shared proximity concept, at least insofar as sector proximity is concerned.

Segment proximity is based on the premise that there are recognized differences between four-year baccalaureate and higher-degree granting institutions and two-year associate-degree granting institutions on educational mission, goals, and programs. Institutions from different segments, there-

Table 3.1
Regionalization Actions by Sector Proximity

Sector	Total N
Public Only	44*
Private Only	1*
Both Public and Private	52
Unclassified	1
TOTAL	98

*Regionalization actions based on shared proximity: 44 + 1 = 45.

Table 3.2
Regionalization Actions by Segment Proximity

Segment	Total N
Four-Year Only	29*
Two-Year Only	12x
Both Four- and Two-Year	56
Unclassified	1
TOTAL	98

*Regionalization actions based on shared proximity: 29 + 12 = 41.

fore, do not generally share proximity. Again, the data show fewer than one-half of the actions to be based on a shared proximity approach (see Table 3.2). In all, forty-one regionalization actions include either four-year institutions only or two-year institutions only.

Program proximity is a bit different. It is based on academic program level—graduate (doctorate, master's first professional), baccalaureate, and associate/certificate (associate and certificate programs, in this presentation,

Table 3.3
Regionalization Actions by Program Proximity

Program	Total N
All Levels	42
Graduate Only	17*
Baccalaureate and Above	8
Baccalaureate and Below	7
Associate/Certificate	21*
Unclassified	3
TOTAL	98

*Regionalization actions based on shared proximity: 17 + 21 = 38.

are considered as one program level). That is, institutions with similar program emphases share proximity. What is different is that two institutions can share proximity on one or more program levels and at the same time not share proximity on others. Using this criterion, only thirty-eight regionalization actions are based on shared proximity (see Table 3.3). In sum, when each of the different types of institutional proximity is considered separately, participating institutions share in only 39 to 46 percent of the regionalization actions identified nationwide; that is, they hold in common a proximity beyond that which is strictly geographic in nature. Further, it can be noted that a shared or commonly held program proximity among participating institutions appears to pose the most serious obstacle to effective interinstitutional cooperation.

Moving to an analysis of two proximities operating at the same time, the data show that the percentage of regionalization actions based on shared proximities diminishes even further (see Tables 3.4, 3.5, and 3.6). Twenty-three to 31 percent of the actions are based on two shared proximities, in addition to the usual geographic proximities present in regionalization. These are actions that include as participating institutions only colleges from the same sector and segment, or only colleges from the same sector where the cooperative arrangement is for one common program level.

Table 3.4
Regionalization Actions by Sector and Segment Proximity

Sector and Segment	Total N	
Public Only		
Four-Year Only	14*	
Two-Year Only	10*	
Both Four- and Two-Year	20	
SUBTOTAL		44
Private Only		
Four-Year Only	1*	
Two-Year Only	0	
Both Four- and Two-Year	0	
SUBTOTAL		1
Both Public and Private		
Four-Year Only	14	
Two-Year Only	2	
Both Four- and Two-Year	36	
SUBTOTAL		52
Unclassified		1
TOTAL		98

*Regionalization actions based on shared proximity: 14 + 10 + 1 = 25.

Finally, when the sector and segment from which participating institutions come and the program levels involved in the regionalization actions are considered simultaneously, it can be reported that only nineteen regionalization actions are based on three shared proximities, beyond those related to geography (see Table 3.7). These are actions that include only colleges from the same sector and segment and where the cooperative arrangement is for one common program level.

These results are quite conclusive. Actions involving different types of institutions and several academic program levels are much more numerous in the states. Regionalization actions for one sector of institutions or one segment or one program level, on the other hand, are fewer in number. This suggests, consistent with Clark's statement on organization in general,

Table 3.5
Regionalization Actions by Sector and Program Proximity

Sector and Program	Total N	
Public Only		
All Levels	15	
Graduate Only	7*	
Baccalaureate and Above	4	
Baccalaureate and Below	4	
Associate/Certificate	15*	
Unclassified	0	
SUBTOTAL		45
Private Only		
All Levels	0	
Graduate Only	1*	
Baccalaureate and Above	0	
Baccalaureate and Below	0	
Associate/Certificate	0	
Unclassified	0	
SUBTOTAL		1
Both Public and Private		
All Levels	27	
Graduate Only	9	
Baccalaureate and Above	4	
Baccalaureate and Below	3	
Associate/Certificate	6	
Unclassified	2	
SUBTOTAL		51
Unclassified		1
TOTAL		98

*Regionalization actions based on shared proximity: 7 + 15 + 1 = 23.

that *regionalization actions based on shared proximities are more complicated and difficult to initiate and institutionalize than regionalization actions
based on geographic proximity but different sector, segment, or program
interests.* Furthermore, as the number of commonly held or like proximities

Table 3.6
Regionalization Actions by Segment and Program Proximity

Segment and Program	Total N	
Four-Year Only		
All Levels	4	
Graduate Only	16*	
Baccalaureate and Above	7	
Baccalaureate and Below	1	
Associate/Certificate	1*	
Unclassified	0	
SUBTOTAL		29
Two-Year Only		
All Levels	0	
Graduate Only	0	
Baccalaureate and Above	0	
Baccalaureate and Below	0	
Associate/Certificate	13*	
Unclassified	0	
SUBTOTAL		13
Both Four- and Two-Year		
All Levels	38	
Graduate Only	1	
Baccalaureate and Above	1	
Baccalaureate and Below	6	
Associate/Certificate	7	
Unclassified	2	
SUBTOTAL		55
Unclassified		1
TOTAL		98

*Regionalization actions based on shared proximity: 16 + 1 + 13 = 30.

increases, the chances of successful interinstitutional cooperation on a regional level diminishes.

The same generalization is supported by the direct observational experience gained in the regional, interstate pilot demonstration projects in the Upper Allegheny and Eastern Gulfcoast Regions. Tensions were greatest

Table 3.7
Regionalization Actions by Sector, Segment, and Program Proximity

Program Level	Public Only				Private Only				Public and Private				UNCLASSIFIED	TOTAL				TOTAL
	4-Yr	2-Yr	4&2-Yr	Total	4-Yr	2-Yr	4&2-Yr	Total	4-Yr	2-Yr	4&2-Yr	Total		4-Yr	2-Yr	4&2-Yr	Total	
All levels	3	0	12	15	0	0	0	0	1	0	26	27	0	4	0	38	42	42
Graduate Only	*7	0	0	7	*1	0	0	1	8	0	1	9	0	16	0	1	17	17
Baccalaureate and Above	4	0	0	4	0	0	0	0	3	0	1	4	0	7	0	1	8	8
Baccalaureate and Below	1	0	3	4	0	0	0	0	0	0	3	3	0	1	0	6	7	7
Associate and Certificate	0	*11	4	15	0	0	0	0	1	2	3	6	0	1	13	7	21	21
Unclassified	0	0	0	0	0	0	0	0	0	0	2	2	1	0	0	2	2	3
TOTAL	15	11	19	45	1	0	0	1	13	2	36	51	1	29	13	55	97	98

*Regionalization actions based on shared proximity: 7+ 11 + 1 = 19.

and inclination toward rivalry rather than cooperation was strongest among institutions of like program level and control sector. The challenge this poses to leaders interested in enhanced regional service from postsecondary education is expressed in the following two paragraphs from an earlier report:

Leadership most interested in a regionalism effort tends to be of two kinds: those from institutions clearly already in strong positions, who are far-sighted enough to see the institutional gain that will accrue in the long run; and those from institutions which are rising (or trying hard to rise) in stature, and see that the benefits of interstate interinstitutional cooperation outweigh its possible disadvantages. Those in leadership positions who involve their institutions only marginally if at all tend to have locally successful operations in a somewhat insulated market; for them cooperation may have more apparent or short-term disadvantages than advantages.

As with all organizations, leaders who are strong, credible, respected and farsighted make the difference in any continuing effort. Action orientation seems to be a key: leadership focused on important and mutually agreed upon purposes, which involves as many as possible in meaningful related efforts, would appear to be essential.[29]

CONCLUSION: IMPLICATIONS FOR STATE-LEVEL POLICY FORMULATION

The implications of these findings for state-level educational policymaking are clear. First, it amounts to a strong statement in support of comprehensive planning efforts—that is, those efforts that attempt to draw all elements of the postsecondary education enterprise into the planning and coordinating processes. Second, and perhaps more importantly, the results reported are a strong indication that such planning must increasingly rest on a body of soundly developed theory related to purposes, outcomes, and anticipated evaluations.

The thrust of these comprehensive planning efforts will likely continue to be to assist each type of institution in establishing its own "turf," but with a new rationality for doing so. In short, the goal is to plan effectively for institutional diversity within the overall framework of statewide interests and needs. The data suggest that a certain tension exists between geographic and other types of institutional proximity, and that regional cooperative arrangements among institutions not sharing these other types of institutional proximities are most successful in accomplishing effective state-level planning. Conversely, the kinds of compromise generally required in interinstitutional cooperative actions appear much more difficult to accomplish when institutions with like proximities are involved. If these kinds of findings continue to emerge, the case becomes very strong for policies and practices in statewide planning that urge more institutional differentiation within a given defined region or locality and less encouragement of "peer" institutional development.

Regionalization actions that are successful in defining and then anchoring differentiated institutional roles should prove effective in countering what has been commonly referred to as "academic drift" and the subsequent duplication and waste that inevitably occur. (Academic drift can be described as the voluntary movement of an institution toward educational programs that are perceived as highest in prestige, or as offering greater rewards financially.[30]) This achievement, however, obviously will not be an easy task. The more postsecondary interests involved, the more complex the process becomes.

Nevertheless, the trend in statewide planning for postsecondary education seems clearly to be toward a more comprehensive approach. As noted here, regionalization undertaking coverage of postsecondary education comprehensively within a specified geographic region is the most common method used in the states. Efforts are now being made to reach out to "nontraditional" educational interests (televised instruction, "open" university programs, field-based instructional centers, etc.), such efforts giving even broader meaning to the notion of comprehensive planning and suggesting a movement toward what S. B. Gould and others have called the American "communiversity."[31] If the thrust of the message here presented is heard by those setting new policies according to this trend—more specifically, using the concept of regionalism in statewide planning—then these policies will call for more than simply the total inclusion in the enterprise of all operating postsecondary educational interests in a region. The policy will also require each of these interests to make clear the philosophic and programmatic bases on which they see themselves as cooperating partners in postsecondary education and the ways in which they wish to be different.

NOTES

1. State Higher Education Officers, "1980, Major Issues of Concern to State Higher Education Agencies," as indicated in "An Analysis of Annual Reports from the States" (Denver: Education Commission of the States, 1980).

2. National Center for Higher Education Management Systems (NCHEMS), *Statewide Planning Measures* (Denver: NCHEMS, 1972).

3. D. K. Halstead, *Statewide Planning in Higher Education* (Washington, D.C.: U.S. Department of Health, Education, and Welfare, 1974).

4. L. L. Leslie and H. F. Miller, Jr., *Higher Education and the Steady State* (Washington, D.C.: American Association for Higher Education, 1974).

5. K. P. Mortimer and M. L. Tierney, *The Three R's of the Eighties: Reduction, Reallocation, and Retrenchment* (Washington, D.C.: Association for Higher Education, 1979).

6. Fred E. Crossland, "Learning to Cope with a Downward Slope," *Change* 12 (1980):18–25.

7. Ronald B. Stafford, "Implications of Regionalism for State-Level Governmental Policies and Possible Legislative Concerns and Actions," in *Study, Talk, and Action: A Report of a National Conference on Regionalism and Regionalization in American Postsecondary Education,* ed. S. V. Martorana and Lawrence A. Nespoli (University Park: Center for the Study of Higher Education, Pennsylvania State University, 1978).

8. Robert Lewis, "The Crazy Dream of a College Trustee," *Chronicle* (November 3, 1980):64.

9. Lewis D. Patterson, *Benefits of Collegiate Cooperation* (University, Alabama: Council for Interinstitutional Leadership, 1979).

10. Robert O. Berdahl, *Statewide Coordination of Higher Education* (Washington, D.C.: American Council on Education, 1971); J. S. Zwingle and M. E. Rogers, *State Boards Responsible for Higher Education 1970* (Washington, D.C.: U.S. Department of Health, Education, and Welfare, 1972); S. V. Martorana, *State Level Planning for Community Colleges: Are the 1202 Commissions Centripetal or Centrifugal Force on Postsecondary Education?* (Iowa City: American College Testing Programs, 1973); Richard Millard, *State Boards of Higher Education* (Washington, D.C.: American Association for Higher Education, 1976); Education Commission of the States, *Coordination or Chaos? Report of the Task Force on Coordination, Governance, and Structure of Postsecondary Education* (Denver: ECS, 1973); Education Commission of the States, *Challenge: Coordination and Governance in the 80's* (Denver: ECS, 1980).

11. John D. Russell and James I. Doi, *Manuals for Studies of Space Utilization in Colleges and Universities* (Athens: Ohio University/American Association of Collegiate Registrars and Admissions Officers, 1957).

12. Halstead, *Statewide Planning in Higher Education.*

13. Warren W. Willingham, *Free Access Higher Education* (New York: College Entrance Examination Board, 1970), p. ix.

14. S. V. Martorana and L. A. Nespoli, *Regionalism in American Postsecondary Education: Concepts and Practices* (University Park: Center for the Study of Higher Education, Pennsylvania State University, 1978), p. 3.

15. Ibid., passim.

16. Jamison Gilder and Jessica Rocha, "Ten Thousand Cooperative Arrangements Serve 1.5 Million," *Community and Junior College Journal* 51 (1980):1117.

17. Martorana and Nespoli, *Regionalism in American Postsecondary Education,* passim.

18. L. A. Nespoli, "State-Recognized Interinstitutional Cooperation in Postsecondary Education: The Relationship between Selected State Characteristics and Support for Regionalism and Use of Regionalization in the States" (Ph.D. dissertation, Pennsylvania State University, 1980), passim.

19. Fred M. Hechinger, "Coming Conditions in Academe: A Backdrop to Regionalism in American Postsecondary Education," in *Study, Talk, and Action,* ed. Martorana and Nespoli.

20. Halstead, *Statewide Planning in Higher Education,* p. 191.

21. John Gardner, *Excellence: Can We Be Equal and Excellent Too?* (New York: Harper and Row, 1961); Barry M. Richman and Richard N. Farmer, *Leadership, Goals, and Power in Higher Education* (San Francisco: Jossey-Bass, 1974).

22. Burton R. Clark, "The Insulated Americans: Five Lessons from Abroad," *Change* 10 (November 1978):28.

23. S. V. Martorana and Eileen Kuhns, *Cooperative Regional Planning and Action to Enhance Postsecondary Education across State Lines*, Final Report to the Fund for the Improvement of Postsecondary Education (FIPSE), March 1983.

24. S. V. Martorana, "Regionalism in Statewide Planning: A Coordination Principle to Counter Chaos," *Proceedings, Conference on Postsecondary Statewide Planning* (Montgomery: Alabama Commission on Higher Education, 1978).

25. Richard R. Johnson, "Leadership among American Colleges," *Change* 10 (1978):50–51.

26. Clark, "The Insulated Americans," p. 29.

27. Kenneth R. Andrews, *The Concept of Corporate Strategy* (Homewood, Ill.: Dow Jones–Irvin, 1971), passim.

28. Rita Braito, Steve Paul, and Gerald Klongdon, "Domain Consensus: A Key Variable in Interorganization Analysis," in *Complex Organizations and Their Environments*, compiled by Merlin Brinderhoff and Philip R. Kunz (Dubuque, Iowa: W. C. Brown, 1972).

29. Martorana and Kuhns, *Cooperative Regional Planning*.

30. Clark, "The Insulated Americans," p. 28.

31. S. B. Gould, *Today's Academic Condition* (New York: McGraw-Hill, 1970), pp. 90–97; S. V. Martorana and Eileen Kuhns, "The Challenge of the Communiversity," *Change* 9 (1977):54–55.

4

Resource Allocation Policies for the Eighties

Barry Munitz and Robert Lawless

"When we have a zero sum mentality," as University of Wisconsin administrator Joseph F. Kauffman has noted, "consensus is often replaced with conflict, and democratic processes of decision making are exceedingly difficult to maintain. The legitimacy of the leader is challenged when resource allocation is the dominant mode for coping with scarce resources. There are few rewards that can be given, no matter how greatly deserved. If across-the-board cuts are made in appropriations or allocations, the most efficient and able administrators may be hurt the most, for they have already eliminated waste."[1]

Over the past decade expenditures for higher education have been increasingly carefully scrutinized throughout the United States. Particular attention has been focused upon those publicly supported institutions that compete for taxpayer dollars through the legislative appropriations process. Although the total resource commitment to higher education always has been a public issue, more recently particular attention has focused on the value of a college education, and the relative benefits of expenditures for it. Lifelong learning potential and ultimate vocational achievements have been weighed carefully against the investment in traditional pre- and post-baccalaureate education.

The seventies saw a shift away from the philosophical foundation that viewed learning as a means to enriching the total life experience, to a view that placed far more emphasis upon education as a "value added experience."

That value was associated directly with enhanced socioeconomic mobility and with strengthened earning potential. This change in the general public attitude has resulted in a much tighter financial environment. The component of higher education administration charged with deploying an institution's resources and with developing reasonable measures to demonstrate value received and productivity gained suddenly finds itself in a small goldfish bowl.

Disenchanted taxpayers have added to the pressure for greater institutional accountability. As the national economy suffered and cries for tax relief grew stronger, more questions were raised about the relative priority for higher education. Administrators, faced with the threat of reduced appropriations and gifts in response to these taxpayer concerns, have sought systematic resource allocation and program evaluation strategies. Ironically, many of those administrators have been interested for some time in a process that would link institutional priorities to the allocation of resources in a way that would ensure that those priorities are achieved in a timely, efficient, and cost-effective manner. They recognized that plans generated internally were far preferable to those imposed by external groups responding to political or other nonacademic motivation. Our general objective has been to replace ad hoc reactions to problems—and their symptoms—with a procedure in which actions are anticipated and danger areas are avoided. The consistent hope has been that this strategy will successfully convert the current prospect of constrained resources and public cynicism into opportunities for a healthy trimming of redundant programs. In addition, energies would be refocused upon a more cohesive, more cost-efficient, and higher quality educational operation.

In other social-policy areas technological and analytical advances have been cited as a means of enhancing the standard of living and increasing the productivity of developed and underdeveloped countries. As economies of scale have been achieved, and the volume of output has been strengthened beyond that formally attributable to manual methods, an increase in the standard of living has been measured in terms of relative earning per unit of production. Many astute observers among and outside our faculty have looked at the modest changes in the administration of higher education, and wondered why comparable efficiencies cannot be achieved in the academic sector. The nature of their concern is reflected painfully in a recent interview with Peter Drucker:

Question: Why does the administration need to be strong?

Drucker Answer: First it must be strong because a lot of difficult decisions have to be made about the shrinking student enrollment. But even if the enrollment wasn't declining, a strong administration is necessary because most of the existing departments in the university are rapidly becoming obsolete.

Question: Pretend that all United States college and university presidents are assembled before you. What would you tell them about how to manage their institutions during the next ten years?

Drucker Answer: First you have the opportunity during the next ten years to think through what the necessary authority of the administration has to be in order for you to do your job and then to push it through again to the faculty.

Final Question: How can a person make a difference?

Drucker Answer: How can you? You have to make time. But do most presidents have time for anything but financial problems? I doubt it. What a waste.[2]

Drucker, a distinguished faculty member for almost fifty years, has spent most of his time examining private enterprise, but his repeated efforts to apply his basic observations to the higher education environment merit the most careful attention.

MEASURING ACADEMIC PRODUCTIVITY

Concepts exploring results obtained for dollars invested in the field of higher education obviously are related to some notion of "academic productivity." This phrase has been subjected to so many different interpretations that its meaning has lost virtually all practical usage in a college or university. However, it is generally recognized that most segments of society approach productivity as a quantity that can be measured. Indeed, they insist that relative efficiencies or inefficiencies can be recognized by comparing productivity at different times. In higher education there are no indices as quantifiably specific as widgets produced per hour of labor, but several new measures are gaining acceptance in the academic environment which can fruitfully be used in a dialogue between individuals inside and outside the academic world. Most critically, they are based upon (rather than being substitutes for) quality and mission issues.

This is a healthy development, since legislators, agency heads, and intellectually curious alumni will continue to press for "certifiable proof" that effectiveness has increased and that their investments in higher education are producing adequate returns. Unfortunately, this accountability issue camouflages in some ways a greater concern about total dollars appropriated for higher education when compared with investments for other social requirements. Nonetheless, clear, concise, and generally applied measures of productivity, stated in terms that nonacademics understand, can provide the basis for enhancing credibility with taxpayers, legislators, and the general public. When joined in a responsible manner, such a demonstration cannot help but increase basic support for higher education in the future.

Developing Resource Allocation Policies

Any resource allocation program begins with the articulation of operational objectives for the institution. These goals evolve naturally from its mission and focus upon areas of institutional strengths and specific targets of opportunity. While qualitative in most aspects, they can be sufficiently quantitative to enable decision makers to evaluate progress and to express publicly the degree of that progress. Quite naturally, such articulation depends upon meaningful faculty participation, an in-depth study of the proposed market "niche" being filled by programs of instruction, and the relative interest felt by various groups in society for those services.

We will propose measures of productivity based on the instructional level, class format, and general pattern of academic delivery for a program. Our analyses ask what a reasonable allocation of resources might be if we wish to support or modify the quality of a given program. Such resources are not restricted to faculty positions. They include the entire range of support mechanisms required for excellent faculty to work at a quality institution. Thus incentives for improving faculty and administration responsibilities are tied to those sources of support.[3] The productivity of the institution is enhanced when students, faculty, and supporting staff who deserve a greater investment in their work receive adequate recognition and support. Therefore, the methodology that enumerates those aspects of efficiency and effectiveness which have received the highest priority from the campus administration, is then tied to the actual educational dollars spent on recognizing and rewarding the finest and most highly motivated faculty, staff, and students. The old-fashioned method of aggregate planning, which projects future programs, likely enrollment, required faculty size, and a "Christmas wish list" of resources, avoids the very components required by any institution that recognizes the reality of resource restraints. The credibility of the policy for allocating those scarce resources will determine whether quality is improved and effectiveness increased.

This tougher look at objectives and their resource requirements cannot disregard the traditional academic governance structure. The fundamental premise of any allocation policy is that resources can be provided to support academic programs in a manner that assures higher overall quality of education and greater cost-efficiency. If this premise is to be met, terms must be identified, discussed, understood, and accepted prior to moving forward with any procedures and criteria. Resource allocation policies should always develop from meaningful discussions with faculty and academic administrators, in order to shape educationally sound goals and to achieve meaningful support for the implementation of those policies. Clearly, allocation policies and reallocation procedures will mean that some departments and academic areas get less. Such a shift creates enormous anxiety. Diversionary techniques and destructive political confrontation are rooted in this anxiety and will undermine the process unless the academic constituency is involved and can make an impact on institutional mission and allocation policy.

Developing Resource Allocation Procedures

Concise definition of criteria is the most sensitive aspect of determining specific productivity measures for any resource allocation policy. Those criteria must be clearly understood, as well as plainly relevant to the chosen conceptual framework for expressing efficiency and effectiveness. Moreover, any assumptions regarding productivity and appropriate levels of funding must be clear to, and supported by, faculty, students, administrators, legislators, and the general public.

Once specific measures of productivity are defined and the basis for criteria analysis is established, it is important to develop a desired or expected level of resource utilization for each of the institution's fundamental activities. These expectations are based upon an identification of attributes, which specifically define the character of a program in terms that encourage and facilitate useful comparisons. Although the examples in this chapter will focus upon academic functions, since they are the heart and soul of any college or university, the same principles apply to an institution's support areas as well. For example, one attribute that can be used for differentiating among programs involves the type and grouping of students in a given discipline. One would expect to find somewhat larger class sizes in predominantly undergraduate instruction than one would normally encounter in instruction devoted principally to the doctoral level. Similarly, courses that have a lecture and discussion format can be significantly larger than those requiring clinical instruction or a high degree of laboratory involvement. Therefore, the format and level of instructional delivery are intersecting variables in an analysis of expected program differences.

THE UNIVERSITY OF HOUSTON MODEL

In the late 1970s the University of Houston–University Park undertook the development of a method for making budget allocations and reallocations among academic departments. It has seven components.

First, a general discussion of academic mission is initiated by the chancellor's office, including the dean's council and certain committees of the faculty senate. The discussion includes the broad educational philosophy and regional characteristics unique to the institution. A focused set of operational objectives gradually evolves from the broader statement of mission. This exploration of campus role and scope has no fixed conclusion. Continued discussion assures the administration that concepts of "quality" and "centrality" are periodically examined and refined.

Table 4.1
Program Priorities Matrix

CENTRALITY TO CAMPUS MISSION

TARGET QUALITY (3-5-year period)	Highly Central (integral to campus mission)	Moderately Central (suportive in substantive ways to campus mission)	Peripheral (Least essential to campus' principal roles but viable demand for programs)
Eminence/ Distinction (consistent high quality)	Most desirable 1	3	6
Strength (solidly and broadly better than average)	2	4	8
Adequacy (sound in many respects, but distinguished in very few if any)	5	7	Least desirable 9

Note: This represents one theoretical assignment of priority rankings to the cells of the academic priority matrix. The matrix establishes the order in which departments will have call on available resources, all other factors being equal.

Second, a current department profile is developed by assigning each department to a particular cell of a nine-cell matrix. The matrix shows current judgments of academic quality as well as a composite evaluation effort to provide preliminary judgments of departmental centrality. In general configuration this matrix is similar to the program priority matrix illustrated in Table 4.1 and discussed in the following step.

Third, a program priority matrix is established. It too is a nine-cell matrix with coordinates representing targeted quality over a three-to-five-year period and shows the same composite sense of centrality to institutional mission. By comparing this pair of matrices, one can visualize the directional quality modification planned over the three-to-five-year period. Targeted quality and current quality of departments may be the same or quite different, depending upon the depth of program problems and the lead time necessary to overcome them. Centrality is, of course, much more fixed. Issues of academic priorities are addressed and resolved by the chancellor's cabinet, composed of the highest level administrators from the divisions of academic affairs, financial affairs, student services, and planning and resource allocation. Advice on such issues is also sought from the dean's council and from standing faculty committees.

The priority rankings in Table 4.1 suggest the general sequence in which faculty and administrators might want to provide resources to advance the quality of their departments while meeting institutional goals. Trade-offs are implicit here. For example, will greater attention be merited by a department that is moderately central and targeted for national distinction, or by a department that is highly central and targeted for broad strength?

Fourth, building upon the initial program evaluation process, as well as the general overview of institutional resources in a context of college and departmental leadership, each department is placed in an appropriate cell of the academic priority matrix. Strictly speaking, the position of a department in this matrix represents both the likelihood of that department making a claim for available new or reallocable resources, and the inverse likelihood that it will be called upon to give up resources needed elsewhere.

Fifth, resource needs are reflected by a matrix that indicates the relative rate of resource consumption by a department's programs. This sixteen-cell matrix (Table 4.2) represents the intersection of the single most significant level of instruction provided by a department during its recent past and the prevalent format of such instruction. The two dimensions of departmental operations that most directly impact its costs per unit of instruction are the program levels it supports and the means of instruction required to deliver these programs effectively. Departments are only rarely engaged exclusively in either undergraduate or graduate instruction. The instructional level axis is divided into four intervals that represent the degree of advanced complexity of its instructional activity. Proportions of course sections offered by levels, semester credit hours generated by levels, and student majors by level serve to indicate the single most appropriate instructional level into which a department is placed.

Similarly, the instructional format axis has also been divided into four intervals. These represent the prevalent form of instructional delivery used in a particular discipline. Some disciplines use the lecture/discussion form of instruction, others require heavy usage of studio/recital classes. Technical disciplines generally prefer laboratory settings in which "hands-on" student experiences are emphasized, while sciences generally favor laboratory courses. Each of these formats has implications for limiting class size, facilities, student-to-teacher ratios, and the necessary composition of support staff. The placement of a department in this matrix indicates its relative costs of operation vis-à-vis other departments.

The resource consumption matrix is intended to portray relative resource needs of departments and not resource allocation priorities. Relative resource needs convey the degree to which normative levels of resources required for a department to operate effectively are actually being fulfilled through

Table 4.2
Financial Priorities Matrix

CENTRALITY TO CAMPUS MISSION

TARGET QUALITY (3-5-year period)		Highly Central (integral to campus mission)				Moderately Central (supportive in substantive ways to campus mission)	Peripheral (least essential to campus' principal roles but viable demand for programs)
		I	II	III	IV		
Eminence/ Distinction (consistent) high quality)	A			Dept D .90			
	B		Dept A 1.10				
	C			Dept E 1.20 / Dept H 1.00			
	D	Dept J .98					
				1		3	6
Strength (solidly and broadly better than average)						Dept B .70 Dept F 1.35 Dept M .95 Dept P .90 Dept R .80	
				2		4	8
Adequacy (sound in many respects, but distinguished in very few if any)				5		7	9

Note: The figures for the featured departments represent the proportion of the normative level of a particular type of resource currently budgeted to departments in two cells of the academic priority matrix. This gives a starting point for deciding reallocation/allocation priorities for this particular type of resource (e.g., faculty positions, staff positions, operating funds, etc.).

current base allocations. The dollar values of the normative resource requirements are established by studying resource requirement levels among similar departments within one's own institution and by comparing these internal requirements with resource allocation patterns of similar departments at other institutions. The relative resource need of a particular department, then, is determined by the proportion of normative resource requirements being met by current budget allocations. Each department's needs are expressed as a coefficient of relative resource requirements.

Sixth, the resource consumption matrix is now overlaid to each cell of the academic matrix. In this way, the relative levels of resource need for each department within each cell of academic program priorities are highlighted (see Table 4.2). The ordering of academic program priorities, discussed in the third step, serves as a guide to the sequence in which the resource allocation (or reduction) decisions would be addressed.

Finally, resource allocation priorities and decisions must be established. It should be noted that some departments may have such urgent resource requirements that their needs must be addressed ahead of those for other departments with higher inherent academic priorities (see Table 4.3). Such an assessment and the consequent resource allocation decision rely heavily on the judgments of key administrators and faculty leaders. Without a sophisticated sense of leadership and management qualities, it is impossible to know whether an investment of additional resources can be put to effective use.

Practical Implications for the Campus

The thirteen colleges were analyzed according to the factors listed in Table 4.4. The assumptions for the process were spelled out to the campus community (and are shown at the bottom of the table) over a period of five years. The resources likely to be available were then identified, and each college received a picture of relative needs and probable support.

Most of the assumptions outlined in Table 4.4 are basic principles of sound administration. For example, you cannot implement the serious reallocation of faculty salary dollars without sufficient lead time to determine the impact of tenure density, the timing of recruitment patterns, and the implications of faculty promotion and salary increment policies. We start with the premise that in a department that is relatively "overstaffed" or that has one or more positions beyond the range required for its sound operation—according to its own objectives and assessment of quality—then the first step is to look very seriously at nontenured faculty positions. Vacancies are examined with great care. An empty position's current location is thoroughly examined, and the places to which it might be reallocated are determined. Such a position-by-position analysis of vacancies results in a departmental, then college, and ultimately campuswide inventory of flexible resources.

Table 4.3
Priorities of Departments to...

Surrender Resources			Receive Additional Resources		
Department	Amount of Need Met	Cell Priority	Department	Amount of Need Met	Cell Priority
Q	1.22	9	D	.09	1
W	1.18	8	G	.85	2
S	1.25	7	I	.92	2
T	1.15	7	_B_	_.70_	_4_
_F_	_1.30_	_4_	K	.92	3
U	1.15	6	R	.80	4
V	1.22	5	P	.90	4
C	1.18	3	L	.83	5
E	1.20	1	N	.77	6
A	1.10	1	_M_	_.95_	_4_
			X	.90	7

Not considered: Departments below 1.10 of normative base

Not considered: Departments above .95 of normative base

Note: Departments in italics shifted positions, either higher or lower, owing to stringency of need relative to other departments in adjacent cells.

Table 4.4
The Enhancement of Productivity through More Efficient Use of Resources

MASTER FORMAT: Reallocation of Faculty Positions

New Biennium for	Pattern	Basic Factors for Allocation Pattern
Education	Major contributor	1. Centrality to institutional mission
HFA	Minor contributor	2. Current and targeted quality
HRM		3. Research consumption matrix which contrasts actual level of instruction
OPT	Remain in current balance	4. Internal and national peer planning models which analyze a series of cost and expenditure ratios
PHARM		
SOC WK		5. A continuous program evaluation process
SOC SCI	Internal redistribution and reorganization	6. Five-year enrollment and student credit hour trends
ENGIN	Adjust current salaries--major	7. Campuswide and college-level faculty workload policies in each college
ARCH	Adjust current salaries--minor plus receive slight new positions	8. Range of curricular offerings in each college
		9. National salary and recruitment markets for faculty and administration
TECH	Combine minor current adjustment with minor base increment	10. Quality of current administrative leadership
LAW	Combine major current adjustment with major recipient after vacancies filled	11. Recent accreditation requirements
		12. State formula adjustments by program
BUS	Major recipient new positions	
NSM	Strongest recipient new positions	

Vital Assumptions for Allocation Pattern

1. The pattern for administrative and operations support for academic units should follow lines analogous to the distribution.
2. The credibility of an allocation process rests upon concomitant analysis of and shifts for nonacademic units and administrative positions.
3. A reasonable lead time is required given the normal faculty recruitment and tenure situations on campus.
4. It makes no sense to go through the planning, analysis, and discussion phases unless there is a firm willingness and ability to implement decisions.
5. The total faculty and salary allocation will include continuing and new positions, budgeted as well as filled positions, graduate students, intern-employees (teaching fellows and teaching assistants), lecturers, and summer session participants.
6. Guidelines for faculty salary increments each year should recognize cost-of-living pressures while they emphasize merit for each category of faculty responsibility. Theoretically each individual on the campus should have access to the total pool of increment dollars.
7. The more faculty added in the current state and national climate, the less flexibility there is to respond to enrollment and financial pressures, and the less relatively well paid the current faculty will be.

The summary table allows us to visualize thirteen colleges on a 30,000-student campus whose enrollment pattern has changed as dramatically as the city within which it is located, and to state the current projected fundamental goals and resource requirements in response to those changes. Houston has moved from a primarily undergraduate and teaching institution to a prestigious graduate and professional university. That transformation has been accompanied by changes in the regional and national marketplace (in terms of job opportunities, student interest, and reward patterns). In the context of student demand, enrollment patterns, market expectation, salary levels, and a shift in our own educational mission and quality target, the faculty resources of two of our thirteen colleges are seriously overbudgeted. Other colleges have moved into a position of needing the resources located in the overbudgeted units. Our task is to devise the specific administrative strategies whereby the reallocation can occur in the least painful and most creative manner.

An equally delicate application of these analyses, which are updated constantly according to tenure ratios, hiring plans, retirement patterns, internal departmental organization, faculty workload policy—all identified in Table 4.4—involves the recruitment of new deans. An aggressive search for appropriate leadership in a given college, and the successful introduction of a new dean to a given college, can be accomplished only within a detailed and candid resource framework.

Although one could argue that such a specific resource picture might discourage certain priority candidates from accepting an administrative leadership position, it would be even worse to bring an excellent person into a confused or misleading situation. Where a college will be surrendering positions in the total reallocation plan over a three-to-five-year period, a new dean must understand the situation before he or she accepts the assignment. Incentives for imaginative leadership leading to the reallocation objectives can be established and should be implemented. The new dean can propose a timetable for surrendering positions, depending upon his or her perception of the trauma induced by varying strategies. The overall goal remains high-quality education. One way to affect productivity in an educational setting is to maintain or enhance quality with the same or fewer resources. This means that we need to know what the available resources are. We also need to examine curricular offerings, workload policies, and staffing ratios, and to identify key leadership.

Regardless of the specific dollar amounts involved, the primary goal is to find a faculty size that is appropriate for the range and the quality of education necessary for the unit and the institution. The campus-level administrator spells out expectations and then has the obligation of balancing available resources so that those expectations can reasonably be met. Needless to say, such decisions are never fixed in concrete. The major themes of the planning process lead to constant updates responding to enrollment patterns, salary market conditions, etc. Thus, a college might wind up gaining additional resources several years after it was identified as a contributor to the resource pool; adjustments are then made accordingly.

Specific strategies flow from those assessments. Sometimes a given college or department badly needs new positions according to our ratio calculations, but has a lower priority for receiving some of those funds because it has a smaller gap to close in reaching its quality target or because it is less relevant to the basic institutional mission. Some colleges have chosen to reorganize their departments in order to reduce administrative and faculty cost. Others have eliminated program components at the graduate level, while still others have attempted to retrain tenured faculty who have some inclination toward programmatic efforts in other areas.

Practical Implications for the Department

Even when faculty positions are available and a tightly squeezed tenure scenario does not prevail, there is a serious question of how much position reduction can be accomplished in a given time frame without severely disrupting the academic offerings and program quality of a department. Implementation requires careful planning, course structuring, and modification so that department members are not demoralized, while at the same time they are being asked to increase their level of productivity.

Since the academic programs must remain the basic component of a resource allocation planning format, it is important to remember our assertion that the desired faculty staffing is principally determined by four attributes: the predominant level of instruction, the prevailing format of instruction delivered, the desired quality of the program, and the centrality of that program to the overall mission of the institution. These defining attributes allow one to look at the faculty staffing goal in terms of the desired semester credit hours generated within the discipline.

Other levels and types of resource support are related to the appropriate faculty staffing. Thus clerical, technical, professional, and administrative support are directly linked to the number of faculty associated with a given program. Likewise, equipment expenditures, operating dollars, travel, and other means of support are also most appropriately tied to the desired faculty staffing within a given department. It follows that related resources cannot be shifted before faculty positions have been shifted. Operationally, as long as the faculty positions remain within the department, the linked resources also remain. When faculty positions can be shifted to a more appropriate department, then the other identifiable supporting relationships and resources are also moved to that program.

To illustrate the implementation complexities, let us assume that the resource model indicates that the desired faculty staffing level in a department is twelve FTE. The current level of staffing is nineteen FTE, or an apparent "surplus" of seven faculty positions. In this particular instance the situation is complicated by the fact that fourteen of the nineteen faculty members are currently tenured, and the other five are "tenure track" faculty. Thus no faculty positions are readily available, and already there are two more tenured faculty than the desired total staffing level. This presents a knotty problem in itself, but it becomes even more intriguing when one realizes that significantly different tenure criteria will probably be applied to the five nontenured faculty. Indeed, it is questionable whether any of these five can attain tenure, since the current tenure density is greater than 100 percent in terms of desired faculty for the department; this despite the fact that any or all of these five may be among the brightest and most productive in the department.

Another complicating factor is the differential among faculty salaries across disciplines. A given faculty position in one department is not necessarily equivalent to a faculty position in another discipline. Some areas with the greatest demand for faculty positions are also those with the highest average rate of compensation. It may be necessary to convert almost two faculty positions in a field such as liberal arts to one in a professional field like law. This simple reality requires linking faculty salary dollars with positions in order to accomplish resource allocation shifts in accordance with the desired productivity-based planning model.

The assumptions addressed above were applied at each of our thirteen colleges and helped them analyze their current use of resources and their priorities for the next five years. In each case we asked the college to prepare a document following the outline shown in Table 4.5. A one-page introduction describing the college's present situation was provided by each dean. After a brief summary of past planning efforts for that college, the dean recapitulated the results of any recent evaluation efforts. These included internal program assessment projects, as well as external reviews and/or formal accreditation visits.

In the next sections of the College Strategic Plan the dean indicated future priorities and projected the types and extent of resources required to meet those priorities. A detailed analysis was made for each department, and then a visual summary for the college indicated the gaps that would have to be filled over the last five years.

The college-level administration then responded to each plan and synthesized the collective responses into a campus document, which integrated program plans with allocation strategies. After indicating the relationship of each college's goals to the general campus planning analyses, the provost and the senior vice chancellor worked with the dean to organize the college's objectives into campus priorities and to identify sources of support for areas that would have to be covered in the future. Considerable conversation was also devoted to the reallocation of internal resources so that the highest

Table 4.5
Model College Strategic Plan

1. General Introduction

2. Past Planning

3. Assessment of Recent Accomplishments

   a. program evaluation: faculty; students; courses; projects
   b. accreditation and/or external review

4. Future Priorities

5. Projected Resources (people, space, equipment, etc.)

6. Detailed Analysis (by department level) and Graphic Summary:

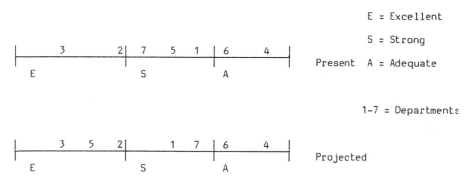

E = Excellent

S = Strong

A = Adequate

1-7 = Departments

RESPONSE FROM PROVOST

7. Relationship of college goals to campus planning analyses

8. Priority order for college objectives, from campus perspective

   A. Centrality goals
   B. Types and extent of resources required
   C. Sources of support

      1. Legislative appropriations
      2. Tuition and fees
      3. Private giving
      4. Grants and contracts
      5. Internal reallocation

objectives for the college and the campus could be met even if external support remained stable, or decreased.

PROGRAM EVALUATION AND RESOURCE ALLOCATION

As a contribution to refined decision making, academic program evaluation provides a necessary, but not sufficient component of responsible planning and resource allocation.[4] It includes a serious look at objectives, resources, and results. The general evaluation process can spell out the institutional mission, explore the human, financial, and physical aspects of an institution which are brought to bear in pursuing that mission, examine the sequence of classroom and laboratory activities, and then determine whether the results correspond to the original objectives. Such an iterative process incorporates the consequences of prior decisions into the shaping of future directions. Program objectives, academic processes, educational products, and institutional resources can increase the return on taxpayer or private investments, and thereby enhance productivity.

While assessment has always been present in the educational environment, pressures for far more systematic resource allocation and public accountability have altered institutional perspectives on program evaluation. Using the method described above, colleges and universities have been able to focus more sharply on both the distinctive and the compatible program objectives and their relation to the larger campus mission. This focus has always been based upon the desire to provide resources that enhance quality and effectiveness. Earlier we emphasized that some disciplines and their programs are more highly central to the achievement of a given institution's objectives than others. Some, by the very nature of their content and instruction format, are more costly to support than others. Educators have always tried to satisfy themselves that they are interpreting current responsibilities, when multiple program opportunities are available, and at the same time carrying them out at a reasonably high quality.

Although it might require a second paper to argue persuasively, public and systematic evaluation for each step of this process is essential if it is to be effective and appropriate. Judgments must be made regarding general strategies and specific allocations, and then factored into planning decisions for the next budgetary cycle. Such a systematic approach to planning and allocation provides some comfort for administrative decisions and an incentive for constituency participation. The resource allocation policy becomes a partner with the traditional reasoned dialogue among students, faculty, and administration which is appropriately preserved at our best institutions of higher education.

Social and economic pressures on colleges and universities are likely to affect how they organize and what strategies they use. Without solid information about the quality of what a college currently offers, no administration can explore or justify the investment required to move toward that college's future. Without an understanding of the results of an institution's current allocation pattern, it is virtually impossible to establish meaningful priorities for a reallocation program. Institutional leaders and their constituencies cannot justify the traditional time-consuming and energy-draining aspects of setting priorities and budgeting dollars in a clandestine or undefined evaluation setting. Instincts may be extraordinarily fine, but without supporting materials studied in a candid setting they can be attacked and subsequently ravaged.

CONCLUSION

American colleges and universities are not likely to find much relief from external pressures during the next ten years. Their health will rest on the ability of faculty members and administrators to devise credible and imaginative responses to those pressures. Campus faculty, as well as department and college administrators, will have to trust in and participate in allocation and program evaluation if it is to be effective. To establish that trust and to sustain that participation, there must be a clear definition of objectives, along with the general context and need for continuing evaluation. Success will depend in significant measure upon the ability to come up with a firm statement of institutional mission, to fulfill that mission through appropriate program selection, and to translate mission priorities into allocation patterns for program improvement.

During this next decade academic administrators must continually ask whether they are recruiting and retaining the brightest young people as students and as faculty members, and whether they are creating an environment conducive to productive learning. The administrator must see to it that decisions made about finding and keeping those people can be publicly justified from the point of view of resource efficiency; they must also be able to maintain that the values received are appropriate and of high quality. To accomplish those goals, we must set meaningful priorities, based upon the relative role each institution plays within its geographical setting and given the national climate. That judgment, in turn, must be based upon historical as well as future considerations and must demonstrate that there is a realistic understanding of the likely impact for each significant investment of scarce resources.

These conditions do not necessarily describe a comfortable setting for many administrators, since their judgments will be implemented more quickly than they would like and will be based upon less information than they will need. Their survival, therefore, will rest substantially on how successful they are in feeling relatively comfortable with the support that underlies their basic decision-making processes. Even with the assistance of a sophisticated institutional research staff, they will never have enough information, they will never have enough time to decide, and they will never be in a position where certainty is even approachable.

In such an administrative milieu, it is essential that academic administrators have negotiating handles for decision making, with reliable indices of current quality, and with comprehensible standards of effectiveness. Ironically, the more inefficiently we allocate our current resources, the weaker our argument for a greater investment from others; the more effective our current allocation pattern, the better justification we have for additional support.

NOTES

1. Joseph F. Kauffman, "Leadership in Higher Education," *Texas Coordinating Board Long Range Plan*, Vol. 2, background papers.

2. "Interview with Peter Drucker," *Educational Record* 62 (Winter 1981):5–7.

3. Munitz has explored this concept in far greater detail by pointing out the relationships to general administrative reward systems; see "The Chief Executive Officer and the Administrative Reward System," *Phi Kappa Phi Journal* 60 (Spring 1980):10–13.

4. This material is drawn from an article by Barry Munitz and Douglas J. Wright, "Institutional Approaches to Academic Program Evaluation," *New Directions for Institutional Research*, No. 27 (1980):21–42.

PART II

ACCOUNTABILITY AND EQUAL OPPORTUNITY

5

Government Responsibility for Quality and Equality in Higher Education

Kenneth C. Green

Declining test scores, rising costs, deteriorating federal research support, and the growing role of postsecondary education in domestic social policy have all contributed to the rise of quality and equality as major policy issues in American higher education.* The academic community, heretofore highly autonomous, has become increasingly concerned about growing government influence over matters pertaining to academic conduct and freedom: the right of the academy "to determine for itself on academic grounds who shall teach, what may be taught, and who may be admitted to study."[1] Concurrently, the institutional, system-wide, and national retrenchment forecast for the 1980s has significant implications for government efforts to maintain and improve both the quality of higher education (training programs and research capacity) and the equality of higher education opportunity.

The transition from elite to mass to universal higher education in the United States during the years following World War II is the result of an expanded governmental presence in the higher education arena. This transition has been marked by a major shift in governmental roles. At the federal level, the role of government has shifted from that of purchaser and consumer of university research to supporter and underwriter of expanded access to and participation in higher education. Similarly, the state role in higher

*This work was supported by grants from the Exxon Education Foundation and the Ford Foundation to the Higher Education Research Institute.

education has changed dramatically from passive provider to concerned underwriter as public higher education has evolved from a limited, low-cost, meritocratic system to one of open and potentially unlimited access to all citizens regardless of age, ability to pay, or previous educational achievement.

Education is not a specific federal responsibility. Both by constitutional design and conscious political choice, education is the responsibility of the individual states. While the federal presence may in some instances be more visible than that of the states, the federal government remains the junior partner—albeit an increasingly influential one—in higher education.[2] The federal role in education is limited and specialized, usually takes the form of categorical grants, and aims to supplement state and local efforts "to solve particularly urgent problems or provide various kinds of assistance and leadership to help . . . improve the quality of education."[3] Because education is primarily a state responsibility, the federal presence has evolved as part of the larger, less explicit—and at least in constitutional terms—federal concern for the commonweal. This commonweal concern has led to federal education policy initiatives linked to a variety of areas: land and agricultural development (the Morrill Act of 1863); veterans' benefits (the GI Bill); scientific development (National Science Foundation); national defense (the National Defense Education Act of 1958); and economic opportunity (the Economic Opportunity Act of 1964). The Higher Education Act of 1965, part of the "Great Society" legislation, was thus the first major federal legislation to address higher education policy. Until then federal initiatives having direct and major impact on American higher education were linked to other, often peripheral, issues and outcomes.

The rapid growth of federal higher education programs since 1965 has tended to overshadow the historical state role and responsibility. The states still have primary responsibility for higher education; the states alone grant charters to both public and private institutions. With regard to funding, state expenditures for higher education continue to exceed those of the federal government (see Table 5.1). In the years following World War II, state governments carried the major burden of broadening college access by providing the bulk of the resources required for institutional and system-wide growth. During the twenty-five–year period beginning in 1950, the number of public colleges and universities, including two-year institutions and branch campuses, increased 228 percent; public institutions, which enrolled roughly one-half of all college students in 1950, accounted for better than 75 percent of all enrollments by 1975. This growth in the public sector occurred at the same time that total degree enrollments were increasing just over 400 percent.[4]

In sum, national higher education policy has been based on two factors: state support for "mortar and brick" issues and federal "carrot and stick" priorities and program incentives.

Table 5.1
Sources of Income for All Colleges and Universities for Educational and General Purposes, 1939–1976

	YEAR			
SOURCE	1939–40	1959–60	1969–70	1976–77
Federal Government	7.4%	24.1%	22.5%	16.4%
State Governments	28.7	32.0	36.6	41.6
Local Governments	4.6	3.5	4.8	5.1
Tuition and Fees[a]	38.1	26.8	26.8	28.2
Gifts, Grants, Endowment, etc.	21.2	13.6	9.3	8.7
	100.0	100.0	100.0	100.0
TOTAL (in billions of dollars)	$0.57	$4.34	$16.2	$32.28

[a]Gross tuition, including student aid.

Source: Carnegie Council on Policy Studies in Higher Education, 3000 Futures
(San Francisco: Jossey-Bass, 1980), p. 140.

THE RESPONSIBILITY FOR QUALITY

Until recently quality was largely the sole jurisdiction of the academic community. Accreditation and peer review were the major vehicles for identifying, assessing, and promoting quality within higher education. Government, with rare exception, was not an active participant. After a controversial attempt by the U.S. Office of Education to rate American universities during the early years of the twentieth century, the federal government ceded the quality issue to the states, the accrediting associations, and the professoriate: Eligibility for federal funding would be determined by state charter, program and/or institutional accreditation, and peer review of research proposals. The states, with rare exception, assumed academic values as their own. During the period of postwar expansion, the states generally viewed quality in terms of students with high test scores and faculty with doctorates, publications, and research grants.[5]

The State Responsibility

D. Kent Halstead indicates that state planning agencies have generally accepted responsibility for providing the leadership to improve the quality of public higher education.[6] Until recently, however, the states generally viewed program quality as depending almost entirely upon student and faculty characteristics. The traditional state perspective is exemplified in the following statement from the 1960 California *Master Plan for Higher Education*, a document that became the model for statewide higher education planning during the 1960s:

> The quality of an institution and that of a system of higher education are determined to a considerable extent by the abilities of those it admits and retains as students. This applies to all levels—lower division, upper division, and graduate. It is also true for all segments, but the emphases are different. The junior colleges are required by law to accept all high school graduates (and even some nongraduates under some circumstances); therefore the junior colleges must protect their quality by applying retention standards rigid enough to guarantee that taxpayers' money is not wasted on individuals who lack the capacity or the will to succeed in their studies. If the state college and the university have real differences of function between them, they should be exacting (in contrast to public higher education in most other states) because the junior colleges relieve them of the burden of doing remedial work. Both have the heavy obligation to the state to restrict the privilege of entering and remaining to those who are well above average in the college-age group.[7]

As this statement makes clear, the California master plan is based on a meritocratic model of program and institutional excellence.

Many states have recently moved beyond this traditional perspective, expanding their list of concerns to include educational process issues as well as student and faculty characteristics as manifestations of quality. This new perspective, motivated by a growing demand for accountability and reflected in the state program review process, has encouraged the states to look beyond traditional measures of quality in evaluating their support for and investment in higher education. Prior to 1970, during the period of growth and expansion, state program review was concerned primarily with assessing the resources required to develop new degree programs; by the mid-1970s, however, the scope of such activities had expanded to include the review of both proposed as well as existing programs.[8]

While state program review has yet to replace accreditation as the primary means of quality assessment and review, accrediting associations and the academic community they represent (and protect) are under growing pressure to cooperate with state and federal agencies. The Division of Institutional Eligibility of the U.S. Department of Education has established requirements for the evaluation criteria of accrediting associations. And in at least one state, Maryland, the state board of higher education and the regional accrediting association have agreed to cooperative efforts in the evaluation and accreditation of public colleges and universities.

A pragmatic acknowledgment of the potential for tension between the state program review process and accreditation is found in the recent Sloan

Commission on Government and Higher Education report. The commission's call for the "periodic review of quality of educational programs at every public college and university to be conducted by academic peer groups, not state employees," recognizes the fiscal realities and political climate in state capitals, yet is also sensitive to the academic community's traditions and concerns.[9] Program review is a fact of life for many public (and some private) institutions. The commission's view that program review is consistent with and complementary to institutional needs and state planning purposes, and that it should make use of existing accreditation structures, may disarm critics who fear uninformed and insensitive governmental intrusion into academic matters. At the same time, the commission's recommendation for periodic review may placate those state officials who demand greater accountability and who might support more drastic and less academically responsive methods.

The Federal Interest

Although the states are primarily responsible for issues pertaining to the quality of education, the federal government too has a major interest and investment in the quality of higher education. Commonweal concerns for national defense, scientific and technological capacity, human resource development, and competent social/medical services provide a rationale for federal R & D expenditures, graduate professional fellowship programs in specific fields (medicine, public health, physical sciences), plus other programs. The proliferation of student aid programs since 1965, culminating in the entitlement provisions of the Basic Grant (now Pell Grant) program of the Educational Amendments of 1972 (as amended), has contributed to federal concern for degree and program quality and integrity, particularly at the undergraduate level and in proprietary institutions. The federal government also funds and coordinates a number of programs to improve the quality of higher education focusing on "national educational problems" beyond the scope and resources of state and local governments (e.g., basic skills programs, international education). While the list of federal quality concerns seems long, no doubt the major focus and impact of federal interest (and funding) has been in the area of university-based R & D capacity and ancillary issues such as scientific and medical training.

THE RESPONSIBILITY FOR EQUALITY

Just as education is the primary domain of the states, so too it would seem that the states are primarily responsible for assuring and providing equality of educational opportunity. Yet the primacy of the state in education and the constitutionally dictated balance of powers among levels and branches of government have inevitably led to conflict over priorities and programs.

Frances Keppel, former U.S. commissioner of education, states, "The conventional wisdom acquired during the 1960s and 1970s suggests that the federal government has set the right agenda on such issues as civil rights, poverty, and policies for minority groups and the handicapped—issues which state governments have generally neglected."[10] Observing that the history of the past two decades shows an "uneasy relationship between federal purpose and state performance" on such educational issues as equal opportunity and desegregation, Keppel notes that policymakers and educators often forget that "the states' willingness to administer a program electively is the key to success of federal programs."[11]

The tensions implicit in the gap between federal priorities and state performance are not new. The growing significance of the federal role in higher education adds to the current tensions and highlights once again the distinct nature of federal and state roles. These tensions are not likely to recede because of the priority/performance gap and because litigation remains the primary form of redress for the perceived failures of state and local governments to meet espoused domestic priorities in the area of equality of educational opportunity.

The State Responsibility

State support for "mortar and brick" issues during the postwar years implicitly addressed the issue of educational access and opportunity long before these concerns were part of the federal policy agenda. Patrick Callan states:

The primary and financial responsibility for meeting the educational needs of the American people resides with the states. For the last two decades state energies and resources in higher education have focused on the expansion of opportunity in response to rapid growth of the college-age population, higher proportions of high school graduates, and increased participating rates. Since the 1960 California *Master Plan for Higher Education*, the first formal state commitment to provide education after high school to all who had the desire and motivation to benefit, the states have been at the forefront of the national movement to improve access. The state master plans developed during the sixties and early seventies were essentially blueprints for increasing access, and they led to dramatic increases in the numbers of programs and institutions of postsecondary education. The approaches used by the states have varied but generally have included some combination of ensuring geographic proximity, enlarging institutions, developing new institutions and programs (most notably community colleges and vocational programs), providing student financial assistance, and increasing institutional support.[12]

Callan adds that, while the federal role has become increasingly important and financially significant, the states are primarily responsible for "the task of linking factors related to access—student aid, various forms of institutional support, and articulation between high schools and colleges . . . ideally working in collaboration with campuses."[13] He notes that although the goal of equal access and opportunity has yet to be fully realized, the progress of the past two decades has been significant.

Not all observers would agree with this assessment. Although the states and their education agencies and institutions are concerned about expanding educational opportunity, a number of other issues appear to have a much higher priority, at least as indicated in annual agency reports.[14] And, although the states did create the structures required to accommodate increasing numbers of postsecondary students, many critics argue that they have not been as successful in dealing with the real heart of the issue of educational opportunity—increasing the entry and retention rates of nontraditional (i.e., low-income, disadvantaged, minority, handicapped) students in public higher education. Federal incentives and aid programs have been responsible for much of the movement of nontraditional students into public colleges and universities. And the *Adams* case, pertaining to the role and mission of historically black public colleges in state systems, serves as a lingering reminder of the discriminatory impacts of previous state policies and practices.

Public policy generally has focused on the issue of access to any postsecondary institution, assuming approximately equivalent impacts and benefits of college attendance, an assumption not supported by nearly three decades of research on college students and institutional impacts.[15] The meritocratic criteria frequently found in state master plans have a policy impact clearly reflected in expenditure patterns across levels of public higher education (see Table 5.2). Financial resources are concentrated at the top of the institutional hierarchy, in the universities. University expenditures for educational and general (E & G) items—perhaps the best measure of an institution's investment in its students—are more than 40 percent higher than in public four-year colleges and almost 60 percent higher than in the community colleges. The extent to which public institutions subsidize their students also varies significantly: Universities have a mean FTE subsidy that is nearly 50 percent greater than that of other institutions. These figures suggest that one important aspect of the equality issue relates to the distribution of educational resources and the concentration of resources in the "least accessible" or more selective institutions.[16]

The expenditure figures reflect, in part, perceptions of the differing costs of equality (at the two- and four-year colleges) and quality (in the universities). Clark Kerr was among the first to describe the quality versus equality debate from the standpoint of the states, warning that they would find it difficult to satisfy the academic community's heightened expectations for program expansion and quality improvement and at the same time accommodate the increasing numbers of high school graduates with degree aspirations.[17] Indeed, the states' interest in and responsibility for educational access and opportunity at all degree levels, and for all citizens—not just

Table 5.2
Mean Expenditures in Public Institutions, Academic Year 1977 (Per Full-Time Equivalent Student)[a]

Expenditure Item	Universities	Institution[b] Four-Year Colleges	Community Colleges
Educational and General	$4,816	$3,358	$3,019
Library	163	136	108
Subsidy[c]	4,334	2,928	2,190

[a]Adjusted to include higher FTE costs of graduate education.

[b]Classification based on Carnegie Council typology.

[c]Subsidy = (Education and General Expenditure) + (Financial Aid) - Tuition.

Source: Special analysis of the 1977 Higher Education General Information Survey (HEIGIS) data by the Higher Education Research Institute.

recent high school graduates—may well conflict with traditional notions of academic quality. However, as previously noted, state perceptions about the attributes of quality are changing. This shift in perspective is in large part a response to the demands from a number of constituencies for an accounting of (1) the resources allocated to public postsecondary education, and (2) the availability and distribution of educational opportunities to various clientele.[18] State program review, with its focus on accountability, equality, and quality—accountability and efficiency in the use of resources, equality of educational opportunity, and quality of education programs—also contributes to a new awareness of the nature of the state responsibility for higher education.[19]

The Federal Responsibility

Since 1965 first blacks and American Indians, and later others—Hispanics, the poor, women, and the handicapped—have been the implicit if not specific beneficiaries of a range of federal programs intended to expand educational opportunity. Both legislation and litigation have contributed to federal concern for equality of educational opportunity.

Prior to 1965 federal forays into higher education were generally linked to areas often only marginally related to higher education. This led to what might be called a contextually defined "quality/equality cycle" in federal higher education policy. Specific "equality" concerns were explicit in the legislation; underlying egalitarian principles were often implicit, and in time would become dominant.

In the 1860s the Morrill Act provided federal incentives for the growth, development, and curricular focus of public higher education. The practical and agricultural curricula stipulated by the legislation reflected egalitarian interests in an era marked by more aristocratic priorities.

By accident or intent, the GI Bill was largely responsible for the immediate surge in college enrollments following World War II. More than two million veterans of the Second World War used their educational benefits to pursue some form of postsecondary education. It brought to the nation's college campuses thousands of former servicemen who otherwise would not have attended college and thus contributed to a tremendous increase in upward social mobility. It is not clear that Congress had such goals in mind when, in 1943, it first passed legislation intended to assist disabled veterans' return to postwar jobs. The scope of the legislation was expanded in 1944 as much to reward returning veterans as to assist in postwar economic recovery.

Harry Truman was the first postwar president to encourage federal support for equality of educational opportunity. Conscious of the traditional state responsibility for education (and of congressional opposition to a federal role in education), Truman advocated using federal funds to reduce inequalities in state educational expenditures. He also appointed the first federal commission charged with the task of examining the goals and functions of American higher education. The 1947 report of the President's Commission on Higher Education espoused a broad set of egalitarian goals and policy objectives, not all of which were warmly received by the higher education community.[20] The commission called for an end to racial and religious discrimination in higher education and advocated the expansion of the public sector, particularly two-year colleges, as an effective way to expand and equalize educational opportunities for all citizens. Truman's public statements and the commission's recommendations underscored growing federal concern for an end to discrimination and for the expansion of educational opportunity.

During much of the postwar period litigation rather than legislation helped to define a federal responsibility for equality of educational opportunity. A series of U.S. Supreme Court decisions, ultimately leading to the historic 1954 *Brown* decision, helped give form and focus to the federal concern for equality.

Beginning in 1964 three sweeping pieces of legislation—the Economic Opportunity Act of 1964, the Civil Rights Act of 1964, and the Higher Education Act of 1965—radically transformed the federal role and presence in higher education. Disadvantaged youth, a major focus of the Economic Opportunity Act, found two federal programs to support their college aspirations: Upward Bound was designed to help them gain college entry, and

Table 5.3
Government Outlays for Higher Education, 1976–1977

	Amount (in billions of dollars)	Percent
Federal Government		
Research	$2.717	9.9%
Student Aid	6.482	23.7
Other	2.532	9.2
State Governments		
Institutional Support	13.426	49.0
Student Aid	.589	2.2
Local Government	1.631	6.0
Total Government Outlays	$27.378	100.0%

Source: Carnegie Council on Policy Studies in Higher Education, 3000 Futures (San Francisco: Jossey-Bass, 1980), Table A-6.

the College Work-Study program provided them with subsidized, on-campus, part-time employment. The Civil Rights Act prohibited discriminatory practices in federally supported programs, and used federal funding as a "carrot and stick" to enforce compliance. And the Higher Education Act espoused a broad set of egalitarian objectives for American higher education.

The federally funded student aid programs, first begun in 1965, perhaps best reflect the extent of federal concern and responsibility for equality. The decision to aid students, rather than institutions, clearly placed the federal government on the side of equality of student access and educational opportunity. The change in federal policy—as manifested in the "all who can benefit" focus of the Higher Education Act of 1965—led eventually to the entitlement provisions of the Basic Grants program established by the Educational Amendments of 1972.

The changing federal role in higher education is reflected in the rapid expansion of student aid and related support programs, coupled with the leveling off of constant-dollar federal R & D funding. These two trends resulted in a dramatic shift in the allocation of federal higher education expenditures; thus in 1967, 65 percent of the expenditures went for insti-

Table 5.4
Total Outlays for Student Aid, 1976–1977

	Amount (in billions of dollars)	Percent
Federal	$6.482	80.2%
State Programs	.589	7.3
Institutional Funds[a]	.659	8.2
Private Sources[b]	.350	4.3
Total Student Aid Outlay	$8.080	100.0%

[a] Total institutional aid expenditures, which may originate from both public and private sources.

[b] Estimated.

Source: Carnegie Council on Policy Studies in Higher Education, 3000 Futures (San Francisco: Jossey-Bass, 1980), Table A-6.

tutional support, largely R & D funding, and student aid allocations amounted to only 35 percent of the total. By 1975 student aid totaled 72 percent of federal higher education expenditures, and institutional support dropped to 28 percent.[21] In the 1976–1977 academic year federal student aid expenditures accounted for almost one-fourth of total (federal, state, local) government expenditures for higher education (see Table 5.3) and for just over 80 percent of total government student aid outlays (see Table 5.4).

The postwar change in federal policy defines the broad context of government concern for equality. Government, and particularly federal government, roles and responsibilities increased, prodded by both litigation and an expanding definition of government responsibility for the commonweal. During the 1960s and 1970s the academic community, "enthusiastically sharing in the national fervor for equal opportunity and social mobility through education," responded to a combination of government directives and incentives designed to expand educational opportunity and promote equality.[22]

SUMMARY AND CONCLUSIONS

The growth of government support for higher education has also affected the government responsibility for quality and equality in higher education. Litigation and legislation have established the federal role and defined the nature of state responsibility for equality; government interest in and concern for quality have been linked implicitly to the federal commonweal concern and to growing public and state government demands for accountability. The likelihood of changing federal education priorities as part of an effort to control the federal budget signals the end of the concurrent state and federal support for both improving quality and expanding equality in higher education. The declining level of real-dollar support for higher education seems certain to increase the implicit competition for funding among the constituencies representing "quality" and "equality" factions.

The fiscal consequences of the anticipated "enrollment crisis" of the 1980s will further complicate government efforts to shift and sort its priorities for higher education. While it may be difficult to retreat from existing commitments to both quality and equality, it may also become very difficult to make new ones.

NOTES

1. Mr. Justice Douglas, opinion, in *Sweezy v. New Hampshire*, 354 US 234 (1957).

2. Frances Keppel, "Education in the Eighties," *Harvard Education Review* 50 (1980):149–53.

3. J. W. Evans, *Dissemination: Current Status and Proposed Initiatives* (Washington, D.C.: Division of Educational Replication, U.S. Office of Education, June 1979), p. 1.

4. Chester E. Finn, Jr., *Dollars, Scholars, and Bureaucrats* (Washington, D.C.: Brookings Institution, 1978), Table 2.1.

5. See William K. Sheldon, *Accreditation* (New York: Harper, 1960); Fred F. Harcleroad, *Accreditation: History, Process, and Problems* (Washington, D.C.: American Association of Higher Education, 1980); and Kenneth C. Green, "Program Review and the State Responsibility for Higher Education," *Journal of Higher Education* 52 (January/February 1981):67–80.

6. D. Kent Halstead, *Statewide Planning for Higher Education* (Washington, D.C.: Government Printing Office, 1974), p. 5.

7. California State Department of Education, *A Master Plan for Higher Education in California, 1960–1975* (Sacramento: California State Department of Education, 1960), p. 66.

8. See Green, "Program Review and the State Responsibility"; Robert J. Barak and Robert O. Berdahl, *State-Level Academic Program Review in Higher Education* (Denver: Education Commission of the States, 1978); and E. C. Lee and F. M. Bowen, *The Multicampus University* (San Francisco: Jossey-Bass, 1975).

9. Sloan Commission on Government and Higher Education, *A Program for Reviewed Partnership* (Cambridge, Mass.: Ballinger, 1980), pp. 16–17, 102–105.

10. Keppel, "Education in the Eighties," p. 149.

11. Ibid.

12. Ibid.

13. Patrick M. Callan, "The State Role after *Bakke*: Toward Collaborative Action," in *Admitting and Assisting Students after Bakke*, ed. A. W. Astin, B. Fuller, and K. C. Green (San Francisco: Jossey-Bass, 1978), pp. 54–55.

14. Richard Millard, *State Boards of Higher Education* (Washington, D.C.: American Association for Higher Education, 1976), p. 59.

15. See Kenneth Feldman and Theodore Newcomb, *The Impact of College on Students* (San Francisco: Jossey-Bass, 1969); Alexander W. Astin, *Four Critical Years* (San Francisco: Jossey-Bass, 1977), Chapter 9.

16. Alexander W. Astin, "Equal Access to Postsecondary Education: Myth or Reality?" *UCLA Educator* 19 (Spring 1977):8–17.

17. Clark Kerr, *The Uses of the University* (Cambridge, Mass.: Harvard University Press, 1963).

18. Callan, "The State Role after *Bakke.*"

19. See Green, "Program Review and the State Responsibility," passim.

20. President's Commission on Higher Education, *Higher Education for American Democracy* (Washington, D.C.: Government Printing Office, 1947).

21. Daryl E. Carson, *Student Access to Postsecondary Education: A Comparative Analysis of Federal and State Aid Programs* (Los Angeles: Higher Education Research Institute, 1978).

22. Finn, *Dollars, Scholars, and Bureaucrats*, p. 23.

6

Higher Education's Evaluation Politics

Richard M. Englert

Many attempts have been made at defining the political aspects of education.[1] The critical question is what differentiates political phenomena from other kinds of phenomena. Several of the most useful ways of answering this question involve such concepts as power, influence, control, government, conflict, policymaking, and authoritative allocations.[2] Various researchers use one or more of these concepts to identify the existence of politics and to analyze its different forms. For example, Gerald Sroufe depicts "politics" most graphically in the following passage:

Politics has to do with the distribution of stakes within a society or group. "Stakes" means jobs, money, prestige, influence, status, or even acceptance of ideas. People care enough about such stakes to try actively to influence their distribution. To this end they develop and husband their influence, and seek to use it wisely to affect the distribution of stakes. "Politics ain't bean bag."[3]

When the above concepts are applied to evaluation, its political nature becomes apparent.[4] Evaluations are derived from biased origins, in the sense that there are often political motivations behind the decision to evaluate something.[5] Moreover, the choice of which program is evaluated is often a result of politics, insofar as politicians create and fund programs to address certain problems and please constituencies.[6] Evaluators themselves have basic political orientations that can influence their conduct during evaluations.[7] Political forces can dictate the kinds of populations sampled, place limitations on the data collected, and influence the design, procedures, and reports of evaluations, as well as affect the impact that evaluations can have.[8] These forces are so prevalent that ultimately methodological considerations are inextricably tied up with political ones so that the evaluator cannot simply be politically neutral in his use of evaluation approaches.[9] In short, from the beginnings of an evaluation to its completion, politics is inescapable at every step.[10]

Yet it is not enough to say merely that external political factors intrude upon the process of evaluation or that participants in evaluations are politically active. Conceptually, the reality of the relationship between politics and evaluation goes even deeper—to the very core of what evaluation is. Lee Cronbach points out that, although evaluation does have a substantial and growing scientific tradition, science is only a subordinate aspect of evaluation: "If evaluation is not primarily a scientific activity, what is it? It is first and foremost a political activity, a function performed within a social system."[11] This political nature of evaluation is based upon a central notion of politics; i.e., politics can be defined as those interactions involved in the authoritative allocation of valued commodities (e.g., money, education) for a society.[12] Since evaluations produce judgments of worth about things or people, such judgments involve the potential or real reallocation of existing "stakes" that people have in various goods and services.[13] Consequently, evaluation is part of the "process of who gets what in the society."[14]

The relationship between evaluation and politics can be depicted in three general ways.[15] One way might be called "politics *in* evaluation." Within this general category would be included any number of power struggles, conflicts, and the like that occur during the actual evaluation process. Such politics usually directly involves the participants in the evaluation (e.g., evaluator, client, staff of program being evaluated, the program's immediate constituencies), and the politics of these participants is often directed at influencing the processes and the outcomes of the evaluation. Attempts by a program staff to socialize or influence the evaluator of the program would be an example of politics *in* evaluation.

A second general category might be labeled "politics *and* evaluation," which refers to the interactions that occur between an evaluation process and various societal political systems. The main political systems that often interact with evaluation processes are the federal government and the governments of individual states. To the extent that these governments, through their officers and agencies, affect and are affected by evaluations, politics *and* evaluation are in evidence. An example would be the federal government's mandate that programs funded by Title I of the Elementary and Secondary Education Act be evaluated.

The third general category, "the politics *of* evaluation," is the foundation of the other two. Since one root meaning of politics is that it involves the authoritative allocation of values for a society, evaluation is political insofar as it is involved in making authoritative allocations. A judgment of worth, i.e., an evaluation, necessarily entails support or lack of support for an allocation of resources. Consequently, an evaluation has at least the potential of affecting the existing and future stakes of various competing interests. For example, I recently was a member of an evaluation team whose responsibility it was to evaluate several projects and to choose one for refunding by the state. In this case, the politics *of* evaluation referred to the allocative nature of the evaluation.

In sum, evaluation is highly political in at least three logically distinct but interdependent ways. Participants in the evaluation attempt to influence the evaluation in directions consonant with their self-interests (politics *in* evaluation). Governmental bodies interact with evaluations (politics *and* evaluation). And evaluation judgments potentially or actually reallocate stakes (the politics *of* evaluation). Each of these kinds of evaluation politics is evident in higher education, though the unique nature of academic institutions affects the ways in which politics is manifest.

ORGANIZED ANARCHY, AUTONOMY, AND MESSY PLURALISM

Three aspects of American higher education are especially noteworthy for an understanding of evaluation politics in academe. Higher education institutions operate quite differently from most organizations in our society. Also, academic institutions have traditionally exercised a great amount of independence from external control. And finally, higher education is noted for its diversity. Each of these characteristics warrants some discussion.

Higher education institutions (specifically universities and colleges) exhibit neither the bureaucratic structures and processes of most other large organizations nor the collegiality that many academics have often claimed. Rather, academic institutions usually fit the patterns of a more political model, one that Victor Baldridge and others term "organized anarchy."[16] Their model entails the following elements, the combination of which makes higher education a unique arena for evaluation politics:

1. Goals are normally vague and multifaceted; highly specific goals are ususally highly contested.

2. The people served by higher education institutions often demand influence over institutional decision making.

3. There is no one "correct" way or technology to accomplish goals.

4. Higher education institutions are dominated by academic professionals who demand considerable autonomy and expect performance reviews to be done only by peers.

5. Academic professionals are not a cohesive group, often having closer ties and

more loyalty to colleagues within the same discipline around the world than to colleagues of different disciplines within the same institution.

6. Within an institution conflict is normal, participation by academics in institutional decision making is highest among those who vie for such power, formal authority is relatively limited, and external interest groups and agencies have a growing influence over institutional decision making.[17]

Since many evaluation approaches focus pointedly upon goals, the inability of higher education institutions to define goals clearly means that academic evaluators are likely to meet considerable resistance. Likewise, the absence of agreement regarding the appropriate means or technologies for meeting goals probably makes the evaluation of the success of any given technology highly controversial. In addition, it might be expected that individuals and interest groups within academic institutions (including professors) would vie for the power to evaluate; at the same time they would resist being evaluated. And the widespread presence of fragmented groups and intra-institutional conflict implies that any potential weapon, such as evaluation, could be employed in the struggles to determine who gets what. Such a political atmosphere cannot help but reinforce the political nature of evaluation.

This organized anarchy exists along with another characteristic feature of academic institutions—their traditional autonomy. As Robert Berdahl has indicated, institutions of higher education have traditionally exhibited three kinds of independence.[18] Intellectual independence (known as "academic freedom") means that faculty have a degree of autonomy from external pressures (especially of the government) in matters related to the exploration, discussion, expression, and teaching of ideas. Faculty tenure is seen by some as a device that insulates academic freedom from political influences. Academic independence ("substantive autonomy") refers to the relative autonomy institutions and facilities have traditionally had in dealing with substantive academic matters such as institutional goals, admissions standards, grading policies, and other concerns at the heart of the academic mission. Most states have adopted through constitutions or legislation some form of a self-denying ordinance, whereby states have agreed to provide funding to higher education while at the same time limiting their own control over how the institutions govern themselves and use those funds. Administrative independence ("procedural autonomy") refers to the degree of autonomy that institutions of higher education have enjoyed in determining the administrative procedures used to meet institutional goals. The extent of each of these three kinds of autonomy has varied from state to state.

Particularly pertinent to this discussion are these facts: 1) the greater the autonomy of an institution of higher education, the less vulnerable it is to outside influence (such as external evaluations by governmental agencies); 2) autonomy usually implies that any evaluations that do occur will be self-evaluations and peer evaluations; and 3) as several authors have noted, the traditional autonomies are being eroded by external pressures, especially as states demand more accountability for their dollars of support, as consumer protection and student protection movements grow stronger, and as the impact of specific governmental mechanisms such as "sunset" legislation, right-to-privacy and confidentiality regulations, and public disclosure mandates are more widely felt.[19] Many of the sources of these external pressures use evaluations as a means of gaining more control over the once autonomous institutions of higher education.

A third characteristic feature of higher education is its diversity. What Berdahl calls a "messy pluralism" is a whole range of profit and nonprofit, public and nonpublic institutions.[20] Baldridge and others classify the many higher education institutions into the following categories (while recognizing that there is considerable intra-category variance): private multiversities, public multiversities, elite liberal arts colleges, public comprehensive institutions, public colleges, private liberal arts colleges, community colleges, and private junior colleges.[21] Moreover, there has been some pressure recently to replace the term "higher education" with a more comprehensive term, "postsecondary education." The latter refers to "an expanding variety of institutions, programs, and delivery systems in many different settings and under various forms of sponsorship."[22]

This "messy pluralism" is particularly evident in the vast array of state, regional, and national coordinating bodies, postsecondary systems, governmental agencies, professional associations, accrediting bodies, and lobbying groups, and it has major consequences for any attempts at evaluation. There is a great deal of competition at all levels of higher education, a competition that often uses evaluation as a political weapon to further certain interests. And there is likely to be a great deal of disagreement regarding appropriate goals and means to attain those goals at the levels of individual institutions, statewide systems, or within higher education as a whole.

By way of summary, organized anarchy, autonomy, and messy pluralism characterize higher education. Whereas evaluation is by nature a political process, the specific political forms manifest in higher education are in large part dependent upon these three characteristics. These specific manifestations can be categorized in three general ways: politics *in* evaluation, politics *and* evaluation, and the politics *of* evaluation.

Politics in Higher Education Evaluation

As is true of most evaluations, evaluation in higher education often involves relationships among three key parties: the evaluator (or evaluation team), the decision maker or sponsor for whom the evaluation is made, and a constituency composed of those who have a stake in what is being evaluated. This conceptualization does not preclude self-evaluation, which conceivably could join all three roles in the same individual or group. For the sake of analysis, these parties are viewed here as existing in different individuals. The particular issues involved in self-evaluation are addressed later.

Politics *in* higher education can be said to comprise the political interactions among these three parties. Evaluation participants attempt to maintain or increase personal or group stakes by influencing the evaluation. For example, one evaluation in which I was involved found the evaluators virtually besieged by letters and phone calls ranging from testimonials in favor of the program being evaluated to veiled threats about possible consequences if the program received an "unsatisfactory" evaluation. Those phoning or writing letters had a stake in the program, and they were trying to secure a favorable evaluation by means of raw political power.

Since the organized anarchy model would lead us to expect political activity, one question that needs to be answered is: In what ways do evaluation participants exhibit political behavior? The answer lies in the nature of the evaluator, the decision maker, and the constituency and the propensity of each to act politically when interacting.

The *evaluator* is a political animal to the same extent that anyone else is. Though she may strive to be objective and rational,[23] her role as evaluator has several political dimensions when she interacts with the decision maker and a constituency. As Carol Weiss notes, the evaluator's basic inclination is reformist.[24] Since social scientists in general tend to be concerned with shaping the future,[25] and since the dominant political orientation of college and university faculty is liberal,[26] those evaluators who are also faculty members may be expected to have a general pattern of political leanings. It is unclear to what extent such leanings actually affect evaluations, but from the viewpoint of political analysis such a general orientation has at least the potential for influencing evaluation results.

One way in which the general political orientation of the evaluator could enter into an evaluation is the evaluator's choice of an evaluation approach. Ernest House describes the political assumptions underlying eight different evaluation models.[27] The choice of one of these models (e.g., accreditation) necessarily involves a choice of certain political assumptions (e.g., the government should have a relatively minor role in evaluating). Similarly, a choice of a given approach to evaluation usually carries with it an implicit assumption about how goals are determined within an institution.[28] The evaluation of a program's success by comparing outcomes with goals implies that the goals have already been set rather than that goals are being constantly renegotiated. In the organized anarchy of higher education, such an assumption might operate to the detriment of certain factions engaged in negotiating institutional goals.

In addition to general political orientations and assumptions, the evaluator also has political motivations of her own that may affect the evaluation. Higher education's organized anarchy necessitates the accumulation of power in order to affect policy decisions and to maintain organizational status. In institutions that pride themselves on respect for knowledge, the accumulation of knowledge has a certain amount of power, and increased power is needed to gain more knowledge. Aaron Wildavsky makes just this point in his commentary on the evaluator (evaluative man): "Evaluative man seeks knowledge, but he also seeks power. His desire to do good is joined with his will to act powerfully. . . . Evaluative man is well off when he can pyramid his resources so that great knowledge leads to enhanced power, which in turn increases access to information."[29] One manner in which the evaluator who is also a faculty member pyramids power in Wildavsky's sense is to be promoted and tenured. Since evaluation is a relatively new field, any evaluator who wishes to establish academic legitimacy by means of the standard criteria associated with scholarship, teaching, and service may find herself forced to emphasize "more respected" lines of scientific inquiry (such as experimental research designs and sophisticated statistical analysis) in evaluations. Yet such research designs, because of the nature of scientific inquiry, may have an inherent conservative bias.[30] The evaluator's attempts to enhance her personal power and prestige may, therefore, result in the rejection of potentially useful solutions to problems because of overly stringent designs or tests. Similarly, findings are often published when they are generalizable to larger populations. Yet evaluations almost always deal with phenomena that are situation-specific and rarely transferable to other settings.[31] It is conceivable that the evaluator could find her need for legitimacy in the eyes of colleagues in conflict with the dictates of the evaluation.

The *decision maker* or sponsor is also a source of potential political activity. In many cases he sponsors the evaluation and takes such action as he sees fit on the basis of the results. In the academic world, the decision maker is often a faculty member who rose to the heights (though many faculty might say fell to the depths) of administration. In the context of organized anarchy, where power is relatively fluid and diffuse, the administrator is regarded as a colleague or peer on temporary assignment rather than a permanent boss. For this reason, the administrator who wants to exercise his authority needs to bolster it by building power coalitions and wielding information. Evaluation thus becomes a source of data as well as a means for building support for a position. It has been my experience that the administrator's decision to evaluate something is frequently more politically motivated than disinterested, and often a means of testing the waters to determine what political support someone or something might have. A comment by House is particularly apropos here: "Evaluation is always derived from biased origins. When someone wants to defend something or to attack something, he often evaluates it. Evaluation is a motivated behavior."[32]

It should not be surprising, therefore, when a decision maker conveys to the evaluator his expectations about what he hopes the evaluation results will be. The evaluator, who is usually hired by or in some way responsible to the decision maker, is then under at least subtle pressure to produce the desired evaluation results. One colleague of mine tells how she was hired to evaluate several campus programs and how the decision maker told her beforehand that he hoped she would find that such a program was indeed the most successful of all. Of course, any evaluator worth her salt, as she was, would not be consciously influenced by such remarks. Interestingly, she did admit she was at least a little relieved when the data clearly indicated that the expected program was the most successful. There is no telling, however, what the unconscious effects of the decision maker's suggestion were.

Just as the decision to evaluate is political, so too is the making of the decision on the basis of the evaluation data. There are many reports of cases in which action was taken on findings that fit academic decision maker's preconceived conclusions, while contrary findings were simply ignored.[33] In such cases, evaluations serve to legitimize beliefs already held, such a legitimization being a very important resource to an academic decision maker in need of a political weapon.

Yet the academic administrator operating in an organized anarchy often does not have the power to act unilaterally. The fluid nature of academic power often demands that a group of faculty (aka a committee) be a decision point for action. Anyone who has worked with committees knows that the group dynamics inherent in committee work can preclude substantive action. Alexander Astin conducted a study in which a sample of higher education institutions was provided with evaluation data. Task forces in each institution were charged with taking whatever action they deemed appropriate given the evaluation data. The results were what Astin termed "academic games," that is, defensive tactics that committees used in order to avoid coming to grips with the data. Such games included "passing the buck" (i.e., leaving the substantive decisions to another committee), "rationalization" (i.e., arguing that bad data are really good if only seen in the proper perspective), and "displacement/projection" (i.e., shifting the attention to some outside source).[34] Such tactics should be anticipated in an environment in which the locus of power is often shifting and power coalitions need to be fashioned continuously.

In addition to an evaluator and decision maker, evaluations often involve a *constituency* for what is being evaluated. In the case of a program that is being evaluated, the constituency would include the program staff and those who derive some benefit from the program. Generally, the constituency tends to view the evaluation as a threat. After all, it is merely human nature that people resent being evaluated.

Constituencies are reluctant to be evaluated because of the possible adverse effects of negative evaluations. House observes that in the case of special, innovative projects in universities, there is a strong potential for a clash between entrepreneurial initiative and evaluations. He argues that it is inevitable for an evaluation to find at least one problem with a project.

The very nature of the funding of special projects almost demands that the project writer cite goals that are not fully attainable. These ideal goals are needed to secure funding, but they never translate into action exactly as written. And once funded, the project takes on a life of its own. Project staff believe the project to be good, and as it matures a myth of success develops. The evaluator, analyzing performance vis-à-vis ideal goals, is bound to identify some degree of lack of fit. The project staff reacts strongly for two reasons. First, their belief system has become very strong. Second, project staff members, especially the director, are usually upwardly mobile entrepreneurs. They realize that they personally need unblemished records if they are to advance. Yet the structure of a university is such that, because the people in the top positions are not more competent than those at the bottom, job contenders are more often excluded because of blemishes on their record than are chosen because of true merit. The evaluator's least hint of failure for a project could potentially damage the entrepreneur's reputation. As House concludes, the case of the evaluation of special projects exemplifies the fact that universities are ill-equipped to handle critical evaluations.[35]

Since constituencies are reluctant to be evaluated, a counteroffensive against the evaluation can be anticipated. This usually comes in the form of either trying to prevent the evaluation or attacking the evaluation if it produces results perceived to be negative. If the evaluation has been sponsored by an academic administrator, he is barraged with appeals to call it off. Copies of these appeals are sent to his superiors or supporters. Data are brandished in keeping with the constituency's belief system that the project is good. Since vocal power blocs are usually powerful within the organized anarchy of higher education, every attempt is made to create an inflated image of the power of the constituency. If the evaluation is mandated by an external funding source or if the tactic of prevention is not successful, then criticism of the evaluation itself (if it is perceived to be negative) is the next tactic. Politically, this can be effective for two reasons. Since evaluations must deal with relatively short-term deadlines and are situation-specific, their methodologies are never pure, in the textbook sense of ideal designs. Also, since the staff of the program being evaluated is probably conversant with research methodology and more knowledgeable about the program than the evaluator, attacks on the evaluation can be both scholarly and comprehensive. These attacks can serve as a rational basis for the political activities of constituencies.

Finally, not all evaluations are necessarily negative. Attempts can be made early in the evaluation to socialize the evaluator into the belief system of the program staff and wider constituency. The evaluator, once socialized, can emphasize the intangibles that the program is affecting and the enthusiasm of staff and constituency.[36] In higher education the likelihood of socialization may be enhanced to the extent that the evaluator and the program staff view themselves as colleagues and peers. And the staff and constituency can use a positive evaluation as a political weapon to increase the image and power of the program.

In brief, politics *in* higher education evaluation can surface in many forms. The evaluator's general orientation, assumptions, and motivations have political bases. The decision maker's decision to evaluate and his prior expectations can influence the evaluation, while his action or inaction affects the impact of the evaluation. The constituency of what is being evaluated is reluctant to have an evaluation occur, and thus tries either to halt the evaluation, attach a negative judgment, or socialize the evaluator into the staff's views of the positive sides of the program.

Politics and Higher Education Evaluation

Whereas "politics *in* higher education evaluation" refers to the attempts by participants to influence an evaluation, "politics *and* higher education evaluation" entails the interrelationships between governmental political systems and the process of evaluation. More specifically, this term emphasizes the ways in which federal or state politics affects evaluations or is affected by evaluations. To analyze "politics *and* higher education," three relationships need to be addressed: the relation between the academic evaluator and the political decision maker, the influence political systems have upon evaluation processes, and the effect that evaluation has on political systems. These relationships are especially complex in higher education because of its long tradition of institutional autonomy and messy pluralism. Government actions are often viewed as intruding upon the academic environment and tending to impose uniform standards that constrain the diversity of higher education institutions.

Evaluators and Decision Makers. To understand the relationship between the academic evaluator and the political decision maker, it is important to realize that each operates on the basis of different values, assumptions, and objectives.[37] Academic evaluators are essentially social scientists. In contrast to political decision makers they tend to be more egalitarian and libertarian, less attentive to the political and monetary costs of situations, more concerned with logic and rationality, and more inclined to support societal change. Moreover, academics are often out of their element in dealing with policy matters.

University researchers are used to choosing their own problems on grounds that derive from the state of their discipline and its theoretical development. They tend to select problems that fit the methods that they know and prefer. They like to take the time to do respectable research, win the plaudits of their colleagues, and gain academic rewards through publication in prestige journals.[38]

But political decision makers do not have the luxury of doing exhaustive research. Because of elections, public officials have relatively short periods of time in which to launch initiatives and produce results. They look for immediate answers and are under too much pressure to gather evidence painstakingly or to conduct adequate assessments. Consequently, tensions and communication gaps develop between the political official and the academic evaluator, with the former trying to push the latter to develop concrete, value-laden recommendations for action and yes-or-no answers. These tensions are intensified by the nature of the political process; new social programs have political origins, embody political priorities, and have political consequences; therefore, any evaluation necessarily enters into the political arena of constituency politics.[39]

Political Systems and Evaluation Processes. Because of the stakes involved, it is no wonder that the political system often influences evaluations. This occurs in many ways. The political system has funded numerous evaluation projects in its attempt to assess performance. Some evaluations are funded by grants from government agencies, the grants being awarded on a competitive basis to individuals after the proposals have been reviewed by a group of peers. Other evaluations are supported by government contracts, although academic investigators normally receive most of their support through grants.[40] Some evaluations are mandated as part of a funded program. For example, a bilingual education resource center is funded by federal funds, but the center is required, or at least expected, to spend some of the money for evaluation purposes to see how well the center is accomplishing its goals. And still other evaluations are required by various pieces of federal legislation that include evaluation components. Thus, Title IX of the 1972 Education Amendments, which forbids sexual discrimination in any educational program receiving federal funds, includes a provision for self-evaluation by institutions to determine the degree of compliance with federal nondiscrimination policies. No matter what the specific vehicle for support, the federal government has initiated, supported, or mandated a large number of evaluation projects, most of which probably would never have been undertaken without federal involvement. This involvement represents a major influence upon higher education institutions, insofar as they must comply with federal requirements or as they voluntarily redirect resources toward federal priorities in order to take advantage of the available funding. Similarly, such federal involvement has provided a great impetus for the evaluation as a whole.

Yet such funding rarely comes without strings, and through numerous strings the government's presence is felt at the institutional level. Forms that are used as part of an evaluation (e.g., to collect data) can be liable to review and clearance procedures by federal agencies, including the Office of Budget and Management. In one documented case, such clearance required in excess of 1,400 pages of paperwork at a cost of over $150,000 in preparation and materials, and months of waiting for federal approval.[41]

Evaluation projects are subject to federal regulations regarding privacy, freedom of information, and protection of human subjects.[42]

Because they involve judgments of worth, evaluations can also involve litigation. For example, in Delaware the dean of an institution that was being evaluated for accreditation sued a member of the accreditation team on the grounds that the latter made defamatory statements in his report.[43] In addition, there have been a number of court cases regarding the evaluation of the performance of professors, especially where tenure and promotion decisions were involved.[44] What emerges, therefore, is the image of a process subject to influence by the political system through an intricate maze of regulations and legal constraints. To the extent that evaluations are so constrained, the results of the evaluations are likely to be affected.

The word that perhaps best captures the notion that politics influences evaluation in higher education is "accountability." Traditionally, academic institutions have been relatively autonomous, even when they have been funded by state dollars. Increasingly, however, state officials have talked of holding higher education more accountable for its use of state funds. Accountability necessarily involves some level of assessment or evaluation of performance.

The first thing that needs to be said about accountability is that it is much more than an economic notion. In fact, accountability is best understood in terms of such political concepts as control, responsiveness, and power. The calls for accountability are essentially attempts to influence the control of higher education, i.e., who has the power to allocate resources, effort, and the like. Attempts to make higher education institutions more responsive imply that they are to be more responsive to someone. Whether that someone is the student, the government, the profession, or the public at large, power is the issue.[45]

Attempts to hold higher education accountable to state government have increased over the last decade. One form of accountability is performance budgeting, which attempts to allocate resources on the basis of performance measure (i.e., outcome and impact measures). When attempts were made to institute performance measures for higher education in Hawaii and Washington, the higher education institutions vigorously resisted. Interestingly, after the performance measures were completed, those in the "poor" institutions argued that they needed more resources to improve, while those in "good" institutions countered that they deserved increased funding because of their fine performance.[46] In short, performance budgeting as an evaluation of higher education institutions proved inherently political as institutions protected autonomy and diversity.

Another mechanism for state-imposed accountability is the performance audit (or post audit) whereby the effectiveness of an activity or institution in achieving its goals is assessed. Traditionally, such audits have been concerned principally with fiscal and management analyses, especially by quasi-independent commissions. By 1975, however, thirty-six states had assigned auditing functions from quasi-independent commissions to the state legislatures, primarily through their staffs. Even more alarming for higher education institutions is the fact that states are indicating a willingness to go beyond traditional auditing concerns and touch upon academic programs in their audits.[47] Such attempts are patently political insofar as the state government is involved (especially a partisan legislature) and a political purpose is being served (increase of legislative control over higher education institutions).

The problem of applying a performance-audit approach to academic programs is that legislative staffs, while expert in fiscal matters, are not attuned to the subtle nuances of academic programs within diverse academic institutions. For this reason, another mechanism has emerged, which holds institutions accountable but still respects the diversity and academic complexities of higher education. Known as statewide coordinating bodies, these agencies have varying degrees of control over academic institutions, depending on the authority invested by each state. These boards are responsible for program review, and the board members are normally quite knowledgeable about the specifics of higher education programs.[48] Although there is considerable resentment by higher education institutions about the power of these boards over individual institutions, some noted authorities have urged the coordinating bodies to assume the key role in academic program review lest state legislative staffs fill the void and attempt to control academic programs under the guise of accountability.[49]

Institutions of higher education have reacted to these attempts by state agencies to increase control over higher education through various evaluation mechanisms with the same political tactics used by other constituencies: prevent the evaluation or, failing that, attack their legitimacy. One way of preventing the external evaluations is to claim that the institutions are already accountable. This argument proceeds as follows. Institutions have claimed that 1) they must already operate within stringent legal and fiscal constraints; 2) they are evaluated regularly by accreditation agencies; and 3) students can vote with their feet by refusing to attend irresponsible institutions. State officials respond that 1) higher education institutions enjoy an autonomy that no other state institutions have; 2) accreditation procedures have questionable rigor; and 3) there are few examples of widespread student dissatisfaction being an effective accountability tool.[50] Here is not the place to resolve this debate, but merely to point out that in essence it is a political issue, with control and power at stake. Such a confrontation influences both the kinds of evaluations employed and their quality. Ultimately, by affecting the means of evaluation, the movement for accountability can influence the nature of the institutions being evaluated. As Melvin George and Larry Braskamp have noted, "Accountability mechanisms can change the fundamental character of the institution being held accountable."[51] If student credit hour production is the basis of a formula for allocating state funding support to individual institutions of higher education, it is likely that admissions standards will be changed to admit more students, course offerings to attract more, and grading policies and academic standards to retain more. These potential consequences alone make the politics of accountability a serious matter for higher education institutions.

Evaluation and Politics—Another View. Not only is academic evaluation affected by politics; at times the political system is itself influenced by evaluations in higher education. Potentially, information can be an instrument for power in politics, and evaluations can be a source of such information. For example, legislators are usually most eager for information about the success or failure of programs. The reality may be somewhat disappointing. There is evidence that although information plays an important role in policymaking, educational inquiry (including evaluations) has had relatively little direct impact on decision making.[52] I suspect that some of the reason for this lies in the different perspectives of policymakers and evaluators: The outputs of the latter are not geared toward the political needs of the former.

The political system can also be affected by evaluation in another, less direct way. Evaluations are conducted by professionals who hope for financial support from state and federal governments for additional evaluation projects and have a stake in the kinds of legislation regulating the conduct of evaluators that is passed. It stands to reason, therefore, that evaluators will attempt to wield political power to lobby for more government funding and fewer governmental constraints. Recent attempts by the American Education Research Association to develop its political arm (the Government and Professional Liaison Committee) reflect such a growing awareness. From a political perspective, it can be expected that this will be a growing trend as evaluators and researchers in general attempt to counterbalance governmental influences by trying to influence government.

In sum, while there is a basic lack of congruence in the approaches of politicians and academic evaluators, the range of the relationships between the two is very wide. The processes and outputs of the political system influence evaluations through extensive mandates, regulations, and demands for accountability. In turn, evaluations have a strong potential for impact on the political system.

The Politics of Higher Education Evaluation

The essence of politics is the authoritative allocation of values. Hence, the critical political issue in academic evaluation is how it affects the distribution of stakes, i.e., education, life chances, prestige, status, resources, and so on. This issue is at the heart of the politics *of* higher education evaluation.

Four common types of evaluation are examined below. Students are assessed by various tests for admission to institutions and throughout their academic programs. The performance of academic personnel is evaluated, especially for promotion and tenure. The institution itself and its academic programs are regularly reviewed. And any number of internal analyses and judgments are made to determine resource allocations within the institutions. Since these evaluations occur in the academic context, their forms depend upon the organized anarchy, autonomy, and messy pluralism characteristic of higher education.

Student Assessment. Professional autonomy demands that academic professionals have considerable control over which students are allowed into an institution and which can successfully complete their academic programs. Normally, this control is exercised through a series of tests and grades, with the criteria for success established by the professionals within each institution. This entire system of student assessment is largely constructed upon normative, competitive, meritocratic foundations. That is to say, the talented are selected and advanced through the system, while the less talented are not. In political terms, some win and some lose.[53]

This win-lose assumption is built into the admissions policies of higher education.[54] Since the various institutions are by no means equivalent, a student's future is determined not only by whether he attends college but also by which college he attends. Admission policies are generally directed at choosing the best students possible, because competition among institutions for status and resources is usually won by those with the best alumni, i.e., most successful and most prestigious. Thus, instead of admitting students they can help the most, institutions select those most likely to succeed. The outcome of such a system is obvious: "Students denied access to the universities and more selective four-year colleges, including a disproportionate share of low-income and minority students, receive substantially less public subsidy for their postsecondary education than students who enter the more selective public colleges and universities."[55]

It is no wonder, then, that admissions tests have come under close public scrutiny recently and are in many instances bitterly contested. In 1979 New York State passed a truth-in-testing law requiring test companies to make public the validity studies on their tests, to inform those who took the tests of the meaning of those tests, and to give copies of test questions and correct answers to consumers after scores have been sent to institutions. And in 1980 the Ralph Nader Report on the Educational Testing Service (ETS) claimed that the ETS tests serve as "gatekeepers" for many of the rewards of society. The report also maintained that the tests have an effect upon students' chances to enter 50 percent of all U.S. colleges and 75 percent of all U.S. graduate programs. The report concluded:

The ETS test system has operated for years as a large, powerful, and entrenched mechanism that served the interests of its managers; offered convenience, prestige, and political justification to its clients; and, as long as consumers were not organized, made no powerful enemies. ETS has an overwhelming economic and political interest in maintaining the current test system.[56]

Such language indicates that testing has entered the political arena, and the contest is not about the educational value of the tests themselves, but about those valued things to which tests provide a measure of access.

Much the same can be said about the use of student evaluations in general, including grading. Some argue that the effects of grading and other evaluations endure for years. And there is some evidence that student evaluations influence student motivation and performance.[57] The main objection to current grading practices is that they are usually relative, i.e., ranking students in relation to each other rather than indicating the amount any one student has learned. One authority has argued that gain scores (indicative of learning and development) should be emphasized more than relative grades. This reduces the emphasis on winners and losers, on the sorting function of colleges in society.[58]

Clearly, there is a growing awareness that student assessment affects many important outcomes. As the *Bakke* case exemplified, admissions procedures can be highly political precisely because some individuals and groups gain at the expense of others. Those who lose are relegated to inferior institutions that offer less opportunity for later success in certain professions and fields. The understanding of this fact should make us much more careful and conscious about the assumptions underlying any particular assessment approach.

Personnel Evaluation. Just as student assessment affects the distribution of stakes in society, so too does the evaluation of personnel in higher education. In any evaluation, since the issue of control is involved, three questions are most important: Who controls the evaluation? What is evaluated? And by what criteria does the evaluation occur? It is instructive to ask these questions about the evaluation processes involved in the promotion and tenure of higher education faculty, since these are central to the institution of higher education.

Academic organizations place great emphasis upon the professional autonomy of faculty. Professionals have traditionally demanded that they be evaluated only by their peers. This professional control is the result of a lengthy struggle over who has control in academic institutions. As one researcher has noted: "One of the long-term developments in American higher education has been the gradual accumulation of professional power plays, both inside a given institution and outside in professional organizations and unions."[59] In institutions that emphasize graduate study and research, peer influence is most strongly felt in promotion and tenure decisions. In undergraduate institutions and especially community colleges, peer pressure is less strong, and administrators have a stronger role in evaluation. Whoever evaluates has a large measure of control in the institution, since academic organizations are labor-intensive. To the extent that evaluations are determined by peers, external influences upon the academic mission can be minimized, and professionals (particularly tenured ones) can be afforded a degree of insulation from nonprofessional interference. Moreover, through peer evaluation tenured professors have a powerful voice in determining who their long-term peers will be.

What is evaluated has serious implications for the nature of an academic institution. Evaluation is part of the reward system, and the principal rewards for academic professionals are promotion and tenure. Evaluation is thus a means of distributing effort, for those activities that receive the highest priority in the evaluation are likely to be most valued in terms of actual effort. Traditionally, activities that have been evaluated include undergraduate teaching, graduate teaching, research, institutional service, and professional service, though never in equal proportion. In most institutions of higher education, undergraduate teaching has highest priority, followed by research and graduate teaching. However, in large public and private multiuniversities (e.g., Harvard) research is accorded the highest priority.[60] There are some indications, though, that the reward system associated with evaluation can be affected by the national economic situation and by pressures for accountability, that it is not totally in the control of academic professionals. One study found a growing emphasis upon on-campus, student-oriented activities such as teaching and student advising, presumably as a result of economic pressures.[61] If this is true for all of higher education, if professional control over what is evaluated is subject to external forces, then peer evaluation may become a mediating influence between powerful forces and allocations of academic effort.

The criteria for evaluation in cases of tenure and promotion are mainly subjective. This is not to say that no data are employed, because a candidate for promotion and tenure typically submits extensive materials documenting his specific achievements. Rather, the criteria are subjective in the sense that in the final analysis quality of contribution is the crucial criterion. Since there is no agreement in academe regarding the best ways to conduct research or teach, peer judgment of the worth of a candidate's achievements is the final arbiter. This subjective peer judgment represents the means by which professionals control the evaluation process. And since the stakes are high, that is, control over who attains the status of tenured professor, the power of peer judgments is carefully protected. The literature (as well as the personal experiences of myself and many colleagues) is replete with instances of bitter struggles involving faculty, students, and administrators regarding who receives tenure in an institution. University administrators have been driven from office on just this issue. And, since the faculty member who is denied tenure is often terminated in an institution within a given number of years, there have been countless court cases to decide whether or not a given faculty member was denied promotion or tenure legally. The stakes are indeed high.

Yet, because the criteria and judgments are subjective, they can be influenced by the political motivations of various individuals and groups. Indeed, one case study of promotion and tenure procedures at select academic institutions found that there were many complaints about departmental politics and other such factors dictating evaluation results.[62] For this reason, there have been numerous attempts to increase the objectivity of the evaluation process. One growing movement is the use of student ratings of teaching performance. There is evidence that such ratings do have some validity.[63] Yet there are warnings that dependence on such ratings may emphasize the wrong faculty characteristics (e.g., entertaining students).[64] In any case, as the control of students over evaluation outcomes increases, control by the faculty decreases. This could be alarming to those who wish professional peers to have maximum control over which activities are to be emphasized in higher education.

Program and Institutional Review. Two evaluation methods are most common in the area of program and institutional review; accreditation and self-evaluation. Though both are aimed at making judgments about academic quality, the former makes use of a visiting accreditation team, while the latter employs an internal evaluation team.

The stakes involved in accreditation are eligibility and respectability. By federal law, accreditation helps academic institutions become eligible for federal funding. Accreditation is not the only means for eligibility, but it is a central one insofar as other prerequisites to eligibility (e.g., state licensing) often directly or indirectly depend upon accreditation. At the same time, most people place a great deal of faith in the accreditation system:

Operationally, . . . state and local governments, hundreds of employers, trade associations, and individuals rely on accreditation. The concept is firmly embedded in our language and thought patterns. . . . We tend to use "accredited" as if it were synonymous with good, respectable, and acceptable—which in fact it is, more often than not.[65]

When the stakes are as considerable as these, the political question becomes: Who controls the distribution of these stakes? In the case of accreditation, the control lies in three sources: the academic peers who serve on the accreditation teams, the member institutions of the accrediting body, and the organizations seeking to control any given accreditation agency. The peer accreditation team has operational responsibility for site visitation, review of the institution's self-study materials, and development of a report. The actual decision on whether to grant accreditation to a program or an institution is made by the accrediting agency based upon the data reported by the review team. But, since the accreditation agency is usually supported by member institutions (i.e., those reviewed for accreditation), since the agency makes its accreditation judgment on the basis of criteria voted on and adopted by these member institutions, and since each institution has a measure of veto power over who will serve on its accrediting team, one could not characterize the accreditation body as a totally impartial, outside party with no stake in the accreditation results. In fact, peer influence and the ties that exist between an accreditation body and its member institutions strongly suggest that current accreditation procedures may be characterized as an internal evaluation rather than an external one. Certainly this is so in comparison with the classic Flexner accreditation study, in which a nonmedical professional evaluated medical institutions as an external evaluator.[66]

The third source of control over accreditation is not as obvious. Control of accreditation bodies at times involves a struggle among special interest groups. It is exemplified by the case of accreditation for teacher education programs. The appropriate accreditation body is the National Council for Accreditation of Teacher Education (NCATE). The National Education Association (NEA), primarily a teacher organization, has recently been actively attempting to gain control over teacher certification. Such control would mean control over entry to the teaching profession, much as the medical association controls entry into the field of medicine. Specifically, NEA hopes to develop field-based, apprenticeship programs for new teachers, controlled by the NEA. On the other side, the American Association of Colleges of Teacher Education (AACTE) counters that NEA's position operates to the detriment of campus-based, more scholarly approaches to pedagogy, i.e., what might be offered by higher education institutions.[67] Total victory by NEA would mean elimination or at least curtailment of teacher education by colleges and universities, which gives an idea of the stakes involved in accreditation.

Determining Resource Allocations. A fourth kind of evaluation worth examining further highlights the manifestations of the politics *of* higher education evaluation. Every institution must develop a budget to distribute revenues among subunits. Various forms of evaluation serve to provide data for such distributions. As Wildavsky has said, "The budget lies at the heart of the political process."[68]

Needless to say, evaluations associated with the internal budgeting of institutions are highly political, because they concern the allocation of scarce resources. An example would be an actual attempt by a major university to make the budgeting process more rational. Two formulas were used, both based upon changes in total student credit hour production within each subunit. One formula calculated the average "productivity" of subunit faculty by dividing total student credit hours by total number of full-time equivalent faculty (FTE) within each subunit. The result was a ratio expressing how many student credits hours per faculty member each subunit averaged. This ratio was calculated for each of five previous years. The second best ratio during that time was considered the criterion. Since trend analysis could "predict" the total number of student credit hours a subunit would have five years in the future, the number of faculty that unit would need in the future could be determined merely by applying the criterion ratio to any given year. The second formula involved a complex relationship of previous cost per credit over five years, projected student credit hours, and use of a criterion cost per credit ratio based on the subunit's historical pattern of costs and credits.

By going to some length explaining these formulas, emphasis is placed on how rational they were (i.e., proceeding from objective data) and how relatively fair (i.e., each subunit was compared not with other units but with its own historical patterns). Even though these formulas seem rational, in fact they were highly political. As can be imagined, the responses of subunits were not rational. The historical data were attacked as fuzzy and inaccurate, the formulas themselves as favoring certain subunits over others, and the future projections as hopelessly simplistic. What in effect had occurred was that rational formulas had invaded the academic autonomy of various subunits. As with any allocation, there were some winners and some losers. The losers quickly coalesced and formed an effective power bloc within the institution. Academic professionals rallied around the cry that no simple formula could capture the nuances of academic programs. In the end, the formulas fell because the countervailing power, under the guise of academic program, proved stronger.

The allocative nature of evaluation is apparent in the way higher education assesses students, evaluates faculty, reviews programs, and makes budgetary analyses. The politics *of* evaluation represents both the distributions that occur as well as the impact those distributions have on those with a stake in the institution. Because there is a politics *of* academic evaluation, there is also a politics *in* academic evaluation and a politics *and* academic evaluation.

IMPLICATIONS

The implications to be drawn from the above analysis are numerous; three merit special note. First, those who participate in evaluations must recognize their political aspects. If knowledge is power, then the recognition that politics is involved could be valuable. Take the case of the formulas for resource allocation discussed above. If those putting forth such formulas wish to have an effect upon budgetary allocation systems, they must recognize the political nature of what they are doing. They can most assuredly expect a political response, and such a response should be recognized as reasonable and appropriate to the situation. Anticipation of such a response should lead to the development of plans for how to deal with it when it occurs and for possible counterresponses.

Second, this chapter implies that we all can (and need to) become more precise in our use of the term "politics." Most people use the term disparagingly and thoughtlessly. It can in fact be used in a more rigorous fashion. Politics *in* evaluation is not the same as politics *of* evaluation, though they are related. Each may indeed demand different skills. And neither necessarily means anything bad or dirty. Conceptual clarity is both worthwhile in its own right and potentially useful in actual situations.

Finally, it needs to be stressed that just because evaluation is inherently political does not imply that it does not involve rational inquiry. House puts it especially well: "Arguing that all evaluations proceed from biased origins . . . does not necessarily invalidate the study. All knowledge is biased but some of it is also true."[69] Evaluations, when properly and intelligently conducted, are invaluable in increasing our knowledge about various phenomena. The fact that an evaluation is political should be viewed as an asset, not a detriment, to its knowledge value. An evaluation that is both scientifically and politically well conceived and conducted can be a valuable tool for increasing our fund of knowledge and in building political support for the application and use of that knowledge.

NOTES

1. Jay D. Scribner and Richard M. Englert, "The Politics of Education: An Introduction," in *The Politics of Education*, ed. Jay D. Scribner, 76th Yearbook of the National Society for the Study of Education (Chicago: University of Chicago Press, 1977), pp. 1–29.

2. David Easton, "Political Science," in *International Encyclopedia of the Social Sciences*, vol. 12, ed. David L. Sills (New York: Macmillan, 1968), pp. 282–98.

3. Gerald E. Sroufe, "Evaluation and Politics," in *The Politics of Education*, ed. Scribner, p. 290.

4. In this article, "evaluation" is used generically to refer to the assessment of programs, personnel, student performance, and institutional effectiveness.

5. Ernest R. House, ed., *School Evaluation: The Politics and Process* (Berkeley, Calif.: McCutchan, 1973), p. 3.

6. Carol H. Weiss, "Evaluation Research in the Political Context," in *Handbook of Evaluation Research*, vol. 1, eds. Elmer L. Struening and Marcia Guttentag (Beverly Hills: Sage Publications, 1975), pp. 13–26.

7. Gideon Sjoberg, "Politics, Ethics and Evaluation," in *Handbook of Evaluation Research*, vol. 2, eds. Struening and Guttentag, pp. 29–51.

8. Henry M. Brickell, "The Influence of External Political Factors on the Role and Methodology of Evaluation," *Evaluation Comment* 5 (December 1976):1–6.

9. Richard A. Berk and Peter H. Rossi, "Doing Good or Worse: Evaluation Research Politically Re-Examined," *Social Problems* 23 (February 1976):337–49.

10. Richard M. Englert, Michael H. Kean, and Jay D. Scribner, "Politics of Program Evaluation in Large City School Districts," *Education and Urban Society* 9 (August 1977):429–50.

11. Lee J. Cronbach, "Remarks to the New Society," *Evaluation Research Society Newsletter* 1 (April 1977):1.

12. David Easton, *The Political System* (New York: Alfred A. Knopf, 1953).

13. Sroufe, "Evaluation and Politics," p. 290.

14. House, ed., *School Evaluation*, p. 3.

15. Iannaccone's description of a politics *of* education, politics *and* education, and politics *in* education served as a general inspiration for the distinction made here; see Lawrence Iannaccone, *Politics in Education* (New York: Center for Applied Research in Education, 1967). See also Lawrence Iannoccone, "Three Views of Change in Educational Politics," in *The Politics of Education*, ed. Scribner, pp. 255–86.

16. J. Victor Baldridge, David V. Curtis, George Ecker, and Gary L. Riley, *Policy Making and Effective Leadership* (San Francisco: Jossey-Bass, 1978). Their use of the term "organized anarchy" is based on the image by Cohen and March; see M. D. Cohen and James G. March, *Leadership and Ambiguity: The American College President* (New York: McGraw-Hill, 1974). Cohen and March wrote: "In a university anarchy each individual in the university is seen as making autonomous decisions. . . . The 'decisions' of the system are a consequence produced by the system but intended by no one and decisively controlled by no one" (pp. 33–34).

17. Baldridge et al., *Policy Making and Effective Leadership*, pp. 19–27.

18. Robert O. Berdahl, "Secondary and Postsecondary Education: The Politics of Accommodation," in *The Changing Politics of Education*, eds. Edith K. Mosher and Jennings L. Wagoner, Jr. (Berkeley, Calif.: McCutchan, 1978), pp. 227–58.

19. John K. Folger, ed., *Increasing the Public Accountability of Higher Education* (San Francisco: Jossey-Bass, 1977); Peter Schotten and Gary A. Knight, "Effects of the Consumerist Movement on the University," *North Central Association Quarterly* 51 (Spring 1977):377–84; James Dunlap Nowlan, *The Politics of Higher Education: Lawmakers and the Academy in Illinois* (Urbana: University of Illinois Press, 1976).

20. Berdahl, "Secondary and Postsecondary Education." p. 229.

21. Baldridge et al., *Policy Making and Effective Leadership*, pp. 58–61.

22. Kenneth E. Young, "New Pressures on Accreditation," *Journal of Higher Education* 50 (March/April 1979):133.

23. For simplicity, the evaluator will be referred to by the feminine gender and the decision maker by the masculine gender.

24. Weiss, "Evaluation Research in the Political Context," p. 40.

25. Daniel Patrick Moynihan, "Social Science and the Courts," in *Evaluation Studies Review Annual*, vol. 4, eds. Lee Sechrest et al. (Beverly Hills: Sage Publications, 1979), pp. 740–59.

26. Everett Carll Ladd, Jr., and Seymour Martin Lipset, *The Divided Academy: Professors and Politics* (New York: McGraw-Hill, 1975).

27. Ernest R. House, "Assumptions Underlying Evaluation Models," *Educational Researcher* 7 (March 1978):4–12.

28. Ibid., p. 10.

29. Aaron Wildavsky, "The Self-Evaluating Organization," in *Evaluation Studies Review Annual*, vol. 3, eds. Thomas D. Cook et al. (Beverly Hills: Sage Publications, 1978), p. 90.

30. Berk and Rossi, "Doing Good or Worse," passim.

31. Ernest R. House, "Justice in Evaluation," in *Evaluation Studies Review Annual*, vol. 1, ed. Gene V. Glass (Beverly Hills: Sage Publications, 1976), p. 96.

32. House, ed., *School Evaluation*, p. 3.

33. Reginald K. Carter, "Clients' Resistance to Negative Findings," in *School Evaluation*, ed. House, pp. 80–95.

34. Alexander W. Astin, *Academic Gamesmanship: Student-Oriented Change in Higher Education* (New York: Praeger, 1976).

35. Ernest R. House, "The Politics of Evaluation in Higher Education," *Journal of Higher Education* 45 (November 1974):626.

36. House, "Politics of Evaluation," pp. 618–27.

37. Weiss, "Evaluation Research in the Political Context"; Carol H. Weiss, "Policy Research in the University: Practical Aid or Academic Exercise?" *Policy Studies Journal* 4 (Spring 1976):224–28.

38. Weiss, "Policy Research in the University," p. 224.

39. David K. Cohen, "Politics and Research," in *School Evaluation*, ed. House, pp. 97–98.

40. Ilene N. Bernstein and Howard E. Freeman, *Academic and Entrepreneurial Research: The Consequences of Diversity in Federal Evaluation Studies* (New York: Russell Sage, 1975), pp. 8ff.

41. Launor F. Carter, "Federal Clearance of Educational Evaluation Instruments: Procedural Problems and Proposed Remedies," *Educational Researcher* 6 (June 1977):7–12.

42. JoAnn Weinberger and John A. Michael, "Federal Restrictions on Educational Research," *Educational Researcher* 5 (December 1976):3–8; Michael and Weinberger, "Federal Restrictions on Educational Research: Protection for Research Participants," *Educational Researcher* 6 (January 1977):3–7; Weinberger and Michael, "Federal Restrictions on Educational Research: A Status Report on the Privacy Act," *Educational Researcher* 6 (February 1977):5–8; Michael and Weinberger, "Federal Restrictions on Educational Research: Privacy Protection Study Commission Hearing," *Educational Researcher* 6 (April 1977):15–18.

43. Thomas J. Flygare, "A Threat to Accreditation: Defamation Judgment against an Accreditation Team Member," *Phi Delta Kappan* 61 (June 1980): 706–707.

44. William H. Holley and Hubert S. Field, "The Law and Performance Evaluation in Education: A Review of Court Cases and Implications for Use," *Journal of Law and Education* 6 (October 1977):427–48.

45. Melvin D. George and Larry A. Braskamp, "Universities, Accountability, and the Uncertainty Principle," *Educational Record* 59 (Fall 1978):345–66.

46. Marvin W. Peterson, "State-Level Performance Budgeting," in *Increasing the Public Accountability of Higher Education*, ed. Folger, pp. 1–34.

47. Robert O. Berdahl, "Legislative Program Evaluation," in *Increasing the Public Accountability of Higher Education*, ed. Folger, pp. 35–65.

48. Robert O. Berdahl, *Statewide Coordination of Higher Education* (Washington, D.C.: American Council on Education, 1971).

49. Berdahl, "Legislative Program Evaluation"; Robert J. Barak, "Program Reviews by Statewide Higher Education Agencies," in *Increasing the Public Accountability of Higher Education*, ed. John K. Folger, pp. 67–90.

50. Folger, ed., *Increasing the Public Accountability of Higher Education*, pp. 91–94.

51. George and Braskamp, "Universities, Accountability, and the Uncertainty Principle," p. 355.

52. David H. Florio, Michael M. Behrmann, and Diane L. Goltz, "What Do Policy Makers Think of Educational Research and Evaluation? Or Do They?" *Educational Evaluation and Policy Analysis* 1 (November/December 1979):61–87.

53. Alexander W. Astin, "Testing in Postsecondary Education: Some Unresolved Issues," *Educational Evaluation and Policy Analysis* 1 (November/December 1979):21–28.

54. Alexander W. Astin, "Equal Access to Postsecondary Education: Myth or Reality?" *UCLA Educator* 19 (Spring 1977):8–17.

55. Ibid., p. 13.

56. Allan Nairn and associates, "The Reign of ETS: A Brief Summary of the Ralph Nader Report on the Educational Testing Service," *Standard Education Almanac*, 10th ed. (Chicago: Marquis Who's Who, 1980), p. 429; See also Allan Nairn and associates, *The Reign of ETS: The Corporation That Makes Up Minds. The Ralph Nader Report on the Educational Testing Service* (Washington, D.C.: Learning Research Project, 1980).

57. Jonathan R. Warren, "Evaluation, Motivation, and Grading," *UCLA Educator* 19 (Winter 1977):22–25.

58. Astin, "Testing in Postsecondary Education," pp. 24–26.

59. J. Victor Baldridge, "Environmental Pressure, Professional Autonomy, and Coping Strategies in Academic Organizations," in *Academic Governance: Research on Institutional Politics and Decision Making*, ed. J. Victor Baldridge (Berkeley, Calif.: McCutchan, 1971), p. 524.

60. Baldridge et al., *Policy Making and Effective Leadership*, pp. 105–113.

61. Peter Seldin, "New Emphases in the Evaluation of Professors," *Phi Delta Kappan* 56, 7 (March 1975):496–97.

62. Baldridge et al., *Policy Making and Effective Leadership*, p. 110.

63. John A. Centra, "Student Ratings of Instruction and Their Relationship to Student Learning," *American Educational Research Journal* 14 (Winter 1977):17–24; Peter W. Frey, Dale W. Leonard, and William W. Beatty, "Student Ratings of Instruction: Validation Research," *American Educational Research Journal* 12 (Fall 1975):435–47; Herbert W. Marsh, "The Validity of Student Evaluations: Classroom Evaluations of Instructors Independently Nominated as Best and Worst Teachers by Graduating Seniors," *American Educational Research Journal* 14 (Fall 1977):441–47.

64. Toby J. Tetenbaum, "The Role of Student Needs and Teacher Orientations in Student Ratings of Teachers," *American Educational Research Journal* 12 (Fall 1975):417–33; Richard D. Shingles, "Faculty Ratings: Procedures for Interpreting Student Evaluations," *American Educational Research Journal* 14 (Fall 1977):459–70.

65. George Arnstein, "Two Cheers for Accreditation," *Phi Delta Kappan* 60 (January 1979):357.

66. Robert E. Floden, "Flexner, Accreditation, and Evaluation," *Educational Evaluation and Policy Analysis* 2 (March/April 1980):35–46.

67. J. Myron Atkin, "Institutional Self-Evaluation versus National Professional Accreditation or Back to the Normal School?" *Educational Researcher* 7 (November 1978):3–7.

68. Aaron Wildavsky, *The Politics of the Budgetary Process* 2d ed. (Boston: Little, Brown, 1974), p. 4.

69. House, ed., *School Evaluation,* p. 46.

7

Accreditation: Issues for the Eighties

Sherry H. Penney

Accreditation is a review process of an institution or a program in line with a given set of standards and criteria, resulting in the rendering of a decision concerning whether or not those standards are met. In the United States it has evolved primarily as a nongovernmental process of self-regulation with peer evaluation as one of its central components. Early in this century institutions began to form voluntary associations with the intent of self-regulating the quality of their endeavors. Professions as well as institutions began to use a similar process and now, by current estimates, there exist in excess of seventy accrediting bodies, either regional or specialized.[1]

Although historically the accreditation process has not been a governmental one, both state and federal agencies have been connected with the process at various stages. In 1975, the two major bodies concerned with accreditation (National Commission on Accrediting and the Federation of Regional Accrediting Commissions on Higher Education) merged into the Council on Postsecondary Accreditation (COPA). The education community wanted COPA to become a central force for coordinating and making sense out of the accreditation morass. COPA also continued to support voluntary accreditation and peer review as opposed to accreditation by governmental agencies. By and large institutions accept this route as preferred and have voiced a growing concern about the possibility of increased governmental involvement in the process.[2]

In recent years many individuals have had rising expectations for accreditation. In the seventies, institutions began to encounter serious problems stemming partially from demographic realities projecting actual or predicted declines in enrollments. Coupled with this problem were those of rising inflation and soaring energy costs. Financial concerns became paramount, and many institutions in turn became hungrier for students and tuition revenue. A variety of new techniques were developed for attracting and retaining students. At the same time, students, parents, and the general public wanted to learn more about institutions and programs in order to make careful choices. Accreditation appeared to many to be an important measure. These questions were posed: Is the institution accredited? If so, for how long? By whom?, and What does it mean to be accredited? It was this latter question that caused agencies to review their methods and many institutions to take the process more seriously.

Difficulty began, however, when the public wanted something that accreditation did not provide. The public appears to want a mechanism to rank institutions—A, B, or C. Moreover, it wishes to know the long-range prospects for strength or, in some cases, survival. Accreditation has always been concerned with quality but that has not been interpreted to mean a ranking system. Instead, the main focus has been on setting standards which are a measure of quality and on examining institutions in line with those standards. A related benefit has been setting goals for institutional improvement.[3] The standards and goals relate to the particular institution, however, and are not intended to provide comparisons.

Gordon Sweet, speaking at the winter COPA conference in 1979, addressed the quality issue and pointed out that the charge is often made that "accreditation has not been very effective in giving guidance to the consumer as to the educational quality of an institution or program." But no one, he argued, has adequately defined quality: "[T]he critics, therefore, have the same problems as do the accrediting agencies with this most important professed function of accrediting: the determination and identification of quality." He continued by disputing the charge that accreditation has failed to identify quality and set minimum standards.[4] However, consumers continue to argue that whatever has been said about quality has not been enough to meet a growing public demand for more information and analysis about institutional functioning.

Throughout its history, the primary purpose of accreditation has been to examine institutions to determine how well they are meeting their stated objectives. Beyond that, the agencies (regional or professional) have standards or criteria which they have developed. Normally included are examinations of the institutional or program purposes and objectives, instructional programs, financial resources, faculty, facilities (including libraries), student services, and ethical standards. More recently accrediting agencies have moved to an "increased concentration on results and learning outcomes."[5]

Adhering to the published standards and having clearly defined objectives are the gauges of quality.

The validity of these criteria usually used by the accrediting bodies has been questioned by some educators. William E. Troutt has pointed out that the quality indicators are concerned with what goes into the educational process and that current research cannot show that outcomes are assured— the effect of the process on the students. Troutt argues quite persuasively that, in general, these indicators have not been tested adequately, and that in cases where they have been, they have not been found to determine quality. He states that "available research cannot substantiate the claim that certain accrediting association criteria assure institutional quality. It also illustrates, however, the difficulty in authoritatively stating that research demonstrates the lack of any relationship between accrediting association criteria and institutional quality."[6] More recently, James Huffman has argued in a similar manner that attention should be shifted from an emphasis on institutional resources to that of the actual learning that students have achieved.[7] Further review of the criteria is needed, as is more emphasis on outcomes. A requirement that institutions develop plans for evaluating outcomes has been adopted by the Southern Association, and institutions in that region are working on strategies to respond. This is but one example that the use of outcomes is receiving more intense review nationwide. However, in the absence of revised standards, the current ones will probably continue to be used for the immediate future while further examination, research, and experimentation with others, including outcome measures, go forward.

U.S. MODEL: REGIONAL ACCREDITATION

In the United States, the regional and professional associations manage accreditation and organize their efforts around the concept of self-regulation. The associations are staffed by professionals, but the review teams are composed of peer evaluators. This process generally proceeds as follows:

- The institution undertakes a thorough self-study following the guidelines and criteria of the particular association (regional or professional). Staff provide assistance to the institution before and during the self-study period.

- The association assembles a team of peer evaluators who review the self-study and other relevant materials and then make an on-site visit.

- During the visit, the team reviews additional materials and meets with administrators, faculty, and students. It looks for possible problem areas and for areas not covered in the self-study which nonetheless need attention. The guidelines, criteria, or standards of the association provide the team with the quality norm.

- The chair and team prepare a report which summarizes the findings and make recommendations. The report is forwarded to the association.
- The relevant board or commission in the association reviews the report and makes its determination for accreditation, reaccreditation, or probation (whichever is appropriate).
- The report and findings are shared with the institution (or program); the institution may then follow the variety of due processes which exist if the report or recommendations appear unwarranted.
- The process starts over as determined by the time schedule of the particular association.

This process is a conventional one for evaluation and review. It is difficult to find fault with the process, and it is one that institutions know and understand. In fact, they have helped to design it—institutional representatives are members of the various association boards. True, institutions are not graded, but some do fail. Those that do not meet minimum standards are put on probation or given show cause orders. Institutions that meet the minimum standards, and the majority do, are given suggestions in order to improve the quality of programs. During the process, it is difficult for institutions to ignore serious problems. As team members meet with faculty, students, and administrators, they pick up signals concerning the health of the institution. These insights are helpful to the institution as it sets future priorities.

In fairness to what does exist, however, it should be pointed out that the process can vary enormously. In some cases it works well, and the institution and its consumers benefit. In most cases the institution meets the minimum standards, and the focus is on improvement. In such instances, the self-study is usually thorough and analytical—the association standards were reasonable, the team was well prepared and worked well together. It reported honestly on strengths and weaknesses that are accepted by the institution as a basis for future planning. In other cases, of course, the result is the opposite. Perhaps the self-study was descriptive rather than analytical. Serious concerns were not identified. Maybe the team was weak or some team members had not received proper orientation. Perhaps the institution was reluctant to cite too many problems out of a fear of losing accreditation. All these things may occur, but it is usually not too difficult to identify the causes of the weakness.

In recent years the process has been stretched to its ultimate in some cases—identifying several problems in an already weak institution such that the institution does not meet the agency standards. A recommendation for probation or termination of accreditation may follow. The institution may be forced to close as a result, but ultimately the consumer benefits precisely because the process did work.

The regional associations as well as institutions are aware of problems which do occur; several steps are underway to address these issues. More comprehensive guides have been developed which delineate standards and help institutions conduct meaningful self-studies. Consultation is provided by the regional staff. Training sessions for team members and chairs are held, sample reports are discussed, and case studies are presented. The team is alerted to potential problems. Moreover, due process provisions are in place to ensure that institutions as well as consumers are treated evenly and fairly.

INSTITUTIONAL SELF-REVIEW

Within the accreditation process, the institutional self-study exercise is usually seen as one of the most valuable parts of the accreditation scenario. Institutions engage in a comprehensive process of self-review which helps them to set priorities and allocate scarce resources.[8] Although some institutions appear to resent accreditation and view it as an effort which diverts scarce resources away from more important tasks, in many instances the process is meaningful for all involved.[9] After all, the self-study exercise provides an opportunity for institutions to examine those very areas that should concern them most. Even strong institutions benefit from critical self-review. What institution can help but be concerned with answering questions such as these:

What are the qualifications of the faculty?

Do the qualifications fit the programs?

What are the policies concerning promotion, termination, and reappointment?

What are the characteristics of the student body? Are they changing? What is the financial aid policy?

What process exists for making changes in the curriculum? Is the curriculum responsive to student interests and needs?

Do new curricular offerings have adequate financial backing?

Are the facilities adequate for the programs?

What happens to students upon completion of their programs?

What has been the value to the students of their educational experience?

Is the financial condition of the institution stable? How will it look three years hence?

Does the institution have an on-going process for review and evaluation? Does it have a long-range planning process?

Are the governance structures appropriate for that type of institution?

Are publications accurate and timely?

What changes has the institution made since the last visit? What changes are contemplated?

The accreditation visit and the self-study provide the impetus for institutions to answer these and other questions and to take a careful look at what and how well they are doing. If the review is thoughtful and responds to significant concerns, if institutions address problems openly and suggest changes where necessary, stronger programs will result.

Case studies buttress these contentions. An analysis was done by the author of twenty some accreditation visits in which she and colleagues participated over the last eight years. The institutions varied in size and complexity. They included coeducational, single-sex, two-year, and four-year colleges and universities. From this sample, it appears the process worked more often than not, and when it did, the institution as well as the student consumers were well served. Except in one case, there was no question that minimum standards were met and improvements were made.

Institution A is a small liberal arts college which had experienced enrollment decline. In preparing the self-study, the institution assembled data on enrollment trends, the changing applicant pool and the like. To counter the decline, the institution tried reaching out to new population groups. This action brought further changes in the applicant pool and forced the institution to revamp some of its programs. These concerns and the planned approaches were honestly addressed in the self-study. The team provided valuable comments concerning the viability of the planned strategy. Program changes were accomplished more readily when it became clear to all those involved how the institution was reshaping its mission and that the goals had been reviewed and confirmed by the team.

In institution B weaknesses were identified in student services. The administrators and trustees had been aware of the problem but had put off dealing with it for budgetary reasons. The weaknesses were confirmed and highlighted by the team, and its recommendations helped in subsequent budgetary decisions when alloctions were determined. A plan was devised for improving the services over a two- to three-year period.

In institution C the team learned of a concern related to minority students that had been addressed only briefly in the self-study report. The institution did not sense the depth of the concern and benefited from the insights of the team. The institution was able to deal with a potential problem before it surfaced as a major issue.

In institution D external reviews had been conducted for each academic department before the visit. The reports from these reviews were made available to the accreditation team so that the two reviews were coordinated. The exercise was cooperative and not duplicative. A useful report emerged which made it possible for the institution to trim some programs and reallocate resources to the few areas where expansion was needed.

Where it worked well, some or all of the following factors were in evidence: a well-prepared self-study, a competent team, and a good fit of the team with the institution. In addition, two other aspects were evident. First, the problems which were identified were ones within an institution's capacity to correct, and second, the institution did not fear change and wanted to improve. Finally, it is worthwhile to note that none of these institutions was extremely weak or about to go under.

To the examples of successes, others can be added where things did not go as well. In these cases, some of the following factors were evident: the self-study tended not to be analytical; the institution wished to gloss over problems with the hope that they would not be noticed; the team was weak or "soft" in that individuals did not wish to be too hard on the institution. To illustrate, in one small institution, the financial situation outlined in the report appeared to be stronger than it was. The team sensed the weaknesses but, lacking enough data to support its concern, simply identified it. The team worried about making things worse for the institution and did not make a major issue of the financial problem which, in hindsight, it should have. The institution was allowed to drift along, and things got worse and worse. What could have helped was a suggestion that a follow-up team be sent in to focus primarily on financial matters.

In another institution, the team identified a weak graduate program with a well-qualified but insufficient faculty, declining enrollments, and inadequate laboratory equipment. Yet the institution wished to hold on to the program for the sake of prestige. In fairness to the students, the program probably should have been placed on probation. In reality it was left to continue while the institution "tried harder." After five years of trying, no improvement was evident, and the institution finally was forced to close it down.

Difficulties may also arise from the process itself. First, institutional representatives will, at times, argue that the standards of the relevant association are too rigid. Is it fair for an institution to lose accreditation or be put on probation for having 150,000 volumes in its library when the standard requires 200,000? This may be an extreme case, but another example includes rigid guidelines on the appropriate breakdown between full and part-time faculty. Institutional officers often will argue that circumstances peculiar to their institution or program mean that deviation from a given standard is acceptable. The argument may be persuasive, especially if the students appear to be doing well in spite of the alleged deficiency. Such situations create problems for the team and for the final ruling by the association. Because the team members are peers, "deviations" that may be acceptable or explainable in terms of final results will probably be permitted. If too many deviations or exceptions occur, the standards need to be reexamined.

Another difficulty is caused by the process. At times institutions are subject to too many accreditation visits, in too short a time, from varying agencies with different standards and reported requirements. When this happens, the institution often does not and cannot take each one seriously. In institution F, the accreditation visit for the theological school took place in the fall, the regional accrediting team was on campus in the spring, and in the duration the nursing association, the chemists, and the engineers also appeared. How much better it would have been for the institution if a coordinated visit could have been arranged among these various agencies.

H. R. Kells has suggested that more coordination is needed between the institutional and specialized reviews, and his suggestion has support from COPA and from several institutional leaders.[10] In cases where such coordination has been attempted, the results have been better for the agencies as well as the institution. In the meantime, while agencies work toward coordination, consumers need to understand that entire institutions as well as individual schools, departments, and programs within them are accredited, and that one institution may be accredited several times.

THE ROLE OF GOVERNMENT AGENCIES

The major accreditation effort is concentrated in the six regional accrediting associations, but the role of the states and the federal government cannot be ignored in program review. States have at least two major functions: chartering and licensure. Incorporation or chartering is a function performed by all states. Not all states, however, have licensure requirements which are imposed as a "condition of offering education within the state."[11] Beyond these two categories, states have other functions related to education, and many operate their own public system of higher education. Some have assumed a variety of quality control roles.[12] In New York, for example, the board of regents registers programs and is also involved in licensure. In the early 1970s, the regents began an exhaustive peer review of doctoral programs in major subject areas at both public and private institutions in the state. At that same time they also conducted a comprehensive statewide review of master's programs. In 1985–1986 master's programs in education were the focus of another review. Louisiana's regents have examined graduate education and have voted to discontinue some master's programs. Other states too, although primarily focusing on public education, have undertaken reviews of graduate education (Florida, Iowa, North Carolina, Texas, and Tennessee).

In his study, Garnet Butch describes the extent to which state boards of higher education now are involved in assessments of quality in public institutions. His findings indicate that the involvement of state agencies is much greater than had been assumed, and, in fact, is growing. It includes:

1. Development of criteria and/or guidelines to assess institutional effectiveness;
2. Encouragement for improvement through continuous self-study;
3. Assurance to the educational community that the institution has met agency standards;
4. Assurance of the effectiveness of the institution in light of its stated goals;

5. Provision of counsel and assistance to established and developing institutions and programs;

6. Protection of the institution against encroachments to academic freedom;

7. Review of the institution when changes or serious problems arise that could affect the institution as a whole;

8. Requirement of a written report of institutional self-study;

9. Requirement of a visit to an institution as part of the evaluation process.[13]

It is predictable that states will be strengthening their efforts in specialized reviews of selected programs, particularly as they face declining enrollments and shrinking resources. It is possible that these reviews may be coordinated with regional reviews or specialized reviews, but either way, states will be more involved in review processes and decisions regarding discontinuing programs.

The 1980 recommendations of the Sloan Commission on Government and Higher Education also discuss state responsibility. In the report of the commission, Carl Kaysen writes, "The decisions the states have to make in the next generation will have a profound impact on the quality, rather than the quantity, of higher education. The big job ahead is retrenchment, and the greatest problem is how to adjust capacity to demand without sacrificing essentials." The report also suggests that states undertake reviews of quality in their institutions and that private institutions be encouraged to be a part of such reviews where feasible.[14] This latter suggestion has been criticized by leaders of some of those private institutions who prefer their own review systems.[15] The extent to which states will assume a more active role in monitoring and evaluating quality (including private institutions) is a primary issue in the eighties. The move in the direction of additional state involvement in concerns related to quality is moving forward. Some states have focused much of their attention on outcomes by "initiating processes for assessing actual educational outcomes, both for assuring competence among graduating students and for rewarding institutions that can demonstrate effectiveness."[16]

Tennessee has incorporated a performance measure into its higher education budgeting process. Northeast Missouri State has engaged in a comprehensive assessment of value added.[17] In other states such as New Jersey, South Dakota and Colorado, similar efforts are beginning.[18]

At the federal level, the secretary of education regularly has compiled a list of authorized accrediting agencies, with the last such list published in 1981–1982. The Division of Eligibility and Agency Evaluation in the U.S. Office of Education developed detailed criteria in order to determine which accrediting agencies the government should approve. This process is sometimes viewed as the way the government accredits the accrediting agencies, and this *Education Directory* was in fact a method by which the Secretary monitored those accrediting agencies whose decisions are used by the federal government.[19] The trend has been for the federal government to rely increasingly on private accrediting bodies for the determination of eligibility to participate in numerous federal programs.[20]

The reauthorization of the Higher Education Act by Congress in the fall of 1980 carried with it a reaffirmation of the federal government's concern with accreditation. Section 1205 established within the Department of Education a National Advisory Committee on Accreditation and Institutional Eligibility, to be composed of fifteen individuals representing professional associations, state education agencies, institutions, and the public. The committee, like its predecessor, assists the secretary in identifying the nationally recognized agencies and associations which are determined to be reliable authorities on the quality of education offered by institutions applying for federal funds.[21]

In the last few years objections have been raised by many in the affected institutions that federal and state officials are trying to assume greater roles in the evaluation process. In the summer of 1980, representatives of institutions as well as accrediting bodies prepared a proposal for limiting the federal government's involvement. Many of the institutions recommended that the federal government rely more on higher education's own system of recognition. Some suggested that if the federal government uses accreditation as the basis for deciding eligibility, it should be guided by COPA's criteria for identifying the appropriate agencies.[22] Subsequent to that meeting, an encouraging spirit of cooperation has been noted between the national advisory committee and representatives at the federal level and those in COPA. An early result of this cooperation was the agreement that the period of recognition be five years and that joint reviews be used when feasible.

WHERE TO GO FROM HERE?

Accreditation does not and cannot do everything that agencies or consumers desire. The public and the consumer need to have appropriate expectations concerning accreditation. What it does do is assure that an institution has met the standards of the relevant regional or specialized association. It also assures the public that the institution has set reasonable goals and is taking steps in line with those. If we reaffirm what accreditation does do as well as what it does not do, misunderstandings can be avoided.

The present system of regional associations, state licensure, and federal listing provides coherence to what is a uniquely American system. Public disclosure and the stimulus given to institutions for ongoing improvement are its strengths. All institutions and agencies must continue to work to improve the accreditation process. Institutions must undertake thorough self-studies to develop academic and financial plans for improving weak areas. They should develop reasonable outcome measures, and they should support the efforts of the accrediting agencies not only by encouraging members of their faculties and administration to serve as evaluators, but also by expressing concern regarding the appropriateness of standards when necessary.

Regional accrediting bodies must continue their efforts to improve training for teams and to revise procedures so that serious situations can be responded to quickly. The 1979 report of the Carnegie Council on Policy Studies in Higher Education, *Fair Practices in Higher Education*, charges the regionals with several steps for improvement, including: 1) placing greater emphasis on reviewing institutional advertising, policies for awarding credit, and catalogs as full disclosure statements; 2) seeking eminently qualified people from around the country to serve on teams; and 3) consulting with other professional associations and societies in developing academic program evaluation criteria.[23] These steps, together with an emphasis on coordination as suggested by Kells and COPA, would result in significant improvements. Several of the regional associations already have taken such steps, and many institutions are committed to making the accreditation process more meaningful.

Like the institutions they review, the associations too are engaging in a continual review process. States also must do this as they expand their roles. If the effort to coordinate accreditation among the regional, specialized, and state agencies can go forward at the same time, and each agency improves its own process, American accreditation can be a positive force for improving institutional functioning and upgrading quality in the decades ahead.

NOTES

1. For summaries of the accreditation process and its history, see Fred F. Harcleroad, *Accreditation: History, Process, and Problems*, Higher Education Resource Report #6 (Washington, D.C.: American Association for Higher Education, 1980); *Journal of Higher Education* 50 (March/April 1979)—this entire issue is devoted to accreditation and provides excellent summaries of many of the issues surrounding the subject; William A. Kaplin, *Respective Roles of Federal Government, State Government, and Private Accrediting Agencies in the Governance of Post Secondary Education* (Washington, D.C.: Council on Post Secondary Accreditation, 1975); Richard M. Millard, Robert A. Scott, and David E. Sumler, "Accreditation," *Change* 15 (May/June 1983):33–37, 53.

2. *Chronicle of Higher Education* (June 16, 1980):1, 10; and (July 10, 1980):13.

3. Jonathan R. Warren, "Is Accrediting Worth the Cost?" *American Association of Higher Education Bulletin* 32 (March 1980):11.

4. Gordon W. Sweet, "Accreditation: Challenge and Change," in Council on Post Secondary Accreditation newsletter, *Accreditation* (Spring 1979):5.

5. *Chronicle* (January 29, 1986):3; *Educational Quality and Accreditation: A Call for Diversity, Continuity and Innovation*, (Washington, D.C.: Council on Post Secondary Education, 1986).

6. William E. Troutt, "Regional Accreditation, Evaluative Criteria and Quality Assurance," *Journal of Higher Education* 50 (March/April 1979):208.

7. James Huffman, "The Role of Accreditation in Preserving Educational Integrity," *Educational Record* 63 (Summer 1982):41–44.

8. Warren, "Is Accrediting Worth the Cost?"

9. Carnegie Foundation for the Advancement of Teaching, *The Control of the Campus* (Washington, D.C.: Carnegie Foundation, 1982), p. 26. The report argues that elite institutions do not always take accreditation seriously.

10. H. R. Kells, "Proliferation and Agency Effectiveness in Accreditation: An Institutional Bill of Rights," and responses to Kells by Robert L. Ketter and William H. Knisely, *Current Issues in Higher Education*, Report No. 2 (Washington, D.C.: American Association of Higher Education, 1980):19–30.

11. Kaplin, *Respective Roles of Federal Government*, p. 3.

12. Robert A. Wallhaus, "Process Issues in State-Level Program Reviews," *New Directions for Higher Education*, No. 37 (March 1983):75–87.

13. *Accreditation* (Fall 1980):7.

14. Carl Kaysen and the Sloan Commission on Government and Higher Education, "New Roles for the States in Monitoring Higher Education Quality," in *Current Issues in Higher Education*, Report No. 6 (Washington, D.C.: American Association of Higher Education, 1980), pp. 21–35.

15. William Friday and James R. Killian, "Dissent to Sloan Recommendation No. 2," in *Current Issues in Higher Education*, Report No. 6, pp. 35–37.

16. Peter Ewell, *The Self-Regarding Institution* (Denver: National Center for Higher Education Management Systems, 1984), p. 2.

17. *Ibid*, pp. 62–69.

18. *Chronicle*, September 18, 1985, p. 16.

19. Kaplin, *Respective Roles of Federal Government*, p. 18; Carnegie Foundation for the Advancement of Teaching, *Control of the Campus*, pp. 22–28.

20. *Chronicle of Higher Education* (June 16, 1980):1, 10.

21. *Accreditation* (Fall 1980):6.

22. *Chronicle of Higher Education* (June 16, 1980):1, 10; and *Accreditation* (Summer 1980).

23. *Fair Practices in Higher Education, Rights and Responsibilities of Students and Their Colleges in a Period of Intensified Competition for Enrollment*, Report of the Carnegie Council on Policy Studies in Higher Education (San Francisco: Jossey-Bass, 1979), p. 72.

8

The Influence of Accreditation on the Development of Traditionally Black Colleges in the Middle States Region

Howard L. Simmons

To date no major studies have been done on the accreditation of traditionally black colleges and universities even though accreditation may have impacted greatly on their development. Among the various references to the issue, one of the more interesting is contained in a Carnegie Commission on Higher Education study, which stressed that "the Negro public colleges have shown significant development as measured by regional accreditation."[1] That study also observed that by 1954 "only two of the associations—the Middle States and the North Central—accredited historically Negro Colleges and admitted them to membership."[2] Another research effort, which assessed the perceptions of black and white chief administrators on the importance of accreditation, concluded that traditionally black institutions attributed such importance to regional accreditation that the accrediting agency "should weigh seriously the possible effects of any student change in its policies which could influence the future destiny of these institutions."[3]

Accreditation is becoming an important issue in higher education. At the same time there is renewed interest in the role of traditionally black institutions in American higher education. The present study focuses on traditionally black higher education institutions accredited by the Commission on Higher Education of the Middle States Association of Colleges and Schools.[4] Although limited to this middle-states area, it concerns policy issues in accreditation that are likely to affect institutions in other regions. The results may also assist agencies and organizations dedicated to the development of research on black colleges and universities. The National Advisory Committee on Black Higher Education and Black Colleges and Universities called for just such a development when it listed among its 1980 priorities the need to make recommendations "in the analysis of and planning for the future role and healthy development of the historically black colleges and their relationship to expanding the number of Blacks enrolled in higher education nationally and regionally."[5]

When the higher education commission at Middle States Association (MSA) issued its first list of accredited institutions in 1921, there was only one traditionally black college to be found on it. Two more were added during the twenties, and in each decade that followed at least one more of these institutions was accorded initial accreditation. As Table 8.1 shows, by 1980 eleven schools had been accredited, and six of these had achieved initial accreditation prior to the 1954 Supreme Court decision on desegregation. It should also be noted that three were established after that date; in other words, they were only recently accredited, which is a normal pattern among these black institutions. The remaining two were initially accredited along with other teachers colleges during the late fifties and early sixties. With few exceptions, these institutions have also had their accreditation reaffirmed at regular ten-year intervals, after this practice was instituted in the 1950s. Only one college was earlier denied initial recognition, and one other had its accreditation withdrawn for a five-year period. At the same time, it should be stressed that some traditionally black institutions within the MSA not only met acceptable standards and were accorded reaccreditation, but were praised for their dramatic progress. An example is provided in the following scenario related to an anonymous black college in the MSA region:

Confidence in the viability of the college was provided in 1967 when the Middle States Association of Colleges and Secondary Schools reaffirmed the college's accreditation and underscored its approval by inviting representatives from other colleges . . . to observe its program as a case study. Whatever merit the observers may have discovered may safely be said to have developed out of a spirit of experimentation, a constant reexamination of program and policies, and a will to respond to academic challenges.[6]

These accreditations and the evaluations which preceded them were based on the same processes, criteria, and procedures used for other MSA institutions.

Notwithstanding the assumed positive impact that the accreditation process had on traditionally black colleges, it was reasonable to suppose that there was also some negative impact on the institutions. It could also be assumed that this negative impact was directly or indirectly related to the inadequacy or inappropriateness of some of the evaluative criteria used by

Table 8.1
Accreditation Actions Related to MSA Black Colleges/Universities

	Highest Degree Level	First Accreditation Date	Reaffirmation Dates	Follow-up Activities
C/U A	B	1945	'57,[4] '62, '72	'59, '64, '75, '76
C/U B	D	1921	'55, '69, '79	'71
C/U C	M	1961	'71	'63, '65, '67, '72, '73, '75
C/U D	M	1962 [1]	'72, '78	'64, '67, '68, '70, '73, '74, '75, '80
C/U E	D	1925	'58, '68, '78	'56, '58, '67, '79, '80
C/U F	B	1980 [2]		('82)
C/U G	M	1937	'66, '76	'72, '78, '79, '81
C/U H	B	1976 [2]		
C/U I	M	1951	'61, '71	'63, '65, '67
C/U J	M	1922	'53, '62, '72	'61, '62, '63, '73, '75, '77, '78, '79, '80
C/U K	A	1976 [3]		('82)

N = 11
[1]Was previously denied
[2]Recently accredited by MSA
[3]Accredited as a unit of other colleges
[4]Accreditation had been withdrawn earlier

C/U A, etc. = Confidential code for colleges
A = Associate
B = Bachelor's
M = Master's
D = Doctorate

the regional accrediting agency. This research study has sought answers to—
or at least insights into—the policy questions raised by these assumptions.
They include questions about the impact of MSA standards, procedures,
processes, and the association's role as a change agent in affecting improvements in the overall development of the traditionally black college or university. For example, should additional guidelines be developed for use in
the evaluation of traditionally black colleges? If so, how and in what areas
would such guidelines differ from current criteria and standards used in
evaluating other colleges and universities? How effective have MSA processes and actions been in improving various aspects of these colleges? How
adequate are the procedures? What more can the agency do to assist in the
orderly development and overall improvement of the traditionally black
institutions?

We start with a look at the accreditation history of the institutions used
in the study.

BACKGROUND

MSA archival information on traditionally black institutions consists of
official correspondence, self-study reports, evaluation reports, follow-up reports on progress, and commission minutes. For the eleven colleges and
universities involved, these documents provide valuable information on actual evaluation and accreditation transactions between MSA and the institutions (see Table 8.1).

More significant than the initial accreditation actions and the reaffirmation,
however, is the degree to which these institutions have been subjected to
follow-up investigations, and the nature of that follow-up activity. Follow-
up actions by MSA usually involve a progress report, as well as a visit by a
staff member or other appointed visitors. An analysis of self-study reports,
evaluation reports, and official action letters indicated that follow-up reports
and/or subsequent visits were expected to focus on a variety of areas requiring
improvement, including 1) physical facilities, 2) library development, 3)
organization and governance, 4) general finances and/or state funding, 5)
undergraduate and graduate program development, 6) developmental programs, 7) planning, and 8) outcomes. In all, forty-two progress reports have
been required from these traditionally black colleges in one or more areas
listed. Some colleges were expected to report on the same area in consecutive
years; some areas showed an even higher frequency of reporting. Thus
physical facilities and library development appear to have significance because reference to them was found in 50 percent or more of the reports.
These areas take on even more significance later in the analysis of the interview and questionnaire data. A study completed in 1979 on library development in the public historically black colleges complements the citations

by the accrediting agency: "The libraries of public black colleges have through the years been forced to operate with fewer, less complete holdings than the better-endowed, predominantly white public higher education institutions . . . [and] . . . many needs are still unmet."[7] Following closely behind were general finances and/or state funding, planning, and program development. All are quite relevant to the accreditation process and in varying degrees may have some impact on an institution's ability to achieve its goals and objectives. Ultimately, this will influence its accredited status.

MSA has subjected all of the traditionally black institutions to the same requirements, consistent with its mission, goals, objectives, clientele, and resources. During the period of their relationship with the association, no special guidelines or different criteria for the evaluation of predominantly black colleges ever existed. Moreover, the institutions themselves have been involved in the development and approval of the standards.

Of equal relevance to this study was the extent to which blacks participated on evaluation teams visiting traditionally black colleges. While the earlier accreditation actions resulted solely from data submitted on questionnaires or from one-person inspection visits, the latter rarely involved black persons as evaluators. However, once evaluations were accomplished as a result of a self-study, all teams visiting black colleges and universities included at least one black educator. In most recent evaluations the teams had from 40 to 85 percent black membership, and on ten occasions the chair of the team has been black. It should be noted that blacks make up less than 10 percent of the total number of persons eligible to serve as evaluators for the Middle States Association. Of course, it was not until 1969 that MSA appointed blacks to serve on its Commission on Higher Education for the review and accreditation of its institutions. Currently, 23.8 percent or five of the twenty-one elected commissioners are black, and one serves on the executive committee. Also, the Middle States Commission on Higher Education has had a black professional staff member since 1974.

FINDINGS: DATA FROM INTERVIEWS AND QUESTIONNAIRES

This section has been divided into four parts: 1) acquaintance of institutional constituencies with MSA; 2) adequacy of standards with respect to the evaluation of traditionally black institutions; 3) effectiveness of accreditation processes and procedures; and 4) the accreditation process as a factor in institutional improvement. In addition to the interview and questionnaire data, appropriate references have been made to the differences in archival information and the perceptions of respondents regarding what occurred.

Acquaintance with MSA Evaluation and Accreditation Procedures

To ascertain the level of awareness among institutional constituencies, interviewees were asked: "Have all relevant constituencies in your institution been sufficiently aware of Middle States evaluation and accreditation procedures?" Of the twenty-two interviewed, twenty (or 91 percent) responded that persons at all levels were aware and involved. These same respondents were consistent in their selection of administrators, staff, faculty, students, trustees, and alumni as being knowledgeable about MSA. Still others indicated that community representatives had received orientation about the association and its relationship to the institution. The question also elicited information about the strategies used to disseminate information about MSA. Among these were 1) use of campus publications, 2) special lectures, 3) general faculty and staff meetings, 4) community council meetings, 5) seminars on accreditation, 6) distribution of Middle States documents, and 7) participation in the self-study/evaluation process itself. One institution, desiring to better acquaint its board of trustees with MSA and its requirements, held a retreat for the board and university representatives.

The two interviewees responding in the negative indicated that not enough had been done on their part in informing various constituencies. They alluded also to the fact that students did not always understand the true purpose of MSA. Overall, then, it appears that the institutional constituencies have had satisfactory exposure to MSA evaluation and accreditation procedures. Naturally, when interviewees and respondents to the questionnaire were asked their perceptions of other aspects of the association, other interesting information was revealed. For example, from 9 to 27 percent of the respondents were unable to answer or had no opinion regarding one or more of the items relating to the question: "How effective are Middle States accreditation processes and procedures regarding your institution?" Of course, these responses may have come primarily from alumni who may not have been in as good a position to answer as were faculty, administrators, and students.

Adequacy of MSA Standards

A number of items in the interview guide and questionnaire were designed to gather perceptions about the adequacy of the standards. The results are shown in Table 8.2. A particularly interesting finding is that no less than 73 percent of the respondents considered all standards at least "essentially adequate." Moreover, only three standards were perceived by more than 10 percent of the respondents as being "not adequate," namely, Plant and Equipment, Innovation and Experimentation, and Resources. While small numbers are involved, and these items are only briefly described in the

Table 8.2
Adequacy of MSA Standards

	Adequate[1]		Not Adequate		No Opinion	
	#	%	#	%	#	%
1. Purposes and objectives...............21		95	0	0	1	5
2. Program...............................22		100	0	0	0	0
3. Outcomes.............................21		95	0	0	1	5
4. Admissions and Student Services.......20		95	2	9	0	0
5. The Faculty..........................21		95	1	5	0	0
6. Organization and Administration...... 20		91	0	0	2	9
7. Board of Trustees....................16		73	1	5	5	23
8. Resources............................19		86	3	14	0	0
9. Library/Learning Center...............20		91	1	5	1	5
10. Plant and Equipment..................16		73	5	23	1	5
11. Financing and Accounting.............17		77	2	9	3	14
12. Innovation and Experimentation........16		73	3	14	3	14
13. Catalogs and Other Publications.......21		95	1	5	0	0

N = 22
[1]For purposes of analysis, "completely adequate" and "essentially adequate" columns from questionnaire are combined.

standards, there may be other reasons for the responses. For example, there may be some relationship to a perceived inadequacy of the standards relating to "Plant and Equipment" and "Resources" and the actual deficiencies noted earlier in the self-study and evaluation reports regarding physical facilities. Also, the negative responses on "Innovation and Experimentation" may be explained further by the fact that two of the institutions considered themselves nontraditional and experimental, and expected greater attention to some of their different practices.

While most respondents agreed that the present evaluative criteria per se are adequate for the evaluation of traditionally black colleges, a more important concern of theirs appeared to be the application of the standards, especially by members of evaluation teams. Several questions were included to elicit information about the adequacy and application of MSA standards. An analysis of responses to these questions indicates at least one area of agreement among respondents: Standards should be the same for all institutions, including the traditionally black institutions. The most frequently stated reason for this view was that any attempt to create separate guidelines or standards would seriously jeopardize the credibility of these institutions. Moreover, the traditionally black colleges may be termed inferior by others. At the same time, a majority of the interviewees made it clear that greater care should be taken in the application of the present standards. While it was recognized that the standards offer some flexibility on missions, goals, and objectives, the diversity of colleges must be given more recognition and careful analysis, especially since black colleges often have fewer resources. Other points advanced by the interviewees with respect to the standards included:

- some modifications are needed in the criteria to respond to traditionally black colleges in periods of transition;
- evaluation team members should receive orientation regarding the cultural heritage of these institutions and what makes them distinctive;
- community participation should receive greater emphasis in the revision and application of criteria;
- the standards are excellent when the institution is viewed vis-à-vis its mission, goals, and objectives;
- the accreditation agency must be sensitive to the lack of equity in funding public colleges and the pressures such colleges feel;
- the present standards demand accountability of all institutions.

With minor exceptions, the interview data revealed that traditionally black institutions would be opposed to separate guidelines or standards, but they would, in some instances, recommend improvements in the content and/or application of specific evaluative criteria. Nevertheless, those interviewed were evenly divided when asked about the desirability of developing additional guidelines for assuring the continuity of traditionally black institutions.

Eleven (50 percent) believed that MSA could or should play some role in preserving the historical mission of these colleges; however, only two concrete suggestions were offered: 1) preparation of a special booklet about the nature and diversity of black colleges and uniquely different institutions; and 2) implementation of briefings for team members regarding the role of the black college or university. The remaining 50 percent in varying degrees took the position that there is nothing more that the association could or should do regarding the "survival" of traditionally black institutions. Seven (30 percent) considered it a political issue and not within the scope of MSA authority or influence, even though these same persons believed that the accrediting agency should be concerned with the maintenance of diversity in American higher education. Still others felt that the very development of additional guidelines for traditionally or predominantly black institutions might be counterproductive and accelerate their demise.

To provide information on MSA's role in the application of its accrediting criteria to traditionally black colleges and universities, interview subjects were asked if the Commission on Higher Education had been an agent in "mainstreaming" their institutions, and if such a practice was desirable. It should be noted that for purposes of the study "mainstreaming" was defined as the practice of applying the same prevailing standards and procedures to all institutions. Fourteen persons, representing 64 percent of those interviewed, indicated that MSA had been in some way an agent in "mainstreaming" their college and perceived this as a desirable situation as long as the institution was able to maintain its traditional and/or historical commitment to the education of blacks. Those providing positive responses conceded that being evaluated on the same terms had resulted in equal prestige and positive advantages when interacting with other institutions. The four who responded in the negative believed that MSA had not been an agent in "mainstreaming" and that it most likely could not be effective in this area. It might be useful here to ponder the observation made by another writer, who argues, "Mainstreaming can . . . be used as a catalyst for change . . . by changing our conceptions of differences in people and by helping people to perceive the potential worth of every member of our multi-faceted society."[8] While the word does have a connotation in this context of attempting to promote integration, interviewees themselves were often ambivalent about the positive or negative effects of the practice, especially since not a single interviewee or respondent wanted black colleges to be given special treatment in the accreditation process.

Effectiveness of MSA Accreditation Processes and Procedures

Data on the effectiveness of the accrediting agency's processes and procedures were collected through interviews as well as questionnaires. The latter sought perceptions on staff and team visits, team selection, written reports and responses, and official actions.

As shown in Table 8.3, all respondents felt that MSA processes and procedures have been either completely or essentially effective in the evaluation and accreditation of their institutions. While there were no negative responses, from two to six persons per item indicated that they had no opinion or were unable to answer. Such responses were most frequently made by persons who were indeed unfamiliar with certain aspects of the accrediting process.

Not surprisingly, staff visits, institutional responses to reports, evaluation team visits, and follow-up reports/visits were considered most effective. Even though commission actions and evaluation team selection were also considered effective by a majority of the respondents (73 and 77 percent, respec-

Table 8.3
Effectiveness of MSA Accreditation Processes and Procedures

	# Effective[1]	%	# Not Effective	%	# No Opinion Unable to Answer	%
1. Middle States staff visits	20	91	0	0	2	9
2. Evaluation team selection.	17	77	0	0	5	23
3. Evaluation team visit(s)	19	86	0	0	3	14
4. Evaluation team report(s).	19	86	0	0	3	14
5. Institutional Response(s) to report(s)	20	91	0	0	2	9
6. Commission on Higher Education Actions	16	73	0	0	6	27
7. Follow-up Report(s)/Visit(s)	18	82	0	0	4	18

N = 22

[1]For purposes of analysis, "completely effective" and "essentially effective" columns from questionnaire are combined.

tively), a closer examination of the data suggests that the respondents who offered no opinion or who indicated an inability to answer may not have been completely satisfied with these areas. When responses to questionnaires were viewed later in conjunction with data from the interviews, it became clear that some respondents believed some improvement in these processes might be desirable, especially in the area of team selection.

Those interviewed felt that team selection was very important in the evaluative processes for all colleges and universities, but especially for the traditionally black schools. A three-part question about minority representation on evaluation teams visiting traditionally black institutions was designed to gather information on past, current, and future practices of MSA. All interviewees agreed that the association had given adequate attention to minority representation on evaluation teams; however, most had little recollection of who was involved prior to their institution's last one or two evaluations. Likewise, all emphasized that qualifications and competence of all visitors were just as important as meaningful representation of blacks on the team. Similarly, those interviewed believed strongly that all teams, especially those visiting traditionally black institutions, should have a preponderance of people who reflect an understanding of the unique nature of the institution being visited. Seven of the twenty-two persons interviewed went even further and said that persons visiting traditionally black colleges and universities should have had experience in another black institution or have some knowledge of minority education. The reason given for this view was that the problems faced by black colleges are often quite different, particularly in the areas of the needs of student clientele, a lower overall level of financial support, and cultural differences.

From another perspective, one respondent cautioned that some team members had come with faulty or preconceived notions about black colleges and universities, and suggested that evaluators should recognize that differences also exist among traditionally black institutions. Overall, the interviewees were satisfied that there had been blacks involved in the evaluation of their institutions but suggested strongly that MSA should find ways of increasing minority participation, provide better orientation to persons visiting black colleges, and continue to expect the same qualifications and expertise of those blacks selected to participate in their evaluation visits.

Participants in the study volunteered that the Middle States Association had been sensitive to their institution's mission, goals, and objectives when they were asked about past evaluators. Only four out of twenty-two indicated that they could not respond because they had no accurate recollection of past evaluations. Except in the case of one respondent, who believed that MSA had not been particularly sensitive to its manner of developing graduate programs, all concluded that the accrediting agency had not only provided an objective appraisal of their institution's status but had also aided in the state agency's better appreciation of their unique characteristics and needs.

The latter could be given even more credence once the data to the question of possible negative impact of Middle States actions had been analyzed. The interviewees were unanimous and unequivocal in their conclusion that they had perceived no negative impact on their institutions because of actions taken by Middle States subsequent to evaluation processes. Although they stated it in various ways, respondents were generally agreed that the processes and results had thus far been positive and perceived that they would continue to be so. At least five persons volunteered that since Middle States always sets a positive tone for evaluations and is well respected, it is these factors that account for the positive reaction to the processes and procedures.

ACCREDITATION AND INSTITUTIONAL IMPROVEMENT

Another crucial task is assessing the extent to which improvements have resulted. This is far more difficult to do. Such improvements may have been the result of an accrediting agency or institutional initiative or a combination of both. Some respondents felt that no improvement had occurred, while others were not sure. Since it was important to determine the areas in which improvement had possibly taken place, the questionnaire was designed to gather such information on institutional programs, boards of trustees' functioning, determination of priorities, governance and organization, funding levels, policies and procedures, planning processes, research, student services, faculty and staff development, resource allocation, facilities, instruction, library resources, and morale.

Not surprisingly, few respondents believed that MSA had been a major factor in improving their institutions and operations, even though one or two believed that to have been the case except in the areas relating to student services and reallocation of resources. More significant, however, was that 68 to 100 percent of the respondents viewed MSA, their own institution's initiative, or a combination of the two as being responsible for some improvement in every area. If one considers that the accreditation process could serve only as a catalyst for change, and that the institution would have to be involved in any improvement activity, it is not surprising that respondents considered joint MSA/institutional or primarily institutional initiative as their choices. As in the case of morale, 41 percent of those responding indicated improvement brought on through primary institutional initiative as opposed to 27 percent who believed that both were causative agents. The same imbalance occurred in the responses related to board functioning and reallocation of resources. One could properly conclude that the respondents considered the institution as the locus of responsibility for such perceived improvements.

Respondents gave larger percentages to the joint initiative of MSA and their institution for improvements in academic programs, policies, procedures, planning, institutional research, student services, faculty/staff development, facilities, instruction, and library/learning resources. When these areas were compared to the previously documented list of areas for improvement noted in the evaluation and follow-up reports, a significant relationship was found, especially with reference to improvements in library resources, physical facilities, academic programs, and planning. Because institutional research and planning have been considered absolutely essential to effective self-study/evaluation processes, it was assumed that these would be placed in the improvement column. Otherwise, these responses would have been considered inconsistent with other findings regarding the effectiveness of the MSA processes and procedures.

Further analysis showed that at least one area—and possibly three—should be examined more closely. In each, 14 to 23 percent of the respondents indicated that no improvement occurred; they were, in order of significance, funding level(s) from sponsor(s), board functioning, and morale. Again, this is not unusual, since they may have been considered beyond the purview of MSA or the institution. Moreover, if those who responded in the negative on morale are combined with those who expressed no knowledge, it could be inferred that no change was necessary or that persons were unwilling to respond. In any case, the majority perceived that improvements had occurred in all categories, regardless of the assumed primary agent or agents.

For more extensive data on the impact of accreditation on institutional improvements, the interview process was designed to incorporate questions regarding the development of the traditionally black colleges and universities, and the role played by the commission in this process.

After the data had been analyzed, fourteen areas emerged as having been significantly improved because of the Middle States accreditation process: 1) ongoing self-assessment procedures; 2) long-range planning; 3) physical facilities; 4) programs; 5) academic management and administrative organization; 6) library resources; 7) faculty morale; 8) instructional equipment; 9) external grants; 10) student transfer; 11) prestige; 12) outcomes assessment; 13) mission statement; and 14) overall quality of life at the college. Considered even more important by a majority (85 percent) of the interviewees, however, was that MSA has provided equitable treatment to all institutions and had helped them focus more clearly on stated goals and objectives. Again, the specific areas mentioned by the respondents are consistent with data from the archives and questionnaires.

On the question of how MSA facilitated the process of getting external resources, twelve (or 55 percent) believed that the agency had been a positive force in securing financial support from state and federal governments, corporations, and foundations. Such support came as a result of recommendations contained in the evaluation team reports or the fact that some organizations required regional accredited status as a prerequisite to the award of grants and contracts. Further, they reported that references to MSA requirements had been included in proposals to the federal government and foundations. Except in the case of Title III federal funds, respondents believed that such support was usually in the form of capital funding related to physical facilities and library resources. Again, this was consistent with other findings when facilities and library resources were highlighted as areas requiring improvement. The remaining 45 percent indicated that MSA had either not been a factor, or only indirectly. With their institution's accredited status already established, these persons believed their "track record" to be of greater importance in the acquisition of external financial resources.

Finally, some effort was made to get data on any special assistance from MSA that might have been perceived by study participants. While fifteen (or 68 percent) believed that staff visits, follow-up activities, prompt response to inquiries, provision of technical support, convention programs, emphasis on financial management, and self-study materials constituted some form of special assistance, only one person stressed that her institution had requested a special consultant to assist in the resolution of a specific problem area. On the other hand, the data reviewed in the Middle States archives gave evidence that such assistance had been requested and handled from three of the institutions in the study. This did not cause alarm, since several of those participating did not have a recollection of all the transactions between their institution and MSA. Indeed, some had experienced only one evaluation and accreditation cycle, even though there had been two or three visits for reaffirmation by the association since the initial status had been granted.

RECOMMENDATIONS AND IMPLICATIONS FOR HIGHER EDUCATION POLICY

This study has revealed the relatively positive view that traditionally black colleges and universities hold of the Commission on Higher Education of Middle States. The high level of participation in the study also added strong support for the assumption that persons in these institutions have high regard for regional accreditation. The study and its results have also attested to the fact that more research on policy issues regarding blacks in higher education is mandatory if these colleges are to be viewed in the proper perspective. Even though there has been an increased focus by public and private agencies—including the federal government—on policy issues relating to the higher education needs of blacks, only limited or indirect attention has been given to the influence of accreditation on traditionally black institutions. For example, a recent report from the National Advisory Committee on Black Higher Education and Black Colleges and Universities made no specific reference to accreditation as a means of achieving higher education equity for black Americans.[9]

A paper delivered at a national meeting of black educators in 1980 set the agenda for this present study. It focused on the responsibilities of the accrediting agency and the black college in promoting access, choice, and parity for blacks in the accreditation process. A major conclusion was that accrediting agencies should develop special guidelines for the evaluation of historically black colleges on the assumption that such guidelines would supplement existing standards.[10] The findings of this study did not support that conclusion. Respondents were strongly opposed to special guidelines or different criteria for the evaluation of traditionally black institutions. It was clear that these institutions would consider such a change in policy as detrimental to their best interests. Since accreditation on the same basis was perceived to be essential for acceptance as equal partners by other colleges and universities, any attempt to create special guidelines or criteria should be approached with extreme caution so that their accreditation would not be viewed by others as second class. Consider, for example, the current pressure from government for public colleges to merge or change their racial makeup. One might assume that special guidelines might alter significantly the mission or threaten the very survival of these traditionally black colleges and universities.

At the same time, respondents also agreed that the application of the present or revised standards was of greater importance than the standards themselves. While all concurred that excellence in the achievement of goals and objectives was the key, there exists a need for sensitivity to the unique characteristics and needs of this group of institutions. As evidence of their concern, respondents placed importance on the future selection of evaluation team members for the improvement of MSA processes and procedures, and concluded that any team visiting a black college should have significant representation of black persons. It was assumed that such a practice would assure respect for the uniqueness of the black colleges as well as for their historical mission and cultural heritage. Therefore, it would be prudent for the accrediting agency to continue the practice of selecting and appointing persons to all evaluation teams based on their competence, expertise, experience, and ability to be sensitive to diversity and pluralism in American higher education. The implications of the foregoing seem self-evident for the continued positive growth and development of traditionally black institutions and for the good relationship which should continue between the Middle States Association and the various institutions it works with.

While the results of this study have been generally positive, there did emerge some specific policy recommendations regarding the evaluation and accreditation of traditionally black colleges. These include the following:

- MSA should find additional ways to orient evaluation team members in the application of its standards to traditionally black colleges;
- when the evaluative criteria are revised, MSA should examine the possibility of giving increased emphasis to community involvement as a criterion of excellence;
- in the application of standards, there should be greater sensitivity on the part of

evaluation teams and the commission to funding realities, clientele served, and unique mission;

- since there appeared to be no consensus on the issue of a possible role for MSA in assuring the continuity of black colleges, caution was recommended in actions of the agency which might hasten the demise of institutions, or involve the agency unnecessarily in political entanglements which might damage its effectiveness;
- MSA should not develop special guidelines or criteria for the valuation of traditionally black institutions, but rather should recognize their unique role in higher education; and
- MSA should continue to stress the self-study and evaluation processes as essential to the improvement of institutional functioning in all areas.

In summary, the study's findings confirmed some practices and suggested slight improvements in others, all of which should prove beneficial to a better accreditation protocol for Middle States institutions, especially traditionally black colleges. It was also clear that improvements did result from the overall evaluation and accreditation process, regardless of the locus of initiative. It is to be hoped that the results will be useful to other regional accrediting agencies and organizations or that they may serve as an impetus for further study.

One significant controversy remains. Should accrediting agencies assist in perpetuating a dual system, or should they work towards strengthening a system that provides greater access and success for a large number of students?

NOTES

1. Frank Bowles and Frank DeCosta, *Between Two Worlds*, Carnegie Commission on Higher Education (New York: McGraw-Hill, 1971), p. 69.

2. Ibid.

3. Amanda Asgill, "The Importance of Accreditation: Perceptions of Black and White College Presidents," *Journal of Negro Education* 45 (Summer 1976):294.

4. The research involved document review and analysis, interviews with chief executive officers, and a specially designed survey instrument. The following schools were included in the study: Delaware—Delaware State College; District of Columbia—Howard University; Maryland—Bowie State College, Coppin State College, Morgan State University, Sojourner-Douglass College, University of Maryland–Eastern Shore; New York—Malcolm-King–Harlem College Extension, Medgar Evers College–CUNY; Pennsylvania—Cheyney State College, Lincoln University.

5. U.S.O.E. National Advisory Committee on Black Higher Education and Black Colleges and Universities, *Third Annual Report, Overview of Committee Research* (Washington, D.C.: Government Printing Office, June 1980), p. 5.

6. Charles H. Thompson, "The Southern Association and Negro College Membership" (Editorial Comment), *Journal of Negro Education* 27 (Winter 1958):3.

7. American Association of State Colleges and Universities, Office of Communications Services and the Office for the Advancement of Public Negro Colleges,

National Association of State Universities and Land Grant Colleges, *Status Report on the Libraries of Historically Black Public Colleges and Universities* (Washington, D.C.: AASCU, September 1979), p. 3.

8. Mara Sapon-Shevin, "Mainstreaming: Implementing the Spirit of the Law," *Journal of Negro Education* 48 (Summer 1979):381.

9. National Advisory Committee on Black Higher Education and Black Colleges and Universities, *Target Date, 2000 AD: Goals for Achieving Higher Education Equity for Black Americans*, vol. I (Washington, D.C.: Government Printing Office, September 1980), p. ix.

10. Howard L. Simmons, "Implications of Accreditation for Promoting Access, Choice, and Parity for Blacks in Higher Education and the Uniqueness of Historically Black Colleges" (Paper delivered at the March 1980 National Association for Equal Opportunity Conference on Blacks in Higher Education, Washington, D.C.), p. 9.

9

The Fall and Demise of Affirmative Action

Robert E. Rucker and Jerry D. Bailey

Because of a complex array of statutes, executive orders, regulations, and court decisions, equal employment opportunity (EEO) is theoretically possible. However, because of the reality of what lies ahead for higher education, the decade of the eighties may very well signal the end of initiatives to promote affirmative action for women and minorities in universities.

Rather than address what William Kaplin calls the "equal employment thicket,"[1] or the successes and failures of EEO efforts, we are going to explore the impact of population trends upon higher education institutions and their faculties, and the resultant consequences for affirmative action. Three specific arguments will be considered:

- Enrollments in higher education in the 1980s will decline, and with this decline will come fewer new professorial openings.
- The percent of tenured faculty in many institutions is high and is rising, thereby further limiting the number of available professorial positions.
- The Age Discrimination in Employment Act Amendments of 1978 (P.L. 95–256) raise, as of July 1, 1982, the mandatory retirement age of faculty members from sixty-five to seventy, further limiting the potential for institutional flexibility in personnel policies.

The logical conclusion, if we are correct, is that those aspiring to professorships will face an increasingly restricted job market throughout the dec-

ade. Moreover, underrepresented groups will continue to have a disproportionately difficult time in accessing the positions which are open.

THE IMPACT OF FERTILITY AND THE "NEW STUDENT" ON ENROLLMENTS

The number of births per year does not have an immediate impact upon
the number of people who go to college. It is, however, the number of
births per year that is the major limiting parameter for college enrollments.
Most people who attend college do so between the ages of eighteen and
twenty-one; the number of births in a given year, therefore, provides the
basic population cohort of college-age people eighteen to twenty-one years
later.[2]

This simple relationship can be used to explain much of the growth in
college enrollments experienced in the 1960s and 1970s. The increased
enrollment during that period was in large part the result of the post–World
War II baby boom, which began in 1947 and reached a peak around 1960.[3]
It was the result of a combination of factors: 1) the GIs returning from the
war, marrying and having families; 2) an increase in the number of children
wanted by families; and 3) a period of relative economic prosperity. The
number of births in 1947 was 2.3 million and increased steadily until it
reached 4.3 million in 1961.[4] From 1961 to 1973 there was a fairly steady
decline, and after 1973 the birth rate leveled off at 3.1 million per year.[5]

One of the results of the postwar baby boom was a dramatic increase in
the number of people attending colleges and universities; in the 1960s undergraduate enrollment more than doubled—from 4 million to 8.6 million.[6]
This growth occurred not only because the college-aged population grew
dramatically but also because a strong economy created a stronger demand
for college-educated people. Moreover, minorities enrolled in larger numbers than ever before. The increases in enrollment began to slow in the
1970s to a growth rate of 2 to 4 percent per year, down considerably from
the 10 percent plus annual increases of the 1960s.[7] Still, enrollments had
increased to 12 million by 1980.[8]

What we saw in the 1970s is an increase in the number of students;
however, this increase occurred at a slower rate than in the 1960s. A partial
explanation for this slowing down is that the number of births per year
during the latter part of the 1950s and the early 1960s reached its zenith
and started downward. The colleges and universities felt the effects of this
fertility decline approximately eighteen years later. Other factors that contributed to the declaration of the growth rates in enrollments include a lower
demand for college graduates and a leveling off of enrollment rates among
older students.[9]

As enrollments increased over the past two decades, so did the demand
for college professors. In the 1959–1960 school year fewer than 400,000

instructional personnel worked in a total of 2,008 institutions. Over 1,000,000 enjoyed positions in 2,785 colleges and universities in the 1976–1977 school year.[10] Faculty growth rates correlate positively with enrollment increases— the number of faculty members increased 116 percent in the decade of the sixties. The percent of women faculty at all ranks in all institutions rose from 22 percent in 1959–1960 to 24 percent in 1969–1970 and to 32 percent in 1976–1977.[11]

Enrollments in colleges were expected to crest at 12.1 million in the fall of 1981.[12] Enrollment projections are tied in part to the traditional eighteen to twenty-one–year–old college-age cohorts. In 1979 there were 17 million people in this group. It is estimated that this figure will drop to 14 million by 1990 and 13 million by 1995.[13] This represents nearly a 25 percent decrease in the age group.

The number of eighteen-year-olds will decline during all of the 1980s and will level off in 1991. The only question affecting this statistic is whether the mortality rate will remain stable. There is usually little change in mortality rates for those between the age of six months and the early thirties. Some authors have suggested that if there is any change it would be an increase in the mortality rate, not a decrease, and there would consequently be fewer, not more, people in this age cohort. (We optimistically are discounting the possibility of major worldwide catastrophe.) Thus most of the enrollment projections we have seen call for at least moderate declines, and some for substantial declines, perhaps as much as 40 percent from 1979 to 1991.[14]

Some believe that new enrollments from older age groups will offset the decline in the eighteen- to twenty-four–year–old group. The enrollment rate of twenty-five– to thirty-five–year–old students did increase by 35 percent from 1970 to 1978.[15] From 1972 to 1978 the largest enrollment rate increase of any group occurred among women aged thirty to thirty-four; their numbers more than doubled.[16] It seems unlikely, however, that these increases can continue at their current rates. University administrators and others looking for alternative client groups to offset precipitous declines in enrollment need to consider that only a small percentage of older students actually obtain degrees, most adults who attend colleges and universities enroll for noncredit or nondegree courses, and it is unlikely "that adults will make up much of the loss of 18 to 24-year-olds in college during the next fifteen years."[17] The period of growth in enrollments for colleges and universities as a group is over for this century, and declines are imminent for most institutions.

The growth in the number of new positions for college faculty is also over. Indeed, it can be assumed that the profile of the American professoriate in 1990 will be the gray-haired mirror image of 1980. The 1973 Carnegie Commission on Higher Education age projections for college and university faculty members showed that those over forty accounted for 55.9 percent of the total in 1970, would be 62.1 percent in 1980, and 87.5 percent in 1990.

At the same time, those under thirty-five totaled 28.2 percent in 1970, would fall to 21.4 percent in 1980, and to 3.8 percent in 1990.[18] It is likely, in other words, that the young faculty members recruited to teach children of the baby boom may also be teaching the grandchildren of the baby boom.

TENURE

One of the key aspects in understanding the problems facing women and minorities as they seek to enter the professoriate is tenure. Tenure follows a period of probation, which is normally five or six years. Once a professor is tenured, he or she is relatively secure (barring fiscal exigency) for the remainder of his or her career. Thus, if a school tenures a large number of faculty, and enrollment drops, it may have more faculty than it can support, especially since tenured faculty members normally earn higher salaries. This as led some to suggest that tenure appointments should be tied to available resources.[19]

One of the significant concerns of university administrations has been the balance of tenured to nontenured faculty. The dramatic growth in enrollments in the 1960s and 1970s resulted in an increase in younger faculty members for whom tenure decisions were made several years after appointment. Currently, 56 percent of all full-time instructional faculty are tenured.[20] The figure for university personnel is 60 percent. Over 80 percent of those tenured in all institutions and nearly 90 percent of those in universities are men.[21]

In most institutions an assistant professor is normally considered for promotion and tenure during his or her sixth year at that rank. Usually the decision occurs when the professor is approximately thirty-five years old, which means that about 80 percent of his or her career could be in a tenured position. This suggests that in a hypothetical situation of uniform age distribution, good health and some intangibles (such as a stable economy and that universities fill all tenure-track lines), one could expect approximately 80 percent of the faculty members at colleges and universities to be tenured. Almost no college or university is eager to accept so high a percentage. Most consider 50–60 percent of the faculty members holding tenure to be a reasonable figure.[22] If promotion and tenure levels are to be maintained at the preferred level, a large percentage (perhaps as many as 60 percent) would need to be denied tenure. It should be kept in mind that these figures do not take into account the impact of declining enrollments.

The aging of tenured faculties does not lend encouragement to new or prospective faculty members, particularly when this information is linked to undergraduate enrollments. If, as we expect, these enrollments decline, it may mean fewer promotions to tenure and fewer replacements of tenured faculty members who resign, retire, or die. It is clear that personnel decisions throughout the remainder of the decade must be made with care, as professors and administrators may well live with their mistakes for the remainder of their professional lives.

MANDATES

The history of federal initiatives to reduce discrimination spans four decades, beginning with President Roosevelt's establishment of a committee on fair employment practices to investigate complaints against companies holding defense contracts (Executive Order 8802, June 1941). At least six executive orders followed during the next quarter century. Then President Johnson initiated 11246 and 11375. These became fully effective in 1968 and are commonly considered the cornerstones of "affirmative action." Shirley McCune and Martha Matthews describe the federal usage of the term as follows:

Affirmative action refers to employer initiated development of a set of specific result-oriented procedures to ensure that job applicants and employees are treated without regard to race, color, religion, sex, or national origin. The term usually implies action taken to overcome the effects of conditions which have resulted in limited participation of minorities and women. This activity, correctly labeled "affirmative action," is distinguished from corrective or remedial action, which is taken by institutions or agencies as a result of the identification of discrimination through required institutional self-evaluation or when mandated after a formal finding of discrimination by a Federal or State agency or court.[23]

Currently, federal antidiscrimination laws, state antidiscrimination laws, judicial decisions, laws regulating collective bargaining agreements, and institutional policies prohibiting discrimination, as well as executive orders, all support affirmative action in employment.

Probably the single most important contribution affirmative action has made over the past few years in higher education is to open up the selection process for new employees. Better choices have been made in many instances as a result of thorough, systematic searches. And in many institutions women and minorities have been considered and employed.

Passage of the Age Discrimination in Employment Act Amendments of 1978 (P.L. 95–256) could work against affirmative action for women and minorities, although its intent is anything but discriminatory. The law changed the age at which tenured employees must retire to seventy. It became effective on July 1, 1982.[24]

The new law will have numerous effects, both direct and indirect. It will allow teachers and other permanent employees to remain in their positions for an additional five years. These faculty members are making more money than at any previous point in their lives; the addition of five more years means that their salaries will continue to take a larger proportion of college and university monies than an assistant professor, or even two assistant professors. Some administrators do not anticipate teachers remaining until they are seventy, since many already take early retirement. Each year that faculty stay on, however, there are fewer positions available at the lower levels.[25]

The legislation raised a tremendous amount of controversy. For one thing, some administrators felt that the four years' lead time did not give them enough time to prepare for the impact of the law. There was also some concern that universities and colleges, already clogged with tenured people, would face an even more difficult situation as enrollments decline and faculty turnover rates slow down even further.

The legislation may also have some indirect effects. It may cause universities to change their retirement programs. Some may try to induce professors to leave their positions voluntarily before they reach the mandatory retirement age. More and more schools may turn to offering monetary incentives to encourage retirement. The schools could benefit by saving money in the long run. However, the professors would benefit from this only if they could find other employment. The ravages of inflation may place great pressure on the professor to remain at the university as long as possible, especially if he or she does not have another job to turn to after retirement.

An indirect consequence of this legislation could be the rethinking of tenure policies by many legislatures, school boards, and college and university governing boards. Thomas Flygare even suggests that this may be the final blow to tenure.[26]

Given current enrollment projections and the fiscal condition of many institutions, P.L. 95–256 could mean that aspiring women and minority candidates will have to wait longer for professorial positions than before. If large numbers of senior professors choose to remain until age seventy, the result can be none other.

CURRENT AND EMERGING QUESTIONS

Currently, one-half of the instructors, one-third of the assistant professors, one-fifth of the associate professors, and fewer than one-tenth of full professors are women. Their average salary for 1979–1980 was about 18 percent less than that of their male colleagues. This gap existed at all levels and types of institutions, although the differences tended to be greater at universities than at four- and two-year colleges. Men on university faculties earned nearly one-third more on the average than their women colleagues. Men also tended to get larger pay raises than women (7.4 percent versus 6.9 percent). Couple this with women's frequently lower salaries, and one can see that they are not as a group closing the gap.[27]

The number of employed full-time instructional male faculty actually decreased from 290,289 to 290,264 from the fall of 1976 to the fall of 1977. At the same time, those holding tenure increased from 177,947 to 181,192 (a total of 3,245 or 1.8 percent). Full-time instructional women faculty grew from 96,589 to 98,769 the same year, with the largest increase at the rank of lecturer. Tenure was awarded to 1,384 women, increasing their numbers from 40,445 to 41,829, or 3.4 percent. Note that women had the largest percentage increase, but 1,861 more men than women received tenure. And during the same year, the number of men who were promoted to full professor increased 1.4 percent, while women in this rank actually decreased .2 percent.[28]

Other major issues affecting this situation should be mentioned but are beyond the scope of this paper. Let us list just a few.

Lyman Glenny has asserted that the primary factor in the maintenance of enrollments may be the "fit" between the values, attitudes, and social mores of the faculty and those of the students they serve. If Glenny is right, what impact, if any, will an aging faculty have on enrollment patterns? Will the professors who were hired in the 1960s and 1970s and who consider themselves "liberals" be out of touch with the increasingly conservative attitudes of the country?

One of the most dramatic changes in the nation during the decade of the seventies was in the numerical growth of the Spanish-origin minority group. The 1970 census counted 9,072,602 persons of Spanish origin; the March 1979 Current Population Survey listed 12,079,000, and increase of 33.1 percent. During this period of time, the Mexican-origin subgroup grew 61.6 percent, from 4,532,435 to 7,326,000.[29] These figures may be seriously underestimated—one estimate of Puerto Rico's population, plus census data and estimates for undocumented workers pointed to a 1978 Hispanic population of 23 million.[30] It is clear, if Hispanics become the largest ethnic minority in the 1980s as is projected, the impact on education (and affirmative action) will be substantial. Are colleges and universities prepared to educate this increasingly sizable segment of our society?

In 1980 the National Center for Educational Statistics predicted that as many as 200 small, private four-year institutions might close during the decade of the 1980s. If so, what happens to their predominantly white, middle-aged male faculty? Will at least some, because of experience, be competitive with young, freshly-minted Ph.D.s—both men and women, majority and minority—for the few positions that will open in the decade?

The impact that Congress and the Reagan administration will have on affirmative action remains unclear. However, it is clear that certain individuals who hold key leadership positions in both the administration and the Senate are not sympathetic to affirmative action.

All of this suggests that, affirmative action notwithstanding, women still face a difficult decade in terms of economic and academic equity. When the factors mentioned previously are considered—declining enrollments, limited openings for new faculty because institutions have become "tenured in," the inclusion of faculty into the Age Discrimination in Employment Act, and the political environment—women faculty members will constitute the largest minority group in academe for the foreseeable future.

NOTES

1. William A. Kaplin, *The Law of Higher Education* (San Francisco: Jossey-Bass, 1979), p. 128.

2. W. Vance Grant, *Survey and Projections of National Center for Education Statistics* (Washington, D.C.: Government Printing Office, March 18, 1980).

3. William Petersen, *Population*, 3d ed. (New York: Macmillan, 1975), pp. 550–57.

4. Howard R. Bowen, "Some Reflections on the Present Condition and Future Outlook for American Higher Education," *Academe* 66 (February 1980):10.

5. There was little change in the total number of births in 1974 and 1975. However, the following years, 1976–1979 saw steady increases. In 1979 the total number of births was up to 3.5 million. The data gathered through October 1980 indicated that the birth rates were up over 4 percent compared with 1979, which would mean a total of 3.6 million births for 1980; see Department of Health and Human Services, *Vital Statistics Report* (January 16, 1981), p. 1. The impact of this increased fertility on college and university enrollments will begin in the middle 1990s. The increase will not be sudden, for the increase in fertility has been a slow one, and will be of no help in alleviating the enrollment problem of higher education in this decade.

6. John A. Centra, "College Enrollment in the 1980s," *Journal of Higher Education* 51 (January-February 1980):18.

7. Nancy Brocklehurst, "College Enrollment in the 1980s," *Academe* 66 (February 1980):16.

8. "Fall Enrollment Sets Record Despite Fewer 18-Year-Olds," *Chronicle of Higher Education* (November 10, 1980):3–4. NCES made a series of high and low projections in 1977 for enrollment in higher education institutions. The low projection for 1980 was 12.1 million, which was slightly higher than the actual enrollment figures of 12.0 million. This may indicate that future enrollments will be even lower than their lowest projections. This possibility does not bode well for new Ph.D.s and those entering Ph.D. programs.

9. Brocklehurst, "College Enrollment in the 1980s," p. 16.

10. W. Vance Grant and C. George Lind, *Digest of Education Statistics 1979* (Washington, D.C.: Government Printing Office), p. 100. It should be noted that this is the total number of different individuals (not reduced to FTE).

11. While it is true that women have become a larger proportion of the people employed in teaching positions at colleges and universities, the figures can be misleading. The vast majority of the positions held by women are nontenured and lower paid than those held by men; see Jack Magarrell, "More Women on Faculties; Pay Still Lags," *Chronicle of Higher Education* 21 (September 29, 1980):8.

12. Nancy B. Dearman and Valena White Plisko, *The Condition of Education* (Washington, D.C.: Government Printing Office, 1980), pp. 96ff.

13. Centra, "College Enrollment in the 1980s," p. 19.

14. Bowen, "Some Reflections on the Present Condition," p. 10.

15. U.S. Bureau of the Census, *Current Population Reports*, Series P–20, No. 321 (Washington, D.C.: Government Printing Office, March 1979).

16. Dearman and Plisko, *The Condition of Education*, p. 104.

17. Lyman A. Glenny, "Demographic and Related Issues for Higher Education in the 1980s," *Journal of Higher Education* 51 (July-August 1980):369.

18. Carnegie Commission on Higher Education, *Priorities for Action: Final Report* (New York: McGraw-Hill, 1973), Table B–10, p. 119.

19. Randall Porter, Robert Zemsky, and Penney Oedel, "Adaptive Planning," *Journal of Higher Education* 50 (September-October 1979):592.

20. Excludes students who assist in instruction, faculty in religious orders if their salaries are not determined and paid by the same common principles as those which apply to lay faculty, faculty for clinical medicine, administrative officers even though they may devote part of their time to classroom instruction, faculty in the ROTC program if their salaries are determined on a different basis than civilian faculty, and faculty on contracts other than nine-ten or eleven-twelve month duration.

21. Dearman and Plisko, *The Condition of Education*, p. 122.

22. Charles B. McLane, "The Malaise of Tenure Decisions: A Proposal for Senior Faculty Reassignment at Sixty," *Academe* 65 (March 1979):134.

23. Shirley McCune and Martha Matthews, *Programs for Educational Equity: Schools and Affirmative Action* (Washington, D.C.: Government Printing Office, 1975), p. 1.

24. "Age Discrimination in Employment Act—Exemption for Certain Tenured Employees at Institutions of Higher Education," *Federal Register* 43 (December 12, 1978):58154–56.

25. Heisner Report, "When Should a Teacher Retire? 55 . . . 65 . . . 70 . . . ?" *Instructor* 87 (May 1978):22.

26. Thomas J. Flygare, "Schools and the Law," *Phi Delta Kappan* 59 (June 1978):711.

27. Magarrell, "More Women on Faculties," p. 8.

28. Carolyn R. Smith, "Women Outpaced Men in Faculty and Tenure Increases between 1976–77 and 1977–78," *Special Report*, National Center for Education Statistics, reprint, June 25, 1980, p. 1.

29. U.S. Bureau of the Census, "Persons of Spanish Origin in the United States: March 1979," *Current Population Reports*, Series P–20, No. 354 (Washington, D.C.: Government Printing Office, March 1979).

30. Robert Anson, "Hispanics in the United States: Yesterday, Today, and Tomorrow," *The Futurist* 14 (August 1980):25–31.

10

Women in Higher Education Administration: Prospects and Institutional Policy Response in the 1980s

Sheila Kishler Bennett

Pessimism is fashionable today within the education community, as is the tendency to look to "policy solutions" for redress of problems beyond the scope of particularistic solutions. Both inclinations are anticipatory, in that both involve a critical and analytic look at the future. The issue of women in higher education administration provides an excellent example: The education policy community and concerned administrators view it with cautionary pessimism and anticipatory interest.

This chapter analyzes trends in the entry, distribution, and advancement of women in higher education administration. It is based on a study of a diverse group of female administrators who have participated since 1976 in the Bryn Mawr/Higher Education Resource Services, Mid-Atlantic, Summer Institute for Women in Higher Education Administration. The summer institute is a four-week residential program offering female administrators, including faculty with administrative or governance responsibility, intensive training in educational administration and management skills. In the period 1976–1980, 365 women took part. Summer institute participants are not in a statistical sense representative of all women in higher education administration, but they do represent a diversity of personal and institutional backgrounds. In this sense they are typical of women seeking careers in the area.

Two broad issues are examined: Who are the women in administration and where do they come from? and What has been the impact of growing professionalization in academic administration and the proliferation of programs? Answers to these questions contain numerous implications for policy leaders and administrators. These include the need to reexamine and renew the commitment to institutional missions, to provide credentialization and in-service training opportunities for teaching and administrative personnel, and to recognize not only equity issues but also the institutional costs and benefits of providing opportunity and advancement to women and other minorities in higher education administration.

WOMEN IN HIGHER EDUCATION ADMINISTRATION

As the numbers and distribution of women in administrative positions attest, higher education administration has remained relatively closed to women—both those who are already in administration and wish to advance through the rank and those who hope to enter the field. For example, in 1977 women held but 16 percent of all administrative positions in higher education and were concentrated in positions of relatively low power and authority.[1] Current information on the career backgrounds of such women is fragmentary at best. However, examination of the positions held by Bryn Mawr/HERS Summer Institute participants, and particularly the detailed entry and advancement histories available for the seventy-six participants in 1980, provide a detailed picture consistent with the scattered information available from other sources. Since participants included both older and younger women, and women more and less established in administrative tracks, it is possible to observe changing avenues of entry and advancement over approximately a twenty-year period.

Women's entry patterns are consistent with both culturally conditioned assumptions regarding "suitedness" and women's particular involvement with and concern for special constituencies. For example, entry into academic advising and student counseling services—from faculty rank and, increasingly, degree programs in psychology and counseling—has been and continues to be a primary channel of entry for women, one consistent with assumptions regarding "suitedness." Women are also found dealing with other women as special constituencies, for example, in developing and administering adult learning and continuing education programs targeted for mature women as "reentry" students. To a lesser degree, professional programs enrolling disproportionate numbers of women and leading to careers themselves progressing toward administrative responsibility have also provided opportunity for entry into administrative positions. Schools of education and nursing provide examples.

The converse of these generalizations is of course that women are disproportionately "staff"—in support positions—rather than "line"—having decision-making authority relative to the larger educational mission itself. They are also significantly underrepresented in the business and development

ends of the institutional enterprise, in those aspects of education administration more "instrumental" than "affective" in their function and more technical in the skills required.

These patterns of distribution are illustrated by the positions held by
recent summer institute participants and by patterns of entry for those participants with a history of involvement in higher education administration.
Of the 173 women who participated during the three-year period (1978–
1980) and who held primarily administrative positions at the time they attended, 45 percent described general administration as their primary area
of responsibility, 24 percent academic affairs, and 21 percent student services. Only three women were involved in business or financial management,
while the number involved in development activities was also small (ten, or
6 percent). The category "general administration" includes a majority of
women involved in the administration and development of programs either
designed specifically to meet the needs of noncampus-based students or
learners, many disproportionately enrolling women. Examples include continuing education programs, "universities without walls," cooperative or
lifelong learning programs, and degree and nondegree community college
programs. Few of these female administrators also held faculty rank.

By way of comparison, the sixty-five participants describing themselves
as "faculty" or as also holding academic rank within an established disciplinary program were entering administrative positions through departmental
or divisional chairs, or through performance of special assignments from
their administration (such as that of equal opportunity officers). These women
resemble in their entry pattern the majority of those others describing their
primary area of responsibility as "academic administration" and whose career
tracks were progressing toward deanships and other offices of academic
governance.

The relative importance of initial entry from the teaching faculty and from
student services and special programs is apparent in the career histories of
those who participated in summer 1980, all of whom held administrative or
governance responsibilities in that year. Half (thirty-seven) assumed their
first administrative position from faculty rank, and a quarter (twenty) entered
directly into student services or through involvement in a special constituency program and from there into administrative positions. The remaining
quarter (nineteen), who entered via a strictly administrative track, include
the majority of those with noneducation backgrounds and technical or business degrees, including business, secretarial, and financial experience.

Cohort-specific patterns are apparent. Women with a career history of
administrative responsibility in higher education are likely to have followed
the established route of promotion into positions of academic governance
and management from faculty rank. Younger women and women entering
education administration more recently (regardless of age) are more diverse
in their experience. Many, but particularly younger women with degree

backgrounds in psychology or counseling, have entered directly through student services—for example, as counselors, residential advisors, and directors of student affairs and activities. Other young women, characteristically with doctorates in the humanities, are finding opportunities as administrative or special assistants to deans, provosts, and presidents. By way of comparison, women in this group of more recent entrants who acquired administrative responsibilities first in special constituency programs tend to be older and to bring to their involvements previous experience in primary or secondary education, social service, or volunteer activity, and to be less conventionally credentialed. The smaller number of women in business and fiscal affairs and development offices are generally younger and come to their positions with more technically job-specific training or experience from outside the academic world.

PROFESSIONALIZATION AND PROLIFERATION

The great variety of institutional situations in higher education must be taken into account, even as we are forced to draw a few generalizations. At one extreme, sectarian and women's colleges have traditionally offered relatively good opportunities to women in institutional governance and administration. Changes in such colleges and the rapid "professionalization" of administrative personnel in even the small, liberal arts institution will, therefore, affect entry and mobility opportunities for women in this sector of higher education. At the other extreme is the large, multicampus university, which resembles a corporation in its organization, with multiple divisions producing diverse products and complexly related to its environments. It is the "multiversity" and its component types of institutions—community colleges, research and comprehensive universities—that both mirror and set the trends in the entry and advancement of women into higher education administration. And it is this area that particularly needs initiatives by senior administrators.

A number of demographic and organizational trends are reflected in the women's experience.[2] First, higher education administration has become both a highly differentiated and a professionalized enterprise. Two broad consequences of professionalization require attention. Historically, "professionalization" has resulted in the relative exclusion of women and minorities in a number of occupational areas. This is because entry has been tied to credentialization, and avenues to credentialization have remained relatively more closed to women than to men.[3] Professionalization in this sense is of course tied also to specialization and the requirement of technical and specialized training—for example, legal training; business training; degree certification in counseling, psychology, or education administration; fiscal expertise; experience in the use of data processing and information management.

An immediate secondary consequence of professionalization and certification is that a traditional avenue of mobility into administrative responsibility is increasingly closed—that from faculty rank. In a period of retrenchment, this means that institutions may feel themselves limited in their ability to retain talented junior faculty committed to the academic enterprise and socialized to academic values and priorities. This affects women and other minorities to a disproportionate degree since they are concentrated in the lower academic ranks.[4] Further, the dichotomization of "faculty" and "administration" is progressively accentuated, as administrative positions are filled by professionally trained individuals with more instrumental commitments to their institutions. Other forces—notably centralization of authority under conditions of fiscal stress—act in the same direction.

The second trend observed in women's entry and advancement histories reflects a variety of forces acting upon institutions of postsecondary education: demographic shifts, changing private rates of return on a college education, redefinition of life-style and educational needs, and the increased "market sensitivity" of educators. This trend is the proliferation of programs, including those that are nondegree and targeted at the adult learner, the mature or "reentry student." It parallels but is in no way restricted to the community college movement. Many of these programs enroll a disproportionate number of women, or are designed specifically to serve their vocational and developmental needs.[5] At the same time, there are increasing numbers of women (and decreasing numbers of men), between the ages of nineteen and twenty-two participating and continuing in such programs. The two forces account for the fact that women now constitute a majority of enrollments in postsecondary education.[6]

While women recognized the need for these programs and have developed and administered them, a variety of factors tend to marginalize them. For instance, many do not easily fit the established disciplinary ethos of the university or liberal arts college. Regular faculty remain uninvolved, with the result that the programs are staffed by part-time or nontenure-track appointments. Moreover, a variety of stigmatizing labels have been applied to them: "women's studies," "nondegree," "housewife," "part-time," "older student," "community outreach." Many are jerry-built appendages to the administrative structure, are understaffed and underfunded, or "pay as you go." Poorly housed, frequently physically removed from central university activity, and administratively hidden in the formal governance structure, these programs and services that were designed to respond to the "new students" of the 1970s and 1980s struggle to acquire recognition and legitimacy.

This situation raises the issue of institutional mission and the legitimacy that is granted to an individual who is recognized as vital to an institution's purpose and identity. All of this is particularly difficult today when institutions of higher education are being increasingly challenged to reassess their position and responsibilities. James Perkins has observed that "the university is asked not only to perform conflicting missions but also to perform them within the framework of an organizational design appropriate to its earliest mission—that of teaching or the transmission of knowledge."[7] Yet even the mission of teaching—and its relation to the demands upon higher education for public service and broadened access—has become a complex matter, for the 1970s saw far-reaching changes in the content of educational programs, the function of higher education in providing manpower needs, the access or entitlement of constituencies, and the provision of lifelong educational opportunities. Clearly, institutions of American higher education are being challenged to reassess their rights and responsibilities.

The challenge to women in academia is even greater. Female administrators who seek admission to the larger administrative and governance structures of their institutions must all too frequently gain recognition for the teaching and service function of their programs, along with the acceptance of their contribution to the acknowledged mission of their institutions.

To some extent, institutional differentiation (and specifically the community college movement) can be viewed as a response to these pressures. Two caveats are in order. With respect to women's access to authority and administrative position, community college faculty and administrators share in important respects the professional socialization of their peers elsewhere and cannot be presumed therefore not to share more general assumptions regarding status, prestige, and rank within their professions and higher education.[8] Secondly, as members of confederated state systems, or as satellite campuses, many public two-year institutions look to a centralized administration and must confront complex questions of resource distribution within this larger system, as well as questions of administrative control. As in other sectors of society, stratification with respect to institutional prestige and broader questions of "missions" may also come to be reflected in control of and access to resources. The female administrator may find herself faced with a double burden of marginality: the marginality of her program and the marginality of her institution.

IMPLICATIONS

Today women are increasingly seeking access to the administrative and decision-making structures of higher education—as students, faculty, advocates, and career administrators. At the same time, it is clear that women must consider several complex issues: whether their leadership in redirecting programs and services toward the new constituencies of the seventies and eighties will be granted recognition and will lead them into the centralized governance and administrative structures of their institutions; whether opportunities for certification and in-service training will be available to academic women and others in entry-level positions, as administrative tracks become progressively more differentiated and professionalized; whether academic women will be recognized as the institutional resource that they are despite retrenchment and the myriad other problems facing higher education institutions. None of the trends described above represents a purposeful policy of exclusion or discrimination. Nevertheless, each represents a change that particularly affects opportunities for entry and advancement to women and other minorities.

The issues of marginality and mission relate directly to the question of whether the leadership positions for women provided by the new constituencies and restructured educational programs will be recognized, rewarded, and incorporated. To a degree not previously experienced in American higher education, institutional development in the coming decade is expected to be "enrollment driven," i.e., students will increasingly demand specific programs and educational services. If the experience of the 1970s is a harbinger of the eighties, these students will be older, more frequently female, less frequently full-time and residential, and more professionally and vocationally oriented.[9]

Questions of educational policy cannot, however, be treated simply as "market" questions. An institution that does so will no longer be able to structure its priorities and allocate its resources, except as a response to the most pressing needs of the moment. Institutional decision makers must be able to confront issues of program development from a clear perspective of institutional commitments and responsibilities. Further, as the programs of the 1970s that have proved to be responsive to the changing needs and demands of "new students" become an integral part of their institutional framework, institutional decision makers must take care to recognize the contributions and talents of those who provided the leadership in their development. Increasing centralization of the administration of formerly peripheral programs must not be allowed to "close out" women and others from administrative and decision-making advancement, any more than institutionalized marginality.

Second, an institution can ill afford the loss of talent, human capital, and commitment—to the academy and to the university as both an ideal and a community—represented by the junior faculty. Today such a loss is almost always from the ranks of women and other minorities. Closing the avenues of administrative entry from faculty rank will surely erode the development of shared sentiments and values, institutional loyalties, and acceptance of a common system of authority among faculty and administrative personnel.[10] At the same time, professionalizing administrative tracks and student services is an adaptive and necessary response to size, complexity, and fiscal pressure which cannot be ignored. Providing certification and in-service training opportunities for junior faculty and other institutionally committed women who would otherwise lack certification is one way of retaining talented women who might otherwise be lost to their institutions.

Finally, institutions of higher education must recognize that access and opportunity for women in higher education administration is not just a matter of equity, of an institution's moral or legal responsibility. Universities and colleges are both businesses and cultural institutions. As a business, each must make efficient use of its personnel to produce the highest quality service in as cost-effective a manner as possible. As a cultural institution, each is responsible for preparing students for their place in society, for meeting immediate and long-term student needs, and for transmitting and producing knowledge. As in a corporation, gender and race are personal attributes that are extraneous to an individual's intellectual and administrative talents. In other words, in the administration of an institution of higher education it is good business to recognize and cultivate ability and commitment.

Beyond the benefits of recognizing administrative talent and commitment, however, lie the responsibilities of the college or university as a cultural institution. At a time when women are achieving parity with men in access and enrollments, and challenging men in both the home and the workplace, are our colleges and universities in fact trying to combat gender role stereotyping and sexism in the learning and living environments they create for their students? It seems clear that an institutional environment in which women can be observed in all manner of leadership positions is one that promotes the career development of female students, perhaps in part simply because in such contexts gender is not a primary personal attribute.[11] The responsibilities of an institution of higher education extend beyond faculty representation and the introduction of women and women's scholarship into the curriculum. They include administrative structure of the university and an administrative commitment to curricular and program innovation.

This chapter has focused primarily on the structural aspects of change in higher education that are likely to affect patterns of movement into positions of administrative and decision-making responsibility, particularly by women and other minorities. The issues of equity (in the sense of policies designed to redress the present effects of past discrimination) and institutional discrimination ("bias that stems from the normal structure and functioning of the institution itself"[12]) have not been addressed. This is not to say that these issues do not exist or need not be considered, or that women in higher education administration differ in their experience from token and highly visible women in other management structures.[13] Rather, this chapter purposely expresses a sense of anticipatory caution for the future in an effort to outline broad contours of change that are less likely to receive attention than the immediate issues of equity and discrimination, but which threaten to be just as important for women's entry and advancement within higher education administration.

NOTES

1. C. Van Alstyne and J. S. Withers, *Women and Men in the Administration of Higher Education Institutions: Employment Patterns and Compensation* (Washington, D.C.: College and University Personnel Association, 1977).

2. For a recent, comprehensive overview of enrollment and institutional trends, see Carnegie Council on Policy Studies in Higher Education, *Three Thousand Futures. The Next Twenty Years for Higher Education* (San Francisco: Jossey-Bass, 1980).

3. A statement of the general case—professionalization related to principles of inclusion and exclusion—is found in Magali Sarfatti Larson, *The Rise of Professionalism. A Sociological Analysis* (Berkeley: University of California Press, 1977).

4. Lilli S. Hornig, "Untenured and Tenuous: The Status of Women Faculty," *Annals of the American Academy of Political and Social Science* 448 (March 1980):115–25.

5. For a prospective view of enrollment composition to the year 2000, see Carnegie Council, *Three Thousand Futures*, pp. 32–54. See also Carnegie Commission on Higher Education, *New Students and New Places: Policies for the Future Growth and Development of American Higher Education* (New York: McGraw-Hill, 1971); K. Patricia Cross, *Beyond the Open Door: New Students in Higher Education* (San Francisco: Jossey-Bass, 1971).

6. Center for Educational Statistics, *Digest of Educational Statistics 1980* (Washington, D.C.: U.S. Government Printing Office, 1980); *Chronicle of Higher Education* (November 10, 1980):4.

7. James A. Perkins, ed., *The University as an Organization* (New York: McGraw-Hill, 1973), p. 3.

8. Howard B. London, "In Between: The Community College Instructor," *Annals of the American Academy of Political and Social Science* 448 (March 1980):62–73.

9. Carnegie Council, *Three Thousand Futures*, pp. 28–31.

10. See, for example, Irwin T. Sanders' discussion, "The University as a Community," in *The University as an Organization*, ed. Perkins, pp. 57–78.

11. See particularly the work of M. Elizabeth Tidball, "Perspectives on Academic Women and Affirmative Action," *Educational Record* 54 (Spring 1973):130–35; and "Women's Colleges and Women Achievers Revisited," *Signs* 5 (Spring 1980):504–517. See also Sheila Kishler Bennett, "Undergraduates and Their Teachers: An Analysis of Student Evaluations of Male and Female Instructors," in *The Undergraduate Woman: Issues in Educational Equity*, ed. Pamela J. Perun (Lexington, Mass.: Lexington Books, 1982).

12. Janice Pottker, "Overt and Covert Forms of Discrimination Against Academic Women," in *Sex Bias in the Schools*, ed. Janice Pottker and Andrew Fishel (Cranbury, N.J.: Associated University Presses, 1977), p. 380.

13. See particularly Rosabeth Moss Kanter, *Men and Women of the Corporation* (New York: Basic Books, 1977).

PART III

HIGHER EDUCATION AND
SOCIETAL NEEDS

11

The Service Function of Higher Education Institutions: A New York Case Study

Martin S. Quigley

In this country higher education has always served a public function. Beginning with the founding of Harvard College nearly three and a half centuries ago and continuing to the present, public service has been a goal—expressed or implied—of every higher education institution.

In the colleges founded before the Revolution the public service needs could be defined precisely and were apparent to all. At that time the first priority was the education of future clergymen. Then other needs of the colonies were addressed, including the collegiate education of young men for future careers as lawyers, government officials, and doctors.

Following the growth of universities in the United States during the second half of the nineteenth century, it became popular in education circles to identify three functions of higher education: teaching, research, and public service. Depending on the times and the nature of each postsecondary institution, the relative weight given each of the functions has differed.

One of these, the public service function, deserves special attention today from all those concerned with the direction of higher education—trustees, presidents, administrators, faculty, students, plus officials in legislative and executive branches of government. Significant administrative changes, as well as different faculty perceptions, will be required before the academic world can fulfill its potential in serving national and local needs.

During recent decades few authorities in higher education have done much more than give lip service to public service. Most universities and colleges act as if a policy decision has been made to leave academic public service to others. However, it is more than likely that few institutions actually have made any policy decision on the subject. With strong competition for facilities, dollars, and manpower, public service projects and programs cannot be developed and maintained in the absence of specific decisions and positive actions by top administrators and faculty decision makers.

The reordering of governmental financial priorities initiated by the Reagan administration confronts higher education institutions with difficult decisions. And funding cuts by federal and state governments will make it more difficult for universities and colleges to maintain existing programs. However, financial exigencies should not deter institutions from giving a proper priority to their public service function. In fact, improved public service may be an effective way to compensate for direct losses of government funding by increasing other types of revenue.

The public service experience of universities and colleges in New York State makes an interesting case study. The Regents of the University of the State of New York, the governing body responsible for all education within the state, public or private, played a leadership role in the effort. The Regents have called attention on a number of occasions to the importance of the service function. This has stimulated individual institutions and has resulted in a sharing of reports on various public service programs.

In the first few years of this decade the Regents of the University of the State of New York have given increasing attention to public service. It also began to include the for-profit sector. Thus, for instance, special attention was paid to areas of high technology and biomedicine, as well as training and retraining programs for business and industry.

WHAT IS PUBLIC SERVICE?

There is no general agreement on exactly what activities of a university or college constitute public service. To the extent that higher education is serving a public function, the mere existence of an institution could be termed public service. In fact, higher education institutions enjoy tax-free status because they are deemed to be promoting a community good.

A report to the Board of Regents of New York by Adelphi University proposed the following definition of public service: "The service role of a university is advice and technical assistance, research in public problems, training and upgrading of community personnel—public and private."[1] A weakness of this definition is that it includes much that is properly a part of the teaching function, i.e., "training and upgrading of community personnel."

A more precise definition has been used by Clifton R. Wharton, Jr., Chancellor of the State University of New York: "Essentially public service means the delivery and application of our knowledge resources to the identification, analysis, and solution of public problems."[2] Wharton points out that public service has been a long-standing feature of a number of the public higher education institutions of the country. It also, of course, has been a "long-standing" feature of some of the more prominent private higher education institutions.

The Commission on Independent Colleges and Universities, the New York State organization for private institutions, in a November 1978 questionnaire to its membership, defined public service as activities that provide "benefits to government agencies, business and industry and/or local communities."

A broader definition is required if the whole range of societal demands on higher education is to be met. In 1979 the Bureau of Postsecondary Planning of the State Education Department prepared studies for the New York State Board of Regents showing how the Regents' priority for public service might be implemented. One report included the following section offering a definition and a clarification of elements of public service in the contemporary context:

Public service consists of those activities of a group of members of an academic community addressed to a targeted problem of the locality, region or the State.

In this precise sense *public service* has the following elements:

1. It must be undertaken with the approval of the institution. Unauthorized, independent or "free-wheeling" activities—even though they may have public benefits—do not constitute public service of an educational institution.

2. It must be carried on by a team or a group from the institution, even if the number involved is only one professor or administrator, supported by his staff. Many targeted problems obviously require the involvement of a number from the academic community, often with personnel drawn from more than one department or discipline.

3. It must be addressed to a societal problem. As important as individual consultation might be to a business or industry—and to the academic person involved professionally and financially—service aimed at benefiting primarily a commercial undertaking should not be included under a postsecondary institution's umbrella of public service.

4. To the extent feasible, public service activities should be carried on with the cooperation and the participation of individuals outside the academic world. The advantages of collaboration include the pooling of a variety of expertise and the enhancement of community awareness of the contributions made by faculty and administrators of the postsecondary institution or institutions involved.

5. Whenever the type of problem and local conditions permit, educational institutions should attempt to work together to assemble the best team available in all the postsecondary institutions in the community or region. *Public service* is one function of higher education at which public and independent institutions may work together fruitfully.[3]

The above definition and the five clarifying points are addressed to conditions in New York State where both public and independent sectors of higher education are important. In areas of the country where the private sector is small, no emphasis would be needed on mutual cooperation in public service activities.

PUBLIC SERVICE IMPLEMENTATION

The Regents of the State University of New York first turned their attention to the "outreach" aspect of public service in a 1972 statement of goals to the year 2000:

> The traditional role of the university has always included the expansion of public service, but the level of involvement with the community has been progressively increasing with the advent of a new era of social responsibility. The opening up of new avenues of communication between school and neighborhood serves to foster an increased awareness of each other's goals and needs, and will result in better understanding of the benefits to be derived from cooperative planning. Both collegiate and non-collegiate post-secondary education must therefore continue to integrate the needs of local communities with their own academic goals in order to realize any degree of social betterment resulting from the interaction of the two entities.[4]

The State University, the controlling body of public universities and colleges outside New York City, responded to the Regents' challenge to give increased priority to public service by saying that: "The State University will seek to bring to bear the expertise of its professional staff upon the public policy problems of the State and its localities."[5]

The City University of New York, which has a long record of public service—beginning with the establishment of its first unit, City College—commented as follows:

> The City University of New York is not only a major agency of the city, but also a part of the social, cultural, and economic fabric of the city. Its urban orientation carries with it the strongest possible commitment to further New York City's development, not only as a marketplace and workshop, but as a home and center of cultural and intellectual energy.
>
> The University expresses its intent to continue and expand this commitment through programs and research, through contractual and cooperative relationships with the public schools, and through services directly provided to other city agencies and to other public and private agencies.[6]

The Regents' final word in the 1972 publication struck a balance that seemed to weaken the call for increased public service:

> The issue of the extent and nature of the role of colleges and universities in relation to the general community is being debated in many quarters. The long held non-partisan position of the academic community, however, must be maintained in order to retain the basic principle of academic freedom as it has been known. The Regents

therefore request that all institutions plan consciously and deliberately the nature and extent of their commitment to their communities in order to realize a feasible degree of involvement.[7]

In view of such a cautious expression from the Regents, it is not surprising that colleges and universities in New York—and in places that look to New York for educational leadership—were slow to develop increased and more diversified public service activities. The suggestion that administrators "plan consciously and deliberately" apparently was widely interpreted as indicating that public service was a low priority for the Regents.

Six years later the State University of New York added a recommendation that "voluntary constituencies" of the colleges and universities become involved:

In achieving better understanding of the problems of the State and campus communities, and in the general enhancement of the usefulness of the University, special effort will be made to further utilize the knowledge and counsel of the voluntary constituencies, including the members of college councils, local boards of trustees, and alumni.[8]

An excellent expression of the challenge to colleges and universities to better serve needs of government was made by Governor Hugh Carey's task force on higher education the year before the Regents' 1976 plan was published:

[Needed are] the expanded provision of technical and policy research services to state and local government units, branches, and agencies. These units of government certainly need the technical and analytical insights of a wide range of professional experts; they cannot possibly maintain permanent staffs covering all the fields of knowledge relevant to government today. Yet the collective faculties of our colleges and universities, large and small, do contain such a broad range of expertise which ought to be made available, as needed, to provide consultative, evaluative, and research services.

The problem is how to develop the mechanisms of communication and mobilization so that government needs can be matched with available university experts, and appropriate teams from the academic community can be brought together with the operating officials of government.

There are other problems, too, in the definition and application of the expertise which the academic community possesses, and in the semantics of communication between the academicians and the practical world of governmental operations and public policy. But these are eminently solvable problems.[9]

In its concluding section, titled "The University as a Problem Solver," the governor's task force report stated: "It is time to take a new look at the role of New York's universities, with a view to developing practical means for the organization and mobilization of intellectual resources to produce policy and technical studies—economic, social and governmental."[10] While Governor Carey's task force was addressing concerns of New York State, the points it made can be applied to every state. Moreover, even though the task force focused on academic assistance to government, needs are equally great in nongovernmental sectors. Those needs continue.

In its section on mission, the Regents 1980 *Statewide Plan* discussed service this way:

> New York colleges and universities must serve our communities, State, and Nation. They must train and retrain workers and professionals to keep them abreast of changing technologies in the workplace and the advance of knowledge in professional fields. Higher education must apply its research capacities to the social and technological problems of our communities and our society and to the economic redevelopment to New York State and the Nation.[11]

The Regents 1982 Progress Report reviewed developments since the issuance of the 1980 plan. It reported that the state's Science and Technology Foundation had commissioned Battelle Columbus Laboratories to study ways the state could stimulate growth in high-technology industry. It was estimated that 10 percent of the employed persons in New York State were in that industry. The Battelle study recommended the direction adopted by the state, viz. concentrate on electronics/information and on the medical/biological area. Some progress has been made.

Public institutions under the Regents of the University of the State of New York and independent universities in the state have organized a wide variety of programs to assist business and industry. By 1982 the first group alone had twenty Development Centers for Business, according to the Regents progress report. Special attention was also directed to training engineers.

Governor Hugh Carey signed a law on July 22, 1982, providing for the establishment of "Centers for Advanced Technology." Ultimately eight centers are to be formed, under the direction of the New York State Science and Technology Foundation. The first, a joint venture, was the Center for Industrial Innovation at Rensselaer Polytechnic Institution.

And finally, one of numerous issues raised in preparing the 1984 *Statewide Plan for the Development of Postsecondary Education* was the development of partnerships between industry and institutions of higher education:

> New York's institutions of higher education have a significant role in the State's future economic growth, especially in the area of advanced technology. Recent studies suggest that the promising technologies which represent the greatest economic opportunity for New York are in the two broad groups Electronics/Information and Medical/Biological. Planning efforts need to be focused on the future potential of these key industries and others that may be identified as of major importance, and

on the programs, research, and service higher education institutions can develop to support growth on a regional and statewide basis.[12]

Tentative objectives included increased instructional research and service activities in the identified technological groups, the establishment by 1988 of eight Centers of Advanced Technology, the development of new models of industry-university collaboration, and a campaign by postsecondary institutions and state agencies to attract and retain industry in New York State. "The campaign will feature the rich contributions of New York's diverse colleges and universities to business and industry."[13]

THE NEW CHALLENGE

The call for public service made by Governor Carey's task force in 1975, and repeatedly thereafter by the Regents of the University of the State of New York, is a challenge to universities and colleges finally to fulfill a long-standing expectation. The public is impatient with both government and higher education for not finding solutions to pressing social and economic problems. In order to effectuate the highest possible order of public service, even assuming that all available resources of the academic world can be mustered, a much improved relationship needs to be developed between educational institutions and other organizations.

Whatever the level of a higher education institution—research university, general university, college, or community college—a variety of internal problems of motivation and of organization should be addressed before the particular institution may effectively organize its public service program and individual public service projects.

One problem is psychological. Frank Macchiarola, former chancellor of the New York City Board of Education, has asserted that a college or university must be ready "to get its hands dirty in the process of doing some practical work." In a 1978 address he said:

The link between what we are doing and what you are doing hasn't been made. And as long as universities are going to address not our problems but the problems that *they* think we have, they are not going to provide the help we need. Unless the university community deals with the questions we have, when we have them, I don't think we are going to improve the relationship between the university and the school at all.[14]

While Macchiarola was talking about elementary and secondary school problems, his point about the academic world addressing what may not be the real problems has general application. Faculty have their own interests and often find it psychologically difficult to adjust to the attitudes and viewpoints of nonacademics, whether they be government officials, business and union leaders, or community spokesmen.

Robert E. Marshak, former president of City College of the City University of New York, made public service a top priority during the eight years of his administration. In his first report, published in 1973, he wrote:

Of course, the College's educational programs constitute the major service to the City. But, in addition, the College must find ways to put the intelligence and expertise of its Faculty to the direct service of the City. By participating in the solution of pressing urban problems, by lending assistance to particular agencies of municipal government, and by serving as a resource for all citizen groups, the College can truly serve the City, thus returning many times over municipal investment in the institution.[15]

During Marshak's administration City College took specific steps to broaden its public service program. One significant action was the creation of the post of vice president for public service. The State University of New York also has an official, the associate chancellor for public service, overseeing public service throughout the universities and colleges forming the SUNY system.

Despite the priority assigned to public service by the New York Regents and the call for action by Governor Carey's task force, many universities and colleges in New York State lack effective programs for a variety of reasons, including the following:

• *No institutional priority for public service.* The call for public service by a state agency or a university system must be made at the campus level, where such action is difficult to implement.

• *Lack of trustee and presidential leadership.* Faculty and administrators tend to be fully involved in teaching and research activities and related support services. Public service is usually overlooked unless there is an expressed commitment from the trustees and president.

• *Lack of faculty interest.* Public service fulfills an institutional function rather than the goals of an individual. Hence, participation by individual members of the academic community depends on direction from the administration.

• *Resistance to interdepartmental and team approaches.* Most social problems cross discipline lines. Since academic institutions and their reward systems are organized into departments, cooperative ventures pose numerous problems.

• *Absence of coordination and evaluation.* Even in institutions with well-developed interdisciplinary programs and a fine interdepartmental spirit, public service projects often require a degree of coordination unusual in a college or university. Many public service projects are set up without regard to evaluation, which tends to obscure the value of the work to the community and to the higher education institution.

• *Shortage of funds.* Even in times of financial prosperity for colleges and universities it was difficult to find funds for public service. In these times of fiscal pressures most institutions lack adequate financing for "normal" operations and resist efforts to allocate monies for public service.

- *No effective method of utilizing students.* While public service projects may employ students for some low-level tasks, the basic thrust is to bring to the outside organization the expertise of the academic institution. That means the utilization of faculty and, if practical, the most highly qualified members, but not students.

- *No public appreciation of services performed.* While there are exceptions, in general public service does not result in community praise. The effects of most projects may not be apparent for some time. In contrast, the effects of teaching are visible, at least to the extent that the numbers of students enrolled and annual graduates can be counted.

To be effective, public service activities by a university or college must take into account the following factors:

- *Strong involvement of board and president.* Since the typical board of trustees includes representative leaders of the community, the board should have an awareness of problems that need attention. Public service is one area in which presidential approval is essential and presidential leadership extremely important.

- *Good linkages to the community and local government.* Public service programs are difficult to design and carry out without participation of members of the community and of local government. The college or university that has strong councils and alumni organizations can assess community needs and develop effective public service strategies.

- *High motivation and commitment to team and interdisciplinary efforts to address complex issues.* Unless participants in public service projects are enthusiastic and dedicated, success is unlikely. Moreover, since most social issues are complex, they require the expertise of academic personnel from more than one department.

- *Institution organized for public service under a well-regarded individual.* In order for the interests of the institution to be protected, as well as for the welfare of specific projects, it is important that the person supervising or coordinating public service enjoy a good reputation in the academic community.

- *Care in project selection.* To be effective, public service programs and projects must be chosen with an eye to available personnel and funding resources.

- *Adequate financial support.* Whether funds for projects come from outside sources or from the higher educational institution (or from some combination thereof), clearly they need to be an amount adequate to the circumstances. While many public service projects may be carried out with low levels of funding, few of them can be accomplished without some money.

LESSONS FROM NEW YORK

The New York experience shows that pressures from outside higher education—from government, business and industry, and community leaders—are mounting. Representatives of the public want the fullest possible measure of results for the tax monies spent in support of colleges and universities. The wisdom of the academic world should be made available to help address and, one hopes, to solve the grave economic and social problems facing all of us.

Higher education institutions need first of all to make a commitment to public service. Once an institutional commitment has been made, difficult questions concerning implementation must be faced. These include:

- How can institutional resources be marshaled most effectively?
- What expertise is available among faculty members and administrators that should be utilized in public service programs and projects?
- How can a college or university work successfully with government officials and community representatives who have different backgrounds and priorities than are common to most academics?
- How do we identify specific projects that are within the capability of available human and material resources?
- How do we evaluate results in public service and suitably reward participants in each successful project?

The fact that finding answers to these questions will be difficult does not detract from the urgency of the task. Public service by a college or university is a political issue in the best sense of the term. As is true of other political issues, leadership in planning and carrying out public service requires human relations skills plus a firm determination to serve the common good. There is no question that colleges and universities have unique resources to bring to bear in the important area of public service. It is also clear that success could be personally and institutionally rewarding. What is lacking now is the coordinated will to forge ahead.

NOTES

1. Board of Regents of the State of New York, *Education beyond High School* (Albany, N.Y., 1972), p. 337.

2. "Priorities for the New Austerity: Public Service," *The News* (State University of New York) 9 (October 1980):3.

3. Martin S. Quigley, "Priority for the 1980s: The Service Function of Postsecondary Institutions" (Report prepared for the Bureau of Postsecondary Planning, State Education Department, Albany, N.Y., 1979), pp. 5–6.

4. *Education beyond High School*, p. 14.

5. Ibid., p. 298.

6. Ibid., p. 319.

7. Ibid., p. 433.

8. *The Regents Statewide Plan* (Albany, N.Y.: State Education Department, 1976), p. 14.

9. *The Final Report of the Governor's Task Force on Higher Education* (New York, 1975), p. 15.

10. Ibid., p. 139.

11. *The Regents Statewide Plan for the Development of Postsecondary Education 1980* (State Education Department, October 1980), p. 10.

12. *The Bulletin of the Regents Statewide Plan for the Development of Postsecondary Education 1984* (State Education Department, December 1982), pp. 26–27.

13. Ibid., p. 27.

14. Frank Macchiarola, *The University and Education in New York City*, address presented October 12, 1978, at Columbia University General Education Seminar (New York: Columbia University Press, 1978), pp. 36–37.

15. Robert E. Marshak, *Problems and Prospects of an Urban University* (New York: City College of the City University of New York, 1973), pp. 157–58.

12

U.S. Science Manpower and R & D Capacity: New Problems on the Horizon

Lewis C. Solmon and William Zumeta

This chapter was first written in September 1980 and revised in February 1981, times when there was much less concern than there is at present with science manpower, R & D capability, and related problems.* Our purpose was to point to signs of emerging shortages of Ph.D.-level scientists, of the erosion of our capacity to train such people and of possible qualitative deterioration, and to analyze alternative policy responses. While awareness of the problems we point to is much greater now, we still await an adequate policy response (the recently announced Presidential Young Investigator Awards program notwithstanding). Thus the policy analysis and recommendations we offer are at least as timely today as they were in 1980. Indeed, we would argue that their urgency is greater now; as the saying goes, "time's a-wasting." As we argue in the paper, the problems are unlikely to disappear as a result of market forces alone.

The ups and downs of the labor market for scientists and engineers are fairly well-known. American science was a very small operation in its embryonic years before the First World War. That war stimulated considerable demand for science and for those who could practice and apply it for patriotic purposes. The war also provided a showcase for the practical utility of science

*The research on which this article is based was supported in part by grants from the Spencer Foundation, the National Science Foundation, and the Ford Foundation.

that carried over into peacetime industrial and medical applications. The 1920s were generally good for science and scientists.

During the thirties science and its practitioners, like everyone else, suffered the effects of the Great Depression. The Second World War brought an unprecedented boom for science—national research and development expenditures increased from $74 million in 1940 to $1.6 billion in 1945— and the ensuing "cold war" ensured continued growth. The use of science and its practitioners in nondefense industries grew rapidly too during the postwar period, due in no small part to technological "spin-offs" from defense spending and to the vast potential for nonmilitary applications demonstrated by wartime science. The boom in science and engineering moved into high gear in 1958 when the Soviet Union launched the first sputnik satellite and a worried America turned to science and technology to lead the way in "beating the Russians."

Alas, as is now widely known, the boom stopped booming in the late 1960s. Industrial R & D spending ceased to grow rapidly, and federal R & D support declined in real terms between fiscal 1968 and fiscal 1975. In the last few years valiant efforts to increase real federal support for research and development have been nearly wiped out by accelerating inflation. Enrollments in colleges and universities, which are a major source of demand for scientists, grew more slowly after 1968 following ten years of very rapid growth. Since 1975 nationwide enrollment growth has averaged only about 1 percent per year and is expected to be zero or negative through most of the eighties and early nineties.

Throughout the postwar boom period, but particularly after sputnik, graduate enrollments and degree production in science and engineering grew rapidly as demand for scientists and teachers of science seemed insatiable, and federal support for their training was plentiful. Graduate enrollments increased from just over 100,000 in 1939–1940 to 278,000 in 1957 to 808,000 in the fall of 1968.[1] Doctoral degree awards grew from some 3,300 in 1940 to nearly 8,800 in fiscal 1958 to almost 23,000 ten years later. Partly because many doctoral students were "in the pipeline" when market demand and federal support for their training began to drop off, the number of annual doctorate awards grew to 33,000 in 1973 before starting to decline. The total was about 31,000 in 1979. Total graduate enrollment leveled off for several years but now may be entering a period of decline.

Our purposes in this chapter are two. First, we seek to give warning of potential problems regarding U.S. science manpower by summarizing the prevailing views in the science community concerning the current and future sufficiency of Ph.D.-level scientists and engineers for the nation's research enterprise. Then we pull together and interpret evidence that suggests a turnaround in Ph.D. labor markets in many science and engineering disciplines even as capacity for Ph.D. production is eroding. And we consider the implications of the inevitable uncertainties surrounding the projections of excess supplies of scientists and engineers. We also explain the basis for the concerns of those who fear that the quality of our future scientists may decline.

In the second half of the paper we sketch in broad strokes several policy approaches for dealing with both the quality and quantity aspects of the potential science manpower problem and consider their merits and drawbacks. We conclude with a proposal that could avoid the errors of both under- and overplanning.

CONVENTIONAL WISDOM ON THE ADEQUACY OF CURRENT SCIENCE MANPOWER

A number of studies in the last several years have projected that prospects for work in their fields for scientists and engineers and others with advanced degrees look bleak for years to come. In addition, there have been numerous reports in the popular press suggesting that many young Ph.D.s are "academic gypsies" wandering aimlessly from one temporary, often part-time job to another with little hope of a permanent faculty post, or (perhaps) worse, that they are working as cabdrivers.

The formal market-projection studies, while cognizant of uncertainties and differences among fields, paint a rather pessimistic picture of "underutilization" of new Ph.D. winners in the sciences and engineering and most other fields. The late Allen M. Cartter, long considered the leading student of the Ph.D. labor market, published his culminating work on the subject in 1976.[2]

Even allowing for market adjustments to the developing abundance of Ph.D.s, Cartter foresaw a sharp decline in the 1980s (from historically low 1970s levels) in the proportion of new Ph.D.s who would find faculty positions, and he was not sanguine about the prospects for an across-the-board boom in R & D spending that would take up the slack. It was, however, his hope that the nation would take the opportunity presented by the circumstances of the 1980s to enrich itself by directing otherwise underutilized faculty resources toward increased efforts to broaden and deepen the level of learning of the populace, and to engage in increased research and public service.

The National Science Foundation and the U.S. Department of Labor's Bureau of Labor Statistics have each recently produced projections of future supply and "utilization" of doctorate-level scientists and engineers both in and outside the academic sector. Their findings are generally quite similar. Jobs in science and engineering are projected to grow less rapidly than the science and engineering Ph.D. labor force between 1977 and 1987 in all the broad discipline groups except the physical sciences, where the growth rates are about equal. The projections include allowance for substantial "enrichment" on the demand side—i.e., the "science/engineering utilization" projections assume that the relative abundance of Ph.D.s will lead to some substitution of Ph.D. holders for persons with less advanced training in science/engineering jobs.

Still, the bottom line is a near doubling between 1977 and 1987—from 9 to 17 percent—in the proportion of Ph.D. scientists and engineers not employed in science or engineering work. This "non-S/E utilization" is projected to represent some 70,000 Ph.D.s in 1987, up from 25,000 in 1977, a base year which was itself a time when the job market for Ph.D. scientists and engineers was generally perceived as being none too strong.

Several other studies with similar conclusions could be cited.[3] Although very little attention is given to the nature of the jobs in the rapidly growing "non-S/E utilization" category, the consensus is clearly that there is a more than ample supply of most types of Ph.D.-level scientists and engineers, and that this excess supply situation is likely to persist for a number of years.[4]

Responses to the Weak Labor Market

It is important to note that there have been supply-side responses to the relatively soft job market conditions facing scientists and engineers in recent years. Ph.D. production in engineering and the physical and mathematical sciences (the latter category includes computer science, where there have been sharp increases in recent years) is down sharply from early peaks (see Table 12.1). Ph.D. production in the life sciences has been essentially level since the early 1970s. Overall in enginering, mathematics, and the natural (i.e., physical and life) sciences, doctorate awards are down some 17 percent from the peak levels of nearly a decade ago. In psychology and the social sciences—fields in which the market decline hit later—Ph.D. output continued to increase quite rapidly until the late seventies. But this growth seems now to have ended and in most of the social sciences even to have reversed itself.

Indeed, data on graduate enrollments give indications that advanced degree production in most of the science/engineering disciplines may well be lower in the next few years. Table 12.2 shows that, according to the National Science Foundation's annual departmental surveys, the number of first-year graduate students in doctorate-granting institutions has declined in three of the last four years. Between 1975 and 1979 these enrollments dropped by more than 9,000 students overall, or 8.3 percent. There were fewer first-year graduate students in 1979 than in 1975 in every discipline group except the health sciences, and even in these "boom" fields the numbers have been virtually level since 1977.

Indications of an even longer-horizon supply response are provided by the data shown in Table 12.3. Each fall the Cooperative Institutional Research Program of the American Council on Education and the University of California, Los Angeles, collects survey data from a nationally representative sample of some 300,000 college freshmen concerning, among other

Table 12.1
New Doctorates Awarded in the Sciences and Engineering, Selected Years, 1967–1979

	Mathematics & Computer Science	Engineering	Physical Sciences	Life Sciences	Total: Natural Sciences, Engineering, Math	Psychology	Social Science	Total: Science & Engineering
1967	828	2581	3478	3116	10,003	1293	3157	14,453
1971	1236	3495	4494	5051	14,276	2116	3039	19,431
1975	1149	2959	3611	5022	12,741	2749	3558	19,048
1977	959	2641	3410	4767	11,777	2960	3544	18,281
1979	977[a])	2494	3321	5076	11,868	3081	3298	18,247
1971–79 N	-259	-1001	-1173	+25	-2408	+965	+259	-1184
%	-21%	-28.5%	-26.1%	+0.5%	-16.9%	+45.6%	+8.5%	-6.1%
1977–79 N	+18[a])	-147	-89	+309	+91	+121	-246	-34
%	+1.9%[a])	-5.6%	-2.6%	+6.5%	+0.8%	+4.1%	-6.9%	-0.2%

[a])The increase in "mathematics and computer science" doctorates between 1977 and 1979 is entirely attributable to sharp increases in computer science Ph.D. production. The numbers in the other mathematics fields as a group have been declining since 1972.

Source: Based on data from tables in National Research Council, Doctorate Recipients from United States Universities: Summary Reports (National Academy of Sciences, 1968–1980).

Table 12.2

First-Year Graduate Students in U.S. Doctorate-Granting Institutions by Broad Field of Science, 1974–1979 (Fall)

	1974	1975		1976		1977		1978		1979	
	N	N	% chg	N	% chg	N	% chg	N	% chg	N	% chg
Engineering	25,078	29,314	16.9	27,745	-5.4	28,882	4.1	25,085	-13.1	24,160	-3.7
Physical Sciences											
Environmental Sciences	3396	3708	9.2	3718	0.3	3840	3.3	3582	-6.7	3559	-0.6
Mathematical Sciences	8112	8615	6.1	8084	-6.2	8184	1.2	7722	-5.6	7572	-1.9
Agricultural Sciences	3896	4329	11.1	4489	3.7	4427	-1.4	3826	-13.6	3555	-7.1
Biological Sciences	12,739	13,433	5.4	13,070	-2.7	13,180	0.8	11,728	-11.0	10,782	-8.1
Health Sciences	10,001	10,751	7.5	11,655	8.4	14,041	20.5	13,967	-5.2	14,188	1.6
Psychology	7816	7765	-0.7	7651	-1.5	7758	1.4	7081	-8.7	6865	-3.1
Social Sciences	24,662	28,260	14.6	26,247	-7.1	28,152	7.3	26,351	-6.4	26,690	1.3
Total, Sciences & Engineering	102,618	113,205	10.3	109,761	-3.0	115,635	5.4	106,121	-8.2	103,840	-2.1

Source: Based on data from tables in National Science Foundation, Academic Science: Graduate Enrollment and Support, Fall 1978. Surveys of Science Resources Series, NSF, 1979, and comparable unpublished data for Fall 1979 obtained from the National Science Foundation, 1980.

Table 12.3
Probable Major for All Freshmen, All Institutions, 1970–1979 (in percentages)

Major	1970	1971	1972	1973	1974	1975	1976	1977	1978	1979
Engineering	8.6	7.2	6.9	6.6	6.6	7.9	8.5	9.3	10.3	10.6
Mathematics, Statistics	3.3	2.7	2.2	1.7	1.4	1.1	1.0	0.8	0.9	0.6
Physical Sciences	2.3	2.0	1.9	2.7	2.6	2.7	2.7	2.3	2.4	2.3
Biological Sciences	3.5	3.6	3.9	7.0	6.7	6.3	6.2	4.7	4.6	4.0
Agriculture, Forestry	2.0	3.2	3.2	2.8	3.8	3.9	3.6	3.6	3.2	3.0
Total Natural Sciences and Mathematics	11.1	11.5	11.2	14.2	14.5	14.0	13.5	11.4	11.1	9.9
Social Sciences (including psychology)	14.3	12.8	11.7	11.5	10.5	9.7	8.7	8.4	8.1	8.1
Total Sciences	25.4	24.3	22.9	25.7	25.0	23.7	22.2	19.8	19.2	18.0
Arts and Humanities	15.7	14.3	14.0	11.0	10.6	9.3	9.3	8.8	8.3	8.6
Education	11.6	9.9	7.3	12.1	10.5	9.9	9.3	8.8	8.0	8.4
Health Professional (Non-M.D.)	7.4	8.8	10.6	10.4	7.5	7.3	6.9	9.1	8.6	7.9
Business	16.2	16.4	15.5	17.7	17.9	18.9	20.9	22.2	23.9	24.3
Other	12.9	16.8	18.2	11.7	17.4	18.0	18.2	17.3	17.1	17.4
Undecided	2.2	2.3	4.6	4.7	4.5	5.0	4.7	4.7	4.6	4.8

Source: Based on data from Alexander Astin, Margo King, and Jerry Richardson, The American Freshman: National Norms, Fall 1970–1979 (Los Angeles: Graduate School of Education, UCLA, 1971–1980).

things, their probable choice of major field in college. Expressed interest in natural science and mathematics majors, as a proportion of all responses, peaked in the mid–1970s and has dropped steadily and substantially since. For these fields taken together, the proportion of prospective majors has fallen from 14.5 percent of all freshmen in 1974 to just under 10 percent in 1979. The proportion of prospective majors in the social sciences (including psychology) has declined from 14.3 percent in 1970 to 8.1 percent in 1979.

The proportion of prospective majors in engineering has increased appreciably in recent years after an earlier decline. However, it is important to note that in engineering, to a much greater extent than in any of the sciences, lucrative professional job opportunities in the field are available to bachelor's and master's degree winners, so that strong job market conditions often lure promising young engineers away from doctoral study. Faculty members in many graduate engineering departments indicate that they are seriously short of graduate students to serve as research assistants (an NSF-sponsored study in 1977 reported similar complaints in some physical science and mathematics departments as well).[5] Moreover, they cannot attract junior faculty members because of competition from industrial firms that offer much higher salaries and better research facilities.[6]

The graduate school entry rate in science and engineering (the ratio of first-year fall graduate enrollments in science and engineering to the previous spring's bachelor's degree awards in the science and engineering fields) declined from a peak level near 65 percent in the mid–1960s to 43 percent in 1976, the most recent year for which this data series is available.[7] The ratio of science and engineering doctoral degrees to bachelor's degrees in these fields awarded seven years earlier has also declined sharply from a peak of 13 percent for 1969–1970 doctorates to 6.4 percent for the most recent doctoral cohort for which the data exist (1976–1977 doctorates).[8] While there are substantial variations in the strength of these trends across disciplines, and it is possible (though unlikely) that the graduate school entry and completion rates have increased in the last two or three years, it does not appear that a given number of undergraduate degree awards in science and engineering will lead to as many doctorates within a reasonable number of years as was the case in the past.

CONCERNS ABOUT THE QUALITY OF FUTURE SCIENTISTS

A number of knowledgeable observers have expressed the fear that, as perceived career opportunities and rewards in research decline, the most able students—generally those with the best choice among career options—may be disproportionately attracted to more promising and financially rewarding careers in law, medicine, business, etc. The theory is that those with unusual talents may be willing to bear a substantial opportunity cost burden for a research career—business and the professions have always paid better than research—but that the price they are willing to pay is not unlimited. The dismal reports about the faculty job market and faculty economic status, and the lengthy, insecure, and poorly paid postdoctoral stint facing young scientists must discourage many who have the talent to succeed in the more promising professional career tracks, so this scenario goes.[9]

There is as yet no direct or comprehensive evidence on this question of the quality or the talent entering the graduate schools in science. For a variety of reasons, we are inclined to be skeptical of the arguments of those who fear the worst. A recent study of career choice patterns of Harvard and Radcliffe graduates over the period from 1957 to 1979 has received considerable attention, however, and illustrates the basis for concern.[10] Graduate study in the arts and sciences immediately upon graduation climbed from 15 percent of the class of 1957 to a high of 30 percent of the classes of 1964 and 1965, before plummeting to just 6.8 percent of the class of 1979. But, of course, many students now postpone graduate study for several years, so the real decline is not measured by these figures.

Perhaps more significantly, of those who chose immediate graduate or professional school, the ratios choosing arts and sciences to those choosing professional schools shifted from two to three in 1958, to one to two in 1966, and to one to four in 1979. Among students who graduated magna or summa cum laude and went on to postgraduate study immediately, in 1964 three-fourths chose arts and science fields, while 20 percent chose law or medicine. In the class of 1979 only a third chose arts and science fields, while over half chose professional programs.

We have developed some data from the UCLA Cooperative Institutional Research Program files on the prospective college majors of freshmen with "A" grade-point averages in high school. One should remember that the pervasive grade inflation of recent years has increased the proportion of students reporting "A" high school averages, so the later group includes a smaller fraction of truly outstanding students. The data show a sharp increase in the proportion of "A" students reporting plans to major in engineering, but a substantial decrease in the proportion planning either natural or social science majors. The arts and humanities fields, where job markets are truly depressed, reported a larger decline than the sciences, while business experienced a large gain in prospective majors among the "A" student group. Although substantial changes in plans may occur between college entry and receipt of highest degrees, these data give cause for concern.

Signs of Capacity Erosion

The deteriorated labor market for Ph.D.s and reduced graduate applicant demand in some areas have already produced policy responses. The federal government long ago began cutting back support for graduate fellowships and institutional support for graduate education, so that federal support for these purposes is now a small fraction of its level a decade ago. Universities, facing economic pressures on a number of fronts and often "encouraged" by state control agencies, have eliminated or sharply cut back substantial numbers of doctoral programs, and have halted many plans for the expansion of existing programs and the creation of new ones. According to the most recent data available from the National Science Foundation's Surveys of Graduate Science Student Support, the numbers of doctorate-granting departments in engineering, physics, chemistry, astronomy, and the agricultural sciences declined between 1974 (the earliest year for which comparable data exist) and 1978. More recent data from the American Institute of Physics indicate that the decline in that discipline continued in the 1979–1980 academic year.

A number of state governments have initiated detailed reviews of the plans and programs of their universities in the area of graduate education, in light of both the general climate of fiscal austerity and the apparently weak job market for program graduates. In some states, most notably New York and Louisiana, the state has established a full-blown state-run review process involving analysis of program, cost and market data, and the use of outside academic consultants. The results of these reviews have led to termination or probationary status for scores of doctoral programs so far.

These detailed program reviews by state governments, though they are controversial on academic autonomy grounds, have generally paid considerable attention to the quality dimension. The programs they have terminated thus far may not have been any great loss to the nation's R & D and R & D training capabilities. Probably of more concern are the effects of the general climate of austerity and skepticism about the continuing need for doctoral education, which leads to pressures down through the system to keep graduate enrollments down. This may be accomplished by virtually eliminating all hope for new program directions, even in potentially important new specialties, and by putting special pressures on high cost—i.e., "hard" science and engineering—disciplines.

In short, there is some evidence that, not only are doctoral enrollments and degrees in the sciences and engineering falling, but also that a substantial part of the capacity for scientific research and graduate training may be on the verge of being dismantled. One countervailing force is the fact that the relatively young age distribution of the present faculty will result in record low rates of death and retirement over the next decade. Thus capacity decline due to natural attrition will be quite insignificant until the early 1990s. Then this short-term gain may turn into a new long-term dilemma.

Relatively few faculty postions have opened up for young scientists and engineers in the last few years, a situation that is expected to continue for a decade or more in most fields. Between 1973 and 1977 the proportion of recent (within seven years) Ph.D.s on the faculties of the leading research universities in science fields dropped from nearly 40 percent to just over 30 percent.[11] Each broad field of science experienced some decline in the proportion of young faculty over this period, and several disciplines experienced sharp declines.

Those who are concerned about this problem fear that continuing declines in the proportion of recent Ph.D.s entering faculty positions threaten the intellectual vitality of academic science and hence, ultimately, all American science. The widely held view that younger scientists are more productive is often cited in this connection, though recent studies show that the evidence on the point is at best mixed. Regardless, a plausible case (though soft in terms of conclusive empirical support) can be made that a richer mix of younger (or at least new) faculty adds both stimulation and new ideas to a research group, as well as increased flexibility for responses to shifting research and student demand trends. Moreover, too thin an inflow of new faculty now may set the stage for an abrupt shortage in the 1990s when annual faculty retirements in most fields are projected to increase sharply, just as college and university enrollments begin to recover. These points were made quite forcefully recently by the National Academy of Sciences' Committee on Continuity in Academic Performance in its report cited earlier.

Holes in the Conventional Wisdom?

We described earlier the consensus view that in general, science Ph.D.s are likely to be in ample, if not excess, supply for some years into the future. This consensus notwithstanding, we believe there is evidence that the market for Ph.D. scientists and engineers in a number of disciplines may be turning around. For the two most recent years for which data are available (1978 and 1979) the number of graduating Ph.D.s in engineering and the "hard" sciences (physical and life sciences, mathematics, and computer science) seeking employment but reporting no definite work commitment in the National Research Council's annual survey of earned doctorates has declined significantly for the first time in many years.[12] The proportion of the Ph.D. cohort seeking work but reporting no definite commitment fell from nearly 25 percent of the 1977 "hard" science and engineering Ph.D.s to about 21 percent of the 1979 group (i.e., by about 400 individuals). There were significant declines in this measure in nearly all the reported discipline groupings within this set of fields.

Consistent with the hypothesis that the market for the services of these scientists and engineers is getting stronger, the proportion of the cohort planning postdoctoral study (in recent years an activity that occupied many when the employment market was relatively soft) declined for the first time in years, while the fraction planning employment increased. Again, this phenomenon occurred in most of the disciplines and discipline groupings, notably engineering, physics and astronomy, chemistry, the earth, environmental and marine sciences, and the "basic medical sciences." In chemistry the trend goes back to 1976. Since that year the fraction of the Ph.D cohort in chemistry reporting plans for immediate postdoctoral study has dropped nearly eight percentage points as more new Ph.D.s have evidently found attractive employment opportunities.

There is no indication that the apparent gains in employment of science and engineering Ph.D.s are the result of jobs that underutilize their talents. The employer category claiming most of the gains in the proportion of the Ph.D. cohort in virtually all the disciplines is "business/industry," and the one consistently growing primary work activity for the new Ph.D.s is "research and development." Both these categories have been claiming increased proportions of the engineering and "hard" science Ph.D. cohort each year since 1976.[13]

Data on recent Ph.D. employment patterns reported by the National Science Foundation (NSF)[14] and the National Research Council (NRC)[15] give little support to the notion that there is a surplus of science and engineering Ph.D.s. NSF reports that between 1973 and 1978 the numbers of employed science and engineering doctorates grew by 37 percent, a 6.5 percent average annual growth rate—considerably more rapid than that of the labor force as a whole. There were 63 percent more employed social scientists in 1978 than in 1973, 46 percent more employed psychologists, just under 40 percent more employed engineers and, at the low end of the scale, some 25 percent more employed physical scientists and mathematicians. According to the NRC, the unemployment rate among scientists and engineers declined slightly from an already very low 1.1 percent of the doctorate labor force in 1973 to 0.9 percent in 1979. Even among recent Ph.D.s (1973–1978 graduates) the 1979 unemployment rate was only slightly higher, and in no discipline category did the rate approach 2 percent of the recently graduated doctorate labor force.

The labor force participation rate for all science and engineering doctorate holders exceeded 96 percent in 1978, a very high participation rate. It appears that the labor market has been able to absorb substantial growth in numbers of science and engineering Ph.D.s in recent years. NSF's most recent report concludes that "these high rates of participation and low rates of unemployment indicate that a very large fraction of S/E [science and engineering] doctorates (about 95%) is being utilized in the labor market."[16] More than 90 percent of those employed were employed in science and engineering jobs. This latter percentage declined between 1973 and 1977 since doctorate employment in science and engineering jobs grew about 5.7 percent per year while doctorate employment in non-S/E jobs grew by more than 17 percent annually. But NSF reports on the basis of its survey data that "almost all of those in non-S/E jobs were there voluntarily because of higher salaries, better promotional opportunities or locational preferences."[17] This is not surprising in an economy where technical skills are increasingly important to management.

The median annual salary of experienced scientists and engineers has grown faster than that for all persons in professional, technical, and kindred occupations in each year since 1975 (through 1978).[18] The average annual salary growth rate between 1974 and 1978 for experienced scientists and engineers was 9 percent, versus 6.6 percent for all professional, technical, and kindred workers.

As educational institutions have reduced the fraction of all Ph.D.s they employ, business and industry and, to a lesser extent, health care institutions have picked up the slack (the latter employ mostly psychologists and life scientists). There is no indication from National Research Council surveys through 1979 of any increase in employment of doctorate holders by categories of employers that might suggest underemployment of these individuals.

The 1980 NSF report cited earlier indicates that between 1973 and 1978 the fraction of doctorate-level scientists and engineers primarily engaged in research and development or its management remained stable at about 44 percent. The distribution of work activities within employment sectors changed significantly, however, as a higher percentage of those employed in academe are not researchers (many as postdoctorals and other nonfaculty research staff), while a smaller proportion of those employed in industry are not primarily engaged in R & D. More of the latter are now in management or consulting jobs or render other kinds of professional services in such areas as production, inspection, testing, marketing, and sales. Again, it should be emphasized that those employed in these latter types of activities are generally at least as well paid as those in R & D, and nearly always indicate they are there voluntarily and that they are utilizing their training and skills.[19] The data just reported do not seem to indicate a "surplus" of science and engineering Ph.D.s. The perception of a "Ph.D. glut" evidently results from serious labor market imbalances in the humanities and a very few specialized science fields, which apparently are overgeneralized to other fields. The fact that many fewer of the traditional tenure-track faculty positions formerly taken by new Ph.D.s are now available leads to frustration and expressions of disillusionment on the part of some of those forced to accept lower status, less secure research positions. These are problems that ought to be addressed, but not by regarding our present situation as simply a general "Ph.D. surplus."

Critical Limitations of Demand and Supply Projections

The demand-side analysis of the labor market prospects for Ph.D.s usually begins with a projection of college and university enrollments. While each projection analyst (or team of analysts) has his or her own enrollment projection model, nearly all agree that enrollments will decline during the early 1980s and will not return to current levels until the early nineties. Faculty retirement rates will probably continue to be quite low for more than a decade, owing mainly to the high proportion of faculty who were hired and tenured during the rapid growth years of higher education and are still relatively young. Incentive programs to stimulate early retirement have not proved to be terribly effective. It appears that real faculty salary deterioration might have a significant effect on faculty job openings for new Ph.D.s in many science and engineering disciplines where experienced faculty suffering serious real salary declines can leave academe for other professional positions. But most projection studies have taken the fragmentary data that exist on this point into account, and the consensus is clearly that demand for new faculty will be very limited throughout the 1980s in nearly all science fields.

There is, of course, much speculation about the aggregate level of enrollments, mostly focusing on the degree of success institutions will have in recruiting working or older students. In its report on future enrollment prospects, the American Council on Education has concluded that aggregate enrollments need not decline,[20] but most observers think that they will.

Much less attention has been paid to the important question of the field distribution of enrollments. There have been substantial recent increases in undergraduate engineering enrollments in response to the strong market for professional engineers. If this trend continues, demand for faculty in engineering will be affected. The current strong student interest in the professions creates a considerable "service" demand for basic courses in the science disciplines that underlie training in the professions, and also for natural and social science Ph.D.s interested in teaching applications of their fields in medical schools and schools of business, education, public health, social work and so on.

More generally, it must be remembered that students' preferences among fields are not stable over time. Unpredictable forces such as shifting tastes, cultural values and social concerns, as well as market forces, affect students' field preferences. In regard to market forces, there is another important point. In most of the science fields, and particularly in engineering, enrollments do show evidence of being market responsive. If demand for scientists and engineers in business, government, and the nonprofit sector exceeds the expectations embodied in current projections, the affected fields will probably attract an increased share of all enrollments, and demand for faculty will consequently rise. Whether or not such increased nonacademic demand will materialize is the question to which we now turn.

In engineering and most of the natural science fields, considerably less than half of all Ph.D. holders are employed as college or university faculty members. In most of these fields the largest number are engaged in research and development or its administration. Substantial numbers are also employed in management positions that go beyond or have nothing to do with R & D matters. Significant (in some fields quite substantial) and increasing numbers are employed in a wide variety of other professional activities such as clinical work (many psychologists, a few other social scientists, some natural scientists in health-related fields); consulting (engineers, geologists, agricultural and environmental scientists, economists, psychologists and some other social scientists); design, testing, inspection, quality control, and production (engineers, physicists, mathematicians and computer scientists, economists); various kinds of mathematical, statistical, and data processing (e.g., for insurance companies and financial institutions); and teaching and training of employees (in virtually all fields and for all types or organizations). Thus the level of R & D activity and the overall state of the economy are more important, but much less predictable over a multiyear period than the level of college and university enrollments in determining the demand for scientists and engineers.

The standard methods for forecasting research and development expenditures are widely acknowledged to be less than satisfactory. Projection analyses typically derive R & D expenditure estimates from simple models based on past trends and relationships between R & D expenditure and economic activity. Obviously, important influences such as macroeconomic and political variables have to be treated as exogenous (if they are treated at all), because there seem to be no adequate models for forecasting their behavior or the magnitude of their impacts accurately, especially for periods beyond a year or two ahead. Thus all projections in this area are subject to wide ranges of uncertainty.

Moreover, most projections are done at the level of highly aggregated groups of fields. But by and large, the key supply decisions (by students and prospective students, academic departments, and funding agencies) are made at the discipline or subdiscipline level where large differences from patterns that appear at more aggregate levels may occur. At this level data on which to base forecasting models are less reliable, and the political and other exogenous forces more apt to produce demand fluctuations of substantial size relative to the size of the labor force and the educational enterprise in the field. This point is illustrated by the impact of the recent sudden surge in R & D expenditures in the energy-related disciplines where it has created something of a boom market. But the impact of this particular new demand on the markets for scientists and engineers in the more aggregated field categories generally used in projection studies has been relatively small.

Additionally, it is important to note that projections, even when they are successful in forecasting market demands, are not designed to tell us what "true" societal needs for research personnnel are—and this is the question public policy analysis should ultimately address. Much of the research carried on in the United States is supported by the federal government rather than by profit-making firms, because it is in the nature of a public good—meaning that no profit-seeking firm would likely support the research, because it could not economically bear the risk or retain enough of the benefits to justify such support. The decisions about how much of this type of research should be supported are made by political, not market, processes. Thus we cannot rely on market demand signals alone to tell us how much research or how many research personnel we should be buying. Even where market signals should theoretically induce firms to invest in R & D that will lead to products people want, we cannot be sure that firms will always be wise enough to read and act upon the market signals in an optimal fashion, at least in the short-to-medium run. So we cannot be sure that even accurately projected market demands for research and researchers will fully reflect all the societal needs that could be efficiently served by research.

Another point that is frequently overlooked in projections is that supply may "create its own demand" in some circumstances. During a period of abundance of Ph.D.s relative to the supply of jobs such persons have traditionally held, we find substantial numbers of them taking "nontraditional" jobs. Educators have always argued that higher education is more than just an imparting of specialized knowledge. It also produces general knowledge, skills, and attitudes that are broadly applicable. Students of professional work and careers have long suggested that successful organizations are willing to adapt jobs to fit the skills of the talent available. Even if some Ph.D. holders in recent years have been employed in jobs that would appear to represent "underutilization"—after much research, we think that relatively few scientists and engineers have been so employed—it is worth asking whether they were able to bring something to these jobs that others could not, and were therefore able to rise more rapidly above them. If Ph.D. holders have successfully demonstrated their unique productivity in nontraditional work settings during a period of their relative abundance, they may have created permanent new sources of demand for their services. These issues surely merit further study and empirical research, for they bear directly on the question of how much advanced science education we should encourage.

A TIME FOR ANALYSIS

We believe that the issues posed by the "young investigator" problem, the uncertainties associated with the available projections, and the declining supplies of (and tighter labor markets for) new Ph.D.s in a number of science and engineering fields indicate it is time to give explicit attention to the options available for assuring adequate supplies and quality of Ph.D.-level scientists and engineers. The available options, of course, include allowing the market to work on its own.

Many will argue that reliance on market forces will be the most effective and efficient way to ensure a sufficient supply of scientists and engineers. In this view policies which create artificial labor market demand, such as postdoctoral fellowships in numbers exceeding currently anticipated future personnel demands, are suspect. When shortages arise in certain areas, the salaries of professionals in these fields should be bid up, more students should enroll, and availability of new scientists and engineers should increase. If government subsidies are required to permit universities to add capacity, it will be time enough to initiate them when the need for them is unambiguously clear. Moreover, higher salaries should encourage some to switch fields to fill shortages in the high-demand areas.

The laissez-faire approach may work well enough where substitution from other fields, or by use of less than optimally trained people, is feasible, or where we can afford to wait the several years generally required for graduate and postdoctoral training programs to be "geared up." However, these conditions may not always be met, and there are potential problems with the laissez-faire approach that must be addressed.

First, we are certain about the market responsiveness of students, prospective students, and professionals with various types of science and engineering training. Although work by Richard Freeman and others has shown quite convincingly that economists, engineers (expecially those with degrees lower than the Ph.D.), and physicists in particular do respond to market forces,[21] we know less about the speed and magnitude of adjustments in other fields, and very little about market responsiveness to shortages (or surpluses) in subfields which might be vital to the pursuit of future national interests. It is clear that most fields are not as supply elastic as engineering. Moreover, in fields such as computer science, engineering, economics, and management, it is already proving difficult to attract students to continue their studies for the number of years required to prepare for research careers when lucrative opportunities for bachelor's and master's holders are expanding at the same time.

Second, even if we could determine that scientists and engineers are reasonably responsive to salary adjustments, it is not obvious that employers today are able to react to shortages by adjusting salaries offered, at least not rapidly. Universities are facing increasingly tight budgets, and at the same time find it difficult to differentiate faculty pay schedules by field. Governments face similar constraints. And even the private sector must make salary decisions in a context of fighting inflation, keeping product prices under control, and achieving some "reasonable" equity between highly trained research staff and unionized production workers. Moreover, in a highly inflationary era, huge dollar increases would be required to achieve "real" increases in purchasing power. If job changes required geographic moves, high costs of housing would be a significant obstacle in many areas. Thus the costs of "letting the market work" may be larger than they at first appear.

Third, the market responsiveness evidenced by most of the research to date involves serious lags. Even if shortages do eventually give rise to adequate salary adjustments (and we have questioned this), it has been shown that the time between salary increases and the influx of new scientists and engineers into the labor force is quite lengthy and variable. It takes considerable time for a high school or college graduate who "responds to the market" by pursuing additional science and engineering training to enter the labor force. For example, the average time in graduate school (not counting periods of nonregistration) for 1979 science and engineering doctorate winners was 5.8 years. By the time this many years have elapsed, whatever damage it caused may have been done and the shortage itself may be over. Freeman has argued that "cobweb" cycles of shortage and surplus have been in part the result of "reactive" government policies.[22] Moreover, institutions may be unable to provide additional seats in high-demand classes on short notice without making serious sacrifices in educational quality.

Fourth, we must question the assumption that those who have been highly trained in science and engineering but are working elsewhere can be lured back by high salaries within the feasible range. Many scientists and engineers leave their fields for administrative posts in academe, government, and industry. These jobs often pay very well. Research positions may never be able to produce sufficient salaries, prestige, autonomy, and status to induce reentry of substantial numbers into research activities. Moreover, those who have moved out of science and engineering research may have obsolete skills that would require substantial investment in retraining before they could be utilized for research during times of need.

Fifth, as we suggested earlier, it is not clear that the types of long-run societal needs we are concerned with here will be reflected, at least not very far in advance, in the labor market. Needs for research—needs in the sense of net social benefits to be derived from it including costs or problems that may be averted by doing it—may not be acted upon or may be acted upon only when the urgency has become very great. But by this time labor supplies may have fallen due to earlier depressed market demand, and some of the capacity for rapid response may have been dismantled. This is the situation we fear is developing today.

Finally, there is the problem of the current and almost certainly continuing small number of junior faculty openings in many of the science and engineering disciplines. There is also considerable concern that limited career opportunities and rewards in research will discourage the brightest prospective graduates from careers in science. While we are not entirely persuaded by the evidence underlying this last line of argument, the situation clearly bears watching.

For all these reasons, we believe that reliance on market forces alone may be a dangerous course. We cannot be assured that adequate numbers of highly trained and high-quality scientists and engineers will become available as national needs get articulated and support funds appropriated. The consequences could, depending on the urgency of the particular "needs" involved, be very serious. Also, when these social costs and the high costs of "crash" programs to produce new R & D capacity rapidly are considered, the laissez-faire strategy is not so clearly the cheapest approach.

"Fine-Tuning" Supplies to Demand Forecasts

The idea of adjusting supplies carefully to the best available information about future demands has obvious appeal. It would seem to give us our best chance to avoid the undesirable consequences of both shortages and surpluses of highly trained scientists and engineers.

The basic idea can be carried out in a more or less centralized fashion. In many countries a federal ministry of education generates official forecasts of "societal needs" for various kinds of workers (not necessarily limited to graduate-level scientists and engineers) and allocates quotas and resources to institutions to produce them. In the United States with its substantial private higher education sector, its fifty state-controlled public higher education systems, and its traditional abhorrence of federal control of education and economic planning, science manpower supply policy has never been monolithic. The federal government has sought to influence supplies by varying levels of specifically targeted support for institutions, programs, students, and postdoctoral scholars. The decisions of students, institutions, and state governments have responded in varying measure to the incentives thus created. Presumably, the same kinds of mechanisms would be used again in any concerted national effort to adjust science and engineering manpower supplies to expected demands. Any more centralized approach is not likely to be politically acceptable in light of the decentralized traditions of American higher education and the current distaste for "big government."

Indeed, some would argue that even this fairly traditional incentive-based approach violates important free-market principles to the extent that it relies on government forecasts to decide how many of which kinds of scientists are needed and how the money will be spent to produce them. Pure ideological dogma aside, the crux of this argument must be that 1) government will do no better (or will do worse) than the unfettered marketplace or some alternative approach in producing appropriate levels of manpower as needed and will create additional costly bureaucracy, and 2) when it is time to reduce or eliminate support for programs and students in some fields, government will prove reluctant to do so. Certainly, there is some validity to the latter point now that higher education interests are better organized in Washington than they have been in the past.

Even if timely market forecasts were possible, it seems likely that the inevitable delays involved in government decision making and execution would cause serious problems. Staff-generated forecasts of impending shortages in particular fields would have to be reviewed and accepted at the policy level in the executive branch and steps to deal with the situation agreed upon. Then, legislation would have to be enacted (this step might not be necessary in each case if a basic program structure covering a range of fields were authorized by Congress initially), and funds would have to be appropriated. Any new program of aid to students and institutions would generate considerable interest in Congress. Appropriations and expenditures would be closely watched by politicians and interest groups, and efforts would undoubtedly be made to "spread the wealth" more broadly among disciplines and institutions than the single-minded pursuit of efficient market articulation would dictate.

Even after all legislative hurdles are cleared and funds are available, considerable time is generally required to expand institutional capacities to enroll additional students. Institutions are understandably reluctant to begin serious planning until funds are assured. More important in the longer run, they will undoubtedly be reluctant to make the long-term commitments usually required to increase capacity substantially or begin new programs without assurances that funds and students will continue to be available. Universities have learned some lessons from the abrupt turnaround in federal support policies that occurred in the late 1960s after they had invested heavily in the faculty and facilities for a long-term commitment to scientific research and advanced education.

Finally, after everything else is in place, it must be remembered that high ability students must be recruited and that it takes nearly six years from graduate school entry to produce a new Ph.D. In many science disciplines, several more years of postdoctoral work are thought to be required to prepare a fully mature independent researcher.

Thus we fear that delay will be a serious drawback for any reactive or "need-response" type science manpower policy approach. As we argued before, urgent shortages may go unmet for years while large resources are put in place in an effort to alleviate them, only to find that when all the newly trained people are available, demand has slackened again. Government policies almost certainly exacerbated natural tendencies in this direction during the post-sputnik period.

INTERVENTION NOW TO STABILIZE AND RATIONALIZE THE SYSTEM

There is an alternative to waiting for needs to be apparent before responding. We could instead move to anticipate future needs/demands by seeking on a selective basis to halt the recent declines in science and engineering Ph.D. production and the dismantling of research and training capacity that has already begun. At the same time we could move to increase the limited number of academic positions available to new Ph.D.s, thus presumably alleviating the problems that may be created by a too limited flow of new blood into academe.

Given the difficulty of anticipating new demands for scientists and engineers and the lags involved in increasing labor supplies once new needs are perceived (and especially once substantial training capacity has been dismantled), we believe it is worth explicitly weighing the costs of supporting some possibly excess capacity against the costs of potential future shortages and "crash" programs to alleviate them. The costs of preventing further declines in science and engineering Ph.D. production and of providing support for a modest number of research positions in selected fields should not be onerous. Moreover, our research on recent Ph.D. labor market adaptations shows little evidence of underutilization of the skills of recent science and engineering Ph.D. holders, although employment patterns have changed somewhat in recent years. Many scientists are currently employed as postdoctoral scholars and nonfaculty academic research staff members on temporary appointments, but in these roles they play a vital role in ongoing research and serve as a kind of "stockpile" available to be tapped for new research efforts in their current fields or for retraining in related fields as new research needs arise. By and large, "surplus" scientists and engineers (compared to the number of teaching and research jobs available) do not seem to have lacked the capacity to adapt and find what appear to be productive managerial and professional jobs.[23]

Clearly, some discrimination would be in order in any expanded government support program, both among fields and among individual graduate and postdoctoral training programs. We would propose a very selective program that would not seek to "bail out" disciplines where future market prospects seemed weak. Rather, it would be targeted at specialties and broader discipline categories (to take into account substitution possibilities and allow for the difficulty of projecting demands for each narrow specialty) where a) future demands in excess of projected supplies seem to be a real possibility; *and* b) where the costs associated with shortages—both the costs resulting from failure to meet needs expeditiously and the costs of efforts to expand Ph.D outputs rapidly—would likely be high.

We do not propose a detailed, fine-tuning approach based upon manpower projections. Rather, we would use projections (as they are usually conceived) as part of a broader kind of policy analysis that would also be concerned with whether future demands both should and would be likely to develop in particular areas of science, and with the respective costs likely to be associated with possible shortages or surpluses in these fields. The objective would not be to develop "definitive" manpower projections, but rather to inform policymakers and thereby reduce the likelihood of costly mistakes. We are concerned in particular, of course, with the long-run cost implications of dismantling or eroding capacity in fields where quite urgent new demands may arise suddenly, but can be met only after lengthy and expensive re-building programs.

One way of developing a first-cut list of disciplines for possible special targeting would be to work backward from a list of key areas of anticipated problems and opportunities over the coming decade. Disciplines related to the energy problem, to environmental conservation, to exploiting possibilities created by recent developments in genetic research and particle physics, and to national defense concerns would seem to be likely candidates for high priority. Other perennial problem areas that are traditionally the province of the social sciences—the urban "crisis," poverty, the problem of racial intolerance, etc.—might qualify for high priority on grounds of societal need, but would probably not fare so well when the probable market demand for and efficacy of having additional social scientists working on them were considered, as they should be. A tight overall budget constraint for the program, together with the criteria proposed, should do much to force effective priority-setting among fields. Moreover, before selecting any particular disciplines, it would be important to project supplies and timetables in each in the absence of additional support to see if the extra resources were warranted.

As for the basis for discriminating among programs within disciplines, the primary criteria should be academic quality and productivity. The most productive scientists do generally come from the leading graduate departments, and there are substantial differences in departments' degree-producing efficiency (especially at the margin) that should be taken into account in deciding where to place the public's funds. In addition, however, policymakers should be aware of the dangers of enriching only those departments and institutions with established reputations at the expense of such values as diversity and competition among programs, innovativeness, and special capabilities. In certain cases such considerations might justify support for a program that seemed to have potential and was attractive to students but did not score as well as some other competitors on the standard quality indices.

It is important to emphasize once again that we are not advocating a blind reliance on field-by-field market projections here, though these should play a part in guiding the decision-making process. We advocate that government, with the aid of formal projection models (but not limited by them), consider the areas in which important new demands not likely to be met by projected output from the graduate schools may arise, and at least move to prevent further declines in Ph.D. production and erosion of capacity in these fields.

One mechanism for accomplishing this implied in the discussion above would be to provide institutional support to selected (according to the criteria indicated) graduate and postdoctoral programs in the manner long used in the NSF and NIH training grant programs. Another, possibly complementary, approach with some attractive incentive features built in would be an expanded program of competitive, merit-based graduate and postdoctoral fellowships, with attached cost-of-education allowances for the institutions chosen by the fellows, in the targeted fields.

But these supply-side measures might well be ineffective in the absence of efforts to stimulate immediate, visible demand in the targeted fields. (Recall that we have argued that current market signals may not reflect legitimate needs/demands.) This may permit us to address simultaneously the widespread concern about the shortage of academic posts for young scientists, assuming that there are indeed serious consequences resulting from low levels of junior faculty hirings.

A variety of approaches to this latter concern have been suggested. Some higher education interests would like to see the federal government provide additional funds to universities to increase the number of faculty positions. Such an approach, however, is likely to be politically unattractive at a time when legislators and the public are aware that enrollments are not increasing, and many are inclined to believe that faculty members do too little teaching already. Unless long-term support were guaranteed (which is difficult to imagine), and perhaps in any case, institutions would probably seek to recruit more students to justify and provide assistance to the additional faculty members. These pressures could lead to additional institutional insensitivity to students' career prospects and thus to the various pathologies associated with graduate enrollments too large for appropriate job markets. It is also not clear how net additions to faculty hiring could be assured without undue interference with academic autonomy, given that institutions could easily reallocate internal funds that would otherwise pay for faculty.

A prestigious committee of the National Academy of Sciences recently recommended a modest program—its cost was estimated at 380 million 1979 dollars over the nineteen-year projected life of the program—of five-year research awards (including salary) to outstanding established academic investigators in disciplines where the "young investigators" problem appears to be most serious. The program is designed primarily to free up faculty positions for young Ph.D.s who would presumably be hired to replace the award winners as teacher-scholars. The reasons for making the awards to established scholars rather than to young Ph.D.s are sound: There is no interference with an institution's faculty hiring processes, and there is less risk that the research awards will not result in productive work. But critics have pointed out that awards to established investigators are also more expensive. Most important, there is no effective mechanism for assuring that universities actually increase their net permanent faculty hiring. Given current circumstances, we might expect many universities to reallocate at least some of the funds freed up by the award to the senior faculty member, and/or to replace him/her with an individual whose employment would last only as long as the senior investigator's award. It would be extremely difficult to avoid such outcomes without imposing and enforcing onerous restrictions on the decision making of "autonomous" academic institutions.

In spite of these difficulties, we think that a program along the lines proposed by the academy committee could, if properly designed, address the problems we are concerned with effectively and efficiently. The key design features are 1) the criteria for targeting disciplines discussed earlier (the criteria in the National Academy–proposed program would produce considerable overlap with our criteria, since many disciplines would qualify on both sets of grounds[24]; and 2) participating departments would have to agree to spend the funds released for the full period of the award (say, five years) on an individual with full faculty status. While there would be no effective way to assure that the new hire were given a real opportunity to compete for a tenured slot, this does not worry us, for we believe that this problem would take care of itself in disciplines where the anticipated new demands actually emerged.

In addition, we would propose that the program of senior awards in selected disciplines be supplemented by at least stable (in real terms) funding of research and postdoctoral fellowships in the targeted fields. In the absence of such stable funding, total demand for young Ph.D.s in research positions in the target fields might well decline, thus vitiating the impact of the senior awards program. Moreover, the research capacities of some current faculty members, which might be needed later, may atrophy. Indeed, in the target disciplines it might be well to provide for more multiyear research awards (and perhaps small institutional support grants) to permit more stability in the planning and conduct of research and young investigators' careers. This should serve to reduce the outflow of trained people from these key fields by providing institutions with more opportunity to improve notoriously inadequate arrangements for junior scholars supported by extramural funds. It should also encourage individuals with less incentive to leave the field of science. Institutions should be encouraged to set up suitable screening processes (analogous to those for faculty) to designate nonfaculty scholars who would be eligible to apply for external support as principal investigators in designated fields of institutional interest.

One additional point should be added to this set of recommendations. The federal government should, especially if it is going to adopt a Ph.D. "stockpiling" strategy, invest in the development of better Ph.D. labor market data and the dissemination of such information to students and prospective students. A properly funded federal forecasting unit and a serious program of research in Ph.D. labor market forecasting would be a good and low-cost investment for federal, institutional, and student planning and decision making. Of course, the question must be raised whether the government could do better and more cost-effective forecasting than could properly funded private scholars.

Dissemination, especially to students, is also critical. While graduate students and prospective graduate students in most science and engineering fields appear to have a reasonably good general picture of the labor market, their information does not appear to be very deep. There is considerable awareness of current market conditions in the chosen field but little awareness of impending changes that may have a profound effect on the individual when he or she completes graduate school five or more years later. Prospective graduate students should also be aware that many of the "teaching and research" positions that a department reports are held by, say, 90 percent of its recent graduates may be temporary, poorly paid jobs not at all like the autonomous faculty roles the student may imagine.

Institutions competing for students have little incentive to provide better quality market information when the job market is not as strong as it once was. But the federal government should, and it has the leverage to require that this be done. This step may complicate the problem of assuring adequate supplies of scientists and engineers in some fields, but it is unconscionable to do otherwise. Moreover, student attrition rates and the exodus of young doctorate holders from research may decline if individuals are made aware of what they are getting into (to the extent we can forecast the future) before they begin graduate school.

CONCLUSION

We have presented evidence that should be interpreted as early warning signs that shortages of Ph.D.-level personnel in a number of science and engineering disciplines *may* develop in the foreseeable future. Our modest proposal offers a relatively low-cost way of making this outcome less likely, while also promising the benefits of additional research and, perhaps, additional vitality in academe as the faculty cadre ages through the 1980s. Inaction will be cheaper for a while, but in the end it may prove far more costly, for we live in a world where new problems—and opportunities— emerge suddenly, and often with great urgency.

NOTES

1. The figures given cover all fields, but the increases for the sciences and engineering alone would be even more dramatic.

2. Allan M. Cartter, *Ph.D.s and the Academic Labor Market* (New York: McGraw-Hill, 1976).

3. For a review of the recent projection studies, see D. J. Hernandez, "A Review of Projections of Demand for Ph.D. Scientists and Engineers," in *Research Excellence through the Year 2000: The Importance of Maintaining a Flow of New Faculty into Academic Research*, National Research Council, Commission on Human Resources, Committee on Continuity in Academic Research Performance (Washington, D.C.: National Academy of Sciences, 1979).

4. Recently it has become quite clear, however, that there are shortages in

computer science and some engineering fields. See National Science Foundation, *Science and Engineering Personnel: A National Overview* (Washington, D.C.: NSF, 1980).

5. B. L. R. Smith and J. J. Karlesky, *The State of Academic Science: The Universities in the Nation's Research Effort* (New York: Change Magazine Press, 1977).

6. National Research Council, *Research Excellence through the Year 2000*, pp. 34–36.

7. National Science Foundation, *Science and Engineering Personnel*, Table B–32, pp. 45–46.

8. Ibid., Table B–33, p. 46.

9. It should be noted, however, that we are now beginning to see evidence, or at least claims, that the peak may have been reached in certain of the higher paying professions: lawyers are having some trouble finding jobs, an oversupply of MBAs is forecast, and so on.

10. C. E. Kruytbosh, "The Future Flow of Graduate Students into Scientific Research: A Federal Policy Issue?" Council of Graduate Schools in the United States, *Communicator* 12 (February 1980):1–3.

11. National Science Foundation, *Science and Engineering Personnel*.

12. All the data cited here are based on the National Research Council's annual publication, *Doctorate Recipients from United States Universities: Summary Reports* (Washington, D.C.: National Academy of Sciences, 1968–1980).

13. It should be noted that most of these trends are also occurring, though somewhat less strongly, in psychology and most of the social science disciplines. In the humanities, however, there is no evidence that Ph.D. output declines have yet "caught up" with falling market demand.

14. National Science Foundation, *Science and Engineering Personnel*.

15. National Research Council, Commission on Human Resources, *Science, Engineering, and Humanities Doctorates in the United States: 1979 Profile* (Washington, D.C.: National Academy of Sciences, 1980); see also the profile for 1977, published in 1978.

16. National Science Foundation, *Science and Engineering Personnel*, p. 11.

17. Ibid., p. 9.

18. "Experienced" scientists and engineers include those in the labor force at the time of the 1970 census. No comparable salary data series for doctoral scientists and engineers alone for the period reported is available, to our knowledge.

19. It is possible that these doctorate holders are displacing persons with less training "unnecessarily" (i.e., the latter could perform the jobs equally well). This hypothesis deserves a systematic test. The available evidence concerning rates of technological change and relative salary trends suggests, however, that at least as many of the Ph.D holders in "nontraditional" jobs seem to be making unique contributions that can plausibly be attributed to their training.

20. American Council on Education, *College Enrollment: Testing the Conventional Wisdom against the Facts* (Washington, D.C.: The Council, 1980).

21. Richard Freeman, *The Labor Market for College-Trained Manpower* (Cambridge, Mass.: Harvard University Press, 1971); Richard Freeman, "Supply and Salary Adjustments to the Changing Science Manpower Market: Physics, 1948–1973," *American Economic Review* 65 (March 1975):27–39; W. L. Hansen, H. B. Newburger, F. J. Schroeder, D. C. Stapleton, and D. J. YoungDay, "Forecasting

the Market for New Ph.D. Economists," *American Economic Review* 70 (March 1980): 49–63.

22. Freeman, "Supply and Salary Adjustments," p. 34–36.

23. The authors are currently conducting several research projects on the adaptations of Ph.D. holders to recent labor market conditions. For a report on some of this research, see L. C. Solmon, L. Kent, and M. L. Hurwicz, *Nonacademic Career Option for Science and Engineering Ph.D.s*, Report to the National Science Foundation (Los Angeles: Higher Education Research Institute, 1980).

24. The committee's major criterion for selecting disciplines is the projected severity of the developing decline in the proportion of recent Ph.D.s on the faculties of the nation's major universities in the discipline. Recall that our criteria focus on avoiding costly future shortages in research personnel.

PART IV

THE INTERNATIONAL PERSPECTIVE

13

"The Hot and Cold Wind of Politics": Planning Higher Education in Africa

Hans N. Weiler

In a field as amorphous as educational planning, a preliminary observation on what is and what is not meant by "planning higher education" in the context of this particular chapter would seem to be in order.[1] The dividing line runs roughly between what is usually labeled "institutional planning" and "national planning." In the former institutional sense, university planning consists of the arrangements made for the governance, financing, admissions, and certification processes of tertiary institutions. Within this domain, a number of important issues clearly require the particular rationality of a formal planning process: the origin, allocation, administration, and projection of financial resources; the distribution of decision-making authority within the institution; the estimation of the shape and size of both student body and teaching staff; the needs of the institution in terms of physical plant, logistic and other support services such as computation facilities and libraries; and so forth. Much of the literature that relates specifically to university planning tends to concentrate on one or more of these issues;[2] but important as they are for the well-being and proper administration of the institution, they will not concern us directly in this chapter.

Instead, the focus here will be on planning and decision processes at the national or subnational level of political authority, which determines the overall shape, direction, resources, and philosophy for the entire higher education system and its relationship to society at large as well as to the rest of the educational system. In addition, we will deal with "planning higher education" under conditions of underdevelopment, more specifically in Africa.[3] However, most of the issues discussed here also apply to the conduct of higher education policy in the rest of the underdeveloped world. This is because there is something inherently problematic in the political economy of underdevelopment as far as the planning of higher education is concerned.

With all due respect to the efforts of planners, this chapter is critical of much of the doctrine and practice of planning in higher education in underdeveloped countries. Some of this criticism is directed at educational planning in general and at some of the key assumptions that have guided its practice over the last few decades; the first main section of this chapter deals with this argument. In addition, there are a number of premises and practices specifically related to higher education planning which require critical scrutiny; these are reviewed in the second part of the chapter. Out of this dual review come a number of considerations which, while recognizing the limitations which the critical assessment of planning in education has revealed, may lead to a different and more appropriate perspective on the task of "planning" higher education under conditions of underdevelopment. The perspective from which these notes have been written is that of a critical and sympathetic observer of higher education in Africa and of the many attempts to expand and improve it. This role has the strength of distance and overview, and the weakness of limited familiarity with detail and context. It is hoped that the article reflects more of the former than of the latter.[4]

THE LIMITS OF EDUCATIONAL PLANNING

Both the notion and actual practices of educational planning—particularly in the context of development strategies in the Third World—have undergone some significant changes over the last three decades.[5] What started out in the fifties as a rather euphoric feeling about the potential utility of various approaches to planning for educational systems is now giving way to a much more skeptical attitude. In the words of Henry Levin, "The process of educational planning is necessarily an exercise in optimism."[6] The new attitude is based in part on experience gained from trying out various forms of educational planning in a variety of national situations and on insights derived from a more complete understanding of the complex dynamics of development and social change, especially in underdeveloped and dependent societies. Whatever the source, it is real and serious, and deserves our attention.

Much of the criticism is the result of discovering that some of the key assumptions that have guided the development of educational planning have either been wrong or have led to an unduly simplified conception of the dynamics of educational and social reality. Cases in point include rather naive notions about the effects of education on both individual and collective economic growth, overly sanguine expectations about obtaining a valid and reliable information base for educational planning and about the responsiveness of educational systems to plans, as well as a general underestimation of the political dynamics of educational development and social change.[7] In the course of this critical assessment a number of particularly serious problems in the conception and practice of educational planning have been identified. The following subsections, which summarize this assessment, concentrate on four of the problems, both because they are particularly crucial and because they seem to have a special bearing on planning in higher education.

Educational Planning: Instrument for Maintaining the Status Quo?

One assumption of this review is that educational planning as we know it tends to reproduce the existing educational system, albeit on an expanded scale. Even where educational planning has been, in a technical sense, successful, its main contribution has been to project a more or less linear expansion of the existing educational system into the future. The close association between the established economic and political order and the educational planning process appears to transmit the former's vested interest in the status quo to the latter, thus favoring a planning process in which, more or less consciously, the preservation and expansion of existing conditions are seen as the least threatening option. As a result, it is difficult to find instances where educational planning has been instrumental in bringing about major structural changes in the system, a significant redistribution of educational services, or qualitative reorientations in the educational process. Notable exceptions notwithstanding, this observation holds true for the field of higher education as well: Such major changes as have occurred in African higher education appear to be conspicuous for the absence of any involvement of the regular educational planning machinery.[8]

On the whole, educational planning has, therefore, effectively demonstrated its role as an instrument of existing centers of power and their desire to maintain existing patterns of economic wealth, political power, and social status. The prevailing "technical" connotation of educational planning has kept planning organizations and planners largely from establishing a political identity of their own, and has effectively co-opted a potential force for reform into the service of maintaining the status quo. It is notable that one of the few instances where the educational planning machinery was actively involved in laying the groundwork for significant changes in university policy was in Tanzania, where the political system as a whole is making a special effort to move away from an inherited social structure.

Hierarchy, Bureaucracy, and Consensus in Educational Planning

Traditionally, and largely as a function of its development within fairly centralized governmental bureaucracies, educational planning has operated very much from the top down. Educational plans are formulated at the central level, usually with modest information input and minimal influence from lower levels of the system, and their implementation is promulgated and directed from the top. On the whole, educational planning does not have a record of involving effectively either lower levels of government and administration or institutions and groups that are not part of the administrative hierarchy, such as teachers, parents, students, and local community groups. In most countries, the process of planning is conducted strictly as an intra-administrative matter and according to criteria and operational rules that are characteristic of bureaucratic organizations. In keeping with these structural conditions, there is a strong consensual quality about the notion and the process of educational planning. If the implementation of a plan is to be feasible within the context of a bureaucratic organization, it has to be predicated upon a fairly uniform set of assumptions; disagreement, dissent, and conflict over the targets of the plan and the ways to achieve them are incompatible with the typical planning operation in most countries.

These two shortcomings—the lack of involvement by anyone outside the central administrative hierarchy, and the inability to accommodate and reflect divergent views on the future of the educational system—are perhaps the most serious criticism of educational planning as a means to facilitate social change.

African countries display considerable variation on this score. David Court, in discussing the University of Dar es Salaam, points out not only the heavy involvement of students and faculty in the university's own planning operations, but also the input provided by the general population through involvement in university planning by party and related organizations.[9] The rich case study material assembled by Aklilu Habte and his team also provides valuable information about several countries on a substantial range of efforts and experiences with different forms and levels of involvement.[10]

Growth vs. Distribution in Educational Planning

Educational planning came into existence when the qualitative expansion of extremely limited educational systems in developing countries was an overriding policy concern for national governments and international organizations alike. From such mandates as that expressed at the 1961 Addis Ababa conference of African Ministers of Education,[11] educational planning in many countries has retained a strong preoccupation with the problems of overall quantitative growth in education. Plan targets are typically expressed as the incremental capacity of the system as a whole or its major sections or levels, usually in terms of percentage growth over the baseline situation.

Given the very limited degree to which formal education opportunities—especially at the postprimary level—were (and continue to be) available to the people in developing countries, this preoccupation seems understandable enough. However, the concern with aggregate growth tends at the same time to distract from another task that looms ever more important on the agenda of educational development policy: the task of providing for and assuring a more equitable distribution of educational opportunities and services across different regional or social subgroups of the population. Given this agenda, educational planning faces formidable and as yet largely unresolved challenges both in introducing distributive categories and models into planning the future development of educational systems as well as in planning major redistributive efforts that may be required to compensate for earlier inequities.

Uneven attention to the educational needs of urban and rural areas indicates only one problem area, albeit one of the most glaring, for educational planning. More complex and differentiated disparities between different regions of a country, different ethnic and/or linguistic groups, and different social classes add further difficulty to a task that not only involves a much more differentiated perspective on forward planning and projection, but also a much more penetrating and sophisticated understanding of the social, economic, and political dynamics that have led to existing disparities.[12]

For planning in higher education, this issue presents itself in a variety of different ways. The most significant appear to be in terms of the geographical distribution of facilities and in terms of access patterns and admissions policies.

It would be particularly interesting to analyze the process through which different countries in Africa have arrived at decisions on the location of their universities or institutions of higher education, especially when there is more than one university, as in Nigeria, or where one national university is set up with campuses in different parts of the country, as in Zaire. In either case, the decision to place a university or a university facility in a particular location would presumably benefit that particular location and its surroundings, and would thus appear as a prime instrument to help remedy existing disparities between different regions of the country. Theoretically, the conditions under which the impact of locating an educational facility could be maximized can be identified as part of a planning process that would take geographic, economic, demographic, and other characteristics of different locations into account.[13] In practice it appears that plans of this kind are conspicuous for the absence of such considerations or, where they exist, for their lack of influence on the actual location decision. Instead the decision is guided much more directly and forcefully by considerations of regional political interests or constituency considerations of various kinds, etc.

The picture with regard to access and admissions is a good deal more complex. The relationship between the (prospective) student's social origin and access to higher education appears less pronounced in Africa than it used to be, and to a large extent still is, in Western Europe and North America, although the pattern seems to be similar. At the same time, differences in regional origin appear to play a significant role in university access, partly, of course, because there is a considerable interrelationship between regional and social background characteristics.

The sociographic and demographic pattern of access to higher education in Africa is an integral part of the stratification pattern of each society, as it is elsewhere. As such it is a function of economic and political factors that are beyond the reach of either education or educational planning. Educational planning could, however, make an effort to clarify the relationship between origin and access and to identify, for the instruction and possible use of those having the power to affect the social structure, those factors that do seem to affect most strongly a person's chances both for access to higher education and for the successful completion of his or her course of study.

Numbers and Content: Planning the Substance of Education

A fourth issue on which educational planning has encountered critical attention has to do with the relationship between quality and quantity in the development of educational systems.[14] To date, educational planning has been largely limited to the quantitative aspects of educational systems—projecting and forecasting increases in the number of students, teachers, classrooms, etc., based on whatever model seemed appropriate at the time. Increasingly, however, educational policy is faced with planning tasks that have less to do with quantitative characteristics of the system and much more with its content and substance. The inappropriateness of much of the colonial substance of African education has become so blatant that the call for thorough substantive reforms of the content of education at every level has become an imporant item on the policy agenda of just about every African country.[15]

Conventional, quantitative planning methods can hardly solve this problem, unless the terms of references are expanded to include much more attention to substantive aspects of education and ways in which major substantive reforms in education can be designed, implemented, and evaluated. Faced with the challenge of such reform, educational planning would also have to come to terms with the need for a new kind of knowledge base according to which new substantive specifications for university development could be designed.[16]

THE POLITICS OF PLANNING IN HIGHER EDUCATION

The preceding section suggests the major shortcomings and limitations of educational planning in its conventional sense. These limitations were inherent in the assumptions on which educational planning was predicated and the models it has used, and have become increasingly apparent as policy priorities in education have shifted. As a result, such concerns as educational reform, participatory forms of development and decision making, equity in educational access and success, and the substantive decolonization of educational systems have been put at the top of the educational policy agenda in many underdeveloped countries. There they have replaced earlier and somewhat more simplistic concerns with the quantitative growth and expansion of educational systems.

This political challenge to the established notion and agenda of educational planning in general applies equally, and in some respects even more forcefully, to the specific tasks of planning for higher education. Even in those relatively isolated instances where higher education systems, in Africa as elsewhere, have begun to adjust to the challenges of reform, participation, and equity, these adjustments have hardly ever come about as part of the regular planning process and mechanisms. Instead, they have been "devised outside the university and later imposed upon it."[17]

If this diagnosis of the state of educational planning is correct, then we face a dilemma: If planning turns out to be such a severely limited instrument for making and implementing policy for educational development and reform, is it worth retaining? On the other hand, can we face the increasingly complex task of dealing with the future of higher education without the systematic exercise of anticipation, projection and, alas, planning?

The next section will suggest that the answer to this dilemma lies in reformulating the notion of educational planning along the lines of what I have called in a similar context "enlightened humility": We must be realistic as well as humble about the limited contribution that educational planning can make to the development and reform of educational systems. At the same time we must develop as thorough and sophisticated an understanding of the conditions and constraints under which certain kinds of developments and changes in education are possible.[18]

The most important part of this "enlightenment" is understanding the political conditions under which changes in higher education systems can be planned and implemented. Unless the relevant political factors are fairly well understood and taken into account, planning in higher education runs the risk of remaining just as unrealistic as it has frequently been in the past. In other words, while it is true that "there must be a well-worked-out and carefully elaborated plan," we must also recognize the political factors involved in the planning process.[19]

The International Politics of Higher Education

One of the most significant political parameters for planning the development and reform of higher education in Africa derives from the many different ways in which higher education in Africa—and in most underdeveloped countries—is tied into a complex international network of linkages, influences, pressures, counterpressures, and dependencies. In Latin America, according to Edmundo Fuenzalida, "incorporation" of the scientific-technological infrastructure of Latin American countries into the "cultural superstructure . . . of transnational capitalism" resulted in the dissociation of institutions of higher education from the national context in which they were established.[20]

Whether or not this is an adequate conceptualization of the issue, there is no question that education in Africa, and higher education in particular, has to be seen "in the context of international economic relations."[21] Moreover, African countries are largely dependent upon a set of economic and political configurations created and controlled by the large industrialized nations of the West. In terms of both structure and content, African universities remain closely attached to their foreign models of origin and/or early patronage. Therefore, the claim that the "external orientation" of African universities has been replaced by a "national orientation"[22] has to be considered with some skepticism.[23] To be sure, the administrative and teaching staff in most African universities has been progressively Africanized, but that "does not guarantee awareness and relevance," as Babs Fafunwa points out:

The local staff member differs only in color, not in attitude, from his expatriate counterpart. Both were probably trained in the same overseas institution, and both have imbibed the same idea of what a university is in an affluent society. Their research orientation and their attitude to teaching and curriculum are those of a developed economy.[24]

To "decolonize . . . colonial mentality" becomes therefore an essential and indispensable condition for arriving at a genuinely national orientation of African universities; the attempt made in Tanzania's "Musoma" policy is a case in point both for the importance of this condition and for the difficulties in establishing it.

Another aspect of the international parameter of African higher education stems from the conflict between national universities and supra-national, regional universities. The idea of "pooling" financial and human resources into a relatively limited number of institutions of higher education, many of which were to serve more than one African country, loomed large in the early deliberations and recommendations of the Tananarive conference.[25] However, political dynamics of national development and self-assertion have all but swept away this concept in favor of independent university institutions on a strictly national basis. Even functioning regional systems of higher education, such as the University of East Africa or the University of Botswana, Lesotho, and Swaziland have not been able to withstand the forces of national independence in higher education, leading Mulageta Wodajo to conclude that "regional universities either do not materialize, or, if they do, do not last long."[26]

The costs incurred from this development are substantial, both in terms of the actual cost of setting up and running an institution of higher education, and in terms of the difficulty of creating institutions with reasonably high standards among the staff and adequate coverage across various fields of university training and research. It is not surprising, therefore, to hear André Salifou raise his voice against the "balkanization of the African university," not only to end what he considers the dissipation of African financial, material, and intellectual resources, but also in order for African states as a whole to become more independent of foreign funds.[27]

Following up on some ideas expressed at the Lagos Conference of African Ministers of Education in 1976, Aimé Damiba develops the notion that even if all or most African countries maintained some form of higher education teaching facility on a national basis, a great deal could be gained from establishing regional "centers of excellence," designed as research and advanced training centers with high-quality staff and facilities, and "responsible for innovating in areas crucial to (African) development, e.g., African pharmacology, solar energy, agricultural research, etc."[28]

Higher Education and Basic Education: Competition for Resources and Attention

A second factor likely to affect future developments in higher education in Africa is the gradual shift in attention from the secondary and higher education level to first-level or basic education. Like all generalizations about as varied a group of countries as one finds in Africa, this statement glosses over a great deal of variation. However, the overall trend clearly suggests that it will be a factor in the future development of higher education in Africa.

A comparison between the two poles of inter-African consultation on educational development, the Addis Ababa Conference of 1961 and the Lagos Conference in 1976, is instructive in this respect. At Addis Ababa a great deal of attention was devoted to the development of postprimary and postsecondary education in addition to the expansion of primary education; indeed, the concern over higher education was so strong that a separate inter-African conference was convened specifically devoted to higher education (Tananarive 1962).[29] By contrast, at the Lagos Conference fifteen years later participants spent almost all of their time discussing two issues: expansion (as close to the point of universal primary education as possible) and the substantive reform of basic or primary education.[30] Clearly, the vastly increased concern with equity education and with the elitist features of postprimary and higher education in many African countries has played an important role in this development. There has also been a certain degree of dissatisfaction and disillusionment over what has been perceived as a gross mismatch between the cost and the developmental effectiveness of higher education. In the early sixties academics and politicians saw a close linkage between education and both individual and collective economic development. This view appears to have given way to a broader perspective on the function of education. According to the final declaration of the Lagos Conference, the task of "raising the intellectual level of the whole society" is clearly more important than "contributing to the economic development of the country." The declaration also stressed that education is "an inalienable right which all should be able to exercise."[31]

This is not just rhetoric. Many African countries are moving vigorously toward some form of universal first-level education. Given the increasing political concern over the enormous share of the national budget devoted to education, the resources required for such an effort are bound to arouse controversy. Politically, this is a hazardous situation for higher education, since popular support seems to side with mass education, a tangible and credible commitment to which has assumed an important role in the legitimation of political authorities.

Autonomy, Relevance, and Accountability

The kinds of political issues arising from concerns with autonomy, relevance, and accountability in higher education form perhaps the most complex and intractable part of the political context of university planning in Africa. When the Association of African Universities held a workshop on "Creating the African University: Emerging Issues of the 1970s" in 1972 in Accra, a great deal of attention was devoted to these issues. Participants came to the conclusion that "the university in Africa occupied too critical a position of importance to be left alone to determine its own priorities," and that it should therefore "accept the hegemony of government."[32] Conversely, it could be argued that, where university autonomy is concerned, one encounters an awkward double standard, especially in the perspective of development assistance agencies. While universities in "donor" countries— the Stanfords, Oxfords, and Heidelbergs—would indignantly reject any attempt to infringe upon their right to determine their own priorities in teaching and research, the same right tends to be considered a luxury in countries that are less amply endowed with resources.[33]

This question requires more empirical investigation and normative reflection than is possible here. It does seem clear, however, that those who hold political power in Africa today tend to disagree with the Ashby Commission which argued for an autonomous university council, claiming that "a university has to be insulated from the hot and cold wind of politics,"[34] and with Alex Kwapong's eloquent defense of university autonomy as the "*sine qua non* for the effective functioning and growth and work of universities."[35] The African Regional Report of the higher education study reported by Kenneth Thompson and Barbara Fogel comes to the conclusion that "the policy direction of the institution has shifted in many places from the autonomous faculty . . . to the ideological control center of the government."[36] The "hegemony of government" has gained increasing control over university policy, claiming that in the nation's interest government has both the legitimacy and responsibility to hold universities accountable for their use of the nation's resources. "The principal problem confronting the universities within these less developed countries," concludes Kwapong, "is how to reconcile autonomy and accountability."[37] But are the two reconcilable? Is it possible to have an autonomous, self-governing university which is held accountable by the government? Can there be a different sufficient consensus on the meaning of "relevance" in a given situation to form the basis for a workable arrangement between the government and a university on priorities in higher education?

Answers to these questions must be found if we are to define the agenda of planning in higher education, because it is often the planner who finds himself in the middle. If planning in higher education is to be more than an empty exercise, it will have to relate the growth and development of higher education to plans for development in other parts of the society; if it is to be effective, it will have to include provisions for making sure that plans are implemented.

If autonomy and accountability can in fact be reconciled, the key elements would seem to be communication and participation. To the extent that there are open channels of communication between the political authority and its planning mechanisms, on the one hand, and the university and its internal, institutional planning efforts, on the other, there may be ways to anticipate and reconcile the agendas that emerge on either side. Participation, in this context, is the other side of the same coin. Coping with the dilemma of autonomy vs. accountability would be easier if the university were not dependent upon the government or a government agency, and if the structure of governance would provide for genuine and effective participation of the full range of interests and needs of the society in the formulation of university priorities. In their descriptions of the University of Dar es Salaam, both A. M. Nhonoli[38] and Court[39] state how such participation can work: on the one hand, the university can bring its independent critical abilities to bear upon the process of setting its own priorities and development targets; on the other, society at large, through its mass organizations as well as its governmental agencies, assures the linkage between overall development policy and setting specific tasks for the university.

There are strong and compelling arguments for developing communication, participation, and governance arrangements so that they will maximize the contribution the university can make toward realizing the kind of future a society has set for itself—arguments, incidentally, which are equally applicable to more prosperous countries. One of the most important of these contributions—and one which only a university can adequately make—is the continuing critical reflection on the choices a society has made, and on the means it employs in pursuing them. Schemes for accountability tend to jeopardize this ability and responsibility to raise a critical voice. Julius Nyerere set up a high standard in expecting from the university "both a complete objectivity in the search for truth, and also commitment to our society— a desire to serve it. We expect the two things equally."[40] The conflict between control and autonomy, between accountability and criticism, seems to be getting more intense all the time.

From "Education and Manpower" to "Education and Work"

One of the remarkable things about the Lagos Conference of African Ministers of Education (especially in comparison with its predecessor at Addis Ababa) was the proportion of attention given the quantitative and qualitative dimensions of African education. Deliberations on the substance (as distinct from the size and structure) of the educational enterprise were guided by two considerations: the link between education and work and the link between development of national cultures. From the point of view of our interest in higher education planning, these two items deserve particular attention, for they represent a policy agenda that has substantial implications for the future role of higher education institutions. In this section, we will deal with the relationship between education and work; the next section will look at the role of higher education in relation to "the politics of cultural revival" in Africa.

Until fairly recently, the relationship between education and the world of economic production had been reduced, for purposes of educational policymaking and planning, to a supply-and-demand model centered on the labor market. The notion of the labor market dealt only with the "modern" sector of production activities, virtually excluding the vast sector of subsistence or semi-subsistence farming and related economic activities. Projections of manpower needs—more or less disaggregated and more or less reliable— became the targets for growth in the area of education. Achieving an equilibrium between the production of graduates and the absorption by the labor market was seen as not only desirable, but possible. This expectation, as I have argued elsewhere, has become one of the more conspicuous fatalities as educational planning has moved from the "age of innocence" to the "age of skepticism," suggesting both the undue simplicity of the original model and the strength of the divergent dynamics of its education and labor elements.[41]

It is partly as a result of this experience and partly as a result of further reflection on the nature of the world of work that we are now encountering a broader notion of the relationship between education and work. Policy developments in higher education in Africa provide some interesting examples. This notion is no longer tied exclusively to the manpower aspect and its cognitive skill elements, but encompasses a whole set of other, noncognitive aspects of the relationship between education and work, such as orientations toward various aspects of the work situation, reactions to different kinds of authority structures in education and work situations, etc. So far, and rhetoric to the contrary notwithstanding, educational programs in most countries—developed and underdeveloped—continue to have a rather tenuous and often condescending relationship to the world of work. The reality of work appears in remote, abstract, and rather bloodless reflections in school curricula and textbooks, but is otherwise conceived very much as a world unto itself and as something with which the student concerns himself after he has taken care of his education.

Changes in this orientation are gradually emerging and are beginning to affect policies relating education and work. The strong emphasis that the new educational policy in Zambia places on the interpenetration of school and work is a case in point, as are similar developments in Benin.[42] As far as higher education specifically is concerned, Tanzania's "Musoma" policy requiring the prior immersion of a potential applicant to the university in the world of work, and of taking the success of that experience into account in deciding on his or her admission, may over time lead to changes in attitudes toward the world of work among university students and graduates.[43] Efforts by other African countries to introduce a national service element into higher education go in similar directions and are guided, as are corresponding programs at the preuniversity level, by an overall policy concern for realizing more fully the wide range of relationships between education and the world of work.

These developments at the policy level have potentially instructive parallels in research. Both the research program associated with the World Employment Project of the International Labour Office,[44] and some recent research on education and the world of work undertaken by the International Institute for Educational Planning,[45] attach particular importance to exploring the noncognitive elements in the relationship between education and work, especially with regard to the nature and structure of the social experience in school and at work.

Higher Education and Cultural Independence

"Authenticity" has become another key term on the political agenda of African education in recent years. Upon the conclusion of the Lagos Conference, Amadou Mahtar M'Bow, director-general of UNESCO, stated that "present day systems of education are a means of perpetuating ways of thought and life that are different from those of the American societies. . . . The full development of cultural identity cannot be ensured unless the educational systems inherited from colonial days are called in question."[46]

While the "decolonization" of education has been a perennial element in African educational rhetoric, it seems that it is at last becoming a political priority, at least in those countries that strongly resent the dependence on alien cultural values in general, and in the substance of the educational process in particular. One of the most important outcomes of this concern so far has been a massive effort at curriculum reform, mainly at the pre-university level, together with a gradual replacement of metropolitan teaching materials. Reviewing the history of this effort, it seems that African universities have at best been only marginally involved in it, and that the main burden of developing, trying out, and introducing new curricula has been carried by para-statal instituitons (such as the Institute of Education in Tanzania or the *IPN* in some of the Francophone West African countries) or by regular departments of the Ministry of Education.

While the reform of school curricula toward a stronger sense of national cultural identity still remains very much on the agenda of educational policy, the parallel issue of the use of national languages may be even more salient. Countries across a rather wide range of political persuasions are committing themselves to major programs of replacing Western languages as the medium of instruction with one or more indigenous languages. Perhaps the boldest effort in this respect so far has been in Somalia where, in a matter of a few years, English and Italian were eliminated in favor of a national Somali language.[47] A number of other African countries are moving, albeit not quite as boldly, in similar directions. While the adoption in principle of national language policies is a major political decision, a number of further and rather difficult political decisions are required for the actual implementation of such a policy—such as which languages from among a wide range of indigenous languages to adopt, how to cope with the costs of retooling an educational system, etc.

One of the most difficult problems, however, would seem to be how to involve the higher education system effectively in such a process of cultural reorientation. As the pinnacle of the educational system, universities would theoretically have a special role to play in such a process; in typical eloquence, Joseph Ki-Zerbo articulates this responsibility when he suggests that the African university cannot hold aloof from the cultural environment in which it is immersed. . . . The university must participate intensively, through exhibitions, festivals and competitions, in the cultural renascence of Africa . . . and in the liberation of the long inhibited indigenous creative genius. . . . The university must not be a mirror diffusing a reflected light but a torch that . . . is fuelled primarily in the hearths and homes of the people.[48]

At the same time, however, the university is typically that part of the educational system in African countries most affected by foreign, non-African ideas and patterns of thought, and would seem to have the greatest difficulty responding effectively to a political mandate that is predicated on a more autochthonous function of the educational system. Universities, observes Damiba, are "seldom in the vanguard of educational reform in Africa."[49] This also holds, one might add, for universities almost everywhere. But it seems that those reforms that call for a stronger orientation to the African countries' cultural tradition and identity are posing particular problems for African universities, and may well become the grounds for further political conflict between political authorities and higher education in some African countries. W. Arthur Lewis, in discussing the role of the university as a "bearer of culture," sums up the problem by saying that "there are senses in which the university, far from transmitting the culture, is rather part of the forces that are eroding traditional society."[50] To the extent that this is and remains true, the political determination of many African states to achieve greater cultural independence may well be on a collision course with higher education's place in a "transnational system" of values and ideas. Whether planning, of whatever kind and form, could avert such a collision is questionable indeed, but deserves some further thought.

TOWARDS A NEW ROLE FOR PLANNING IN HIGHER EDUCATION

The limitations and failures that traditional notions of planning in education have encountered and the political determinants of higher education development in Africa that we discussed in the last section raise the question of whether there is any place left for planning in the future arsenal of policymaking in education. At the most general level, the answer would almost by definition have to be affirmative: Some form of more or less systematic anticipation of future developments is bound to be part of any reasonable policymaking process, especially for such a complex system as higher education.

But what kind of planning? Clearly not the kind on which the Ashby Commission in Nigeria in the early 1960s was predicated, or the kind that characterized many of the deliberations and projections at the Addis Ababa

Conference, even though some of the techniques and procedures involved will retain their utility.

There is a future for planning in education, and recent discussions have begun to clarify certain aspects of that future.[51] Given the kinds of experiences and conditions discussed thus far, educational planning is likely to include three notions: planning as research, as communication and participation, and as advocacy.

Planning as Research

One of the most significant weaknesses of planning in its conventional form has been the inadequacy of its knowledge base. Baseline, and even more, target information has suffered from problems of validity and reliability and has rarely been sufficiently detailed and disaggregated to allow for adequately differentiated planning. If problems of this kind affect the relatively narrow form of planning we have today, information and knowledge needs clearly take on a tremendous importance within the context of a broader kind of planning that is also more cognizant of the complex set of contextual determinants of educational development and change. Moreover, the knowledge will have to be oriented not primarily toward forecasting, but toward understanding the dynamics inherent in the existing social and educational fabric and, on that basis, toward identifying the constraints which alternative future developments in education would be likely to encounter. The complexity of causal linkages in the relationship between education and social, economic, and political change requires a substantially improved understanding of the political economy of development in terms of the distribution of economic wealth, political power, and social status in a society, and the factors and processes that help sustain this distribution.

Most of the research needed to provide and sustain that kind of knowledge base will have to address issues that lie outside the strict limits of the educational system: the determinants of regional disparities, the political processes facilitating or hindering reform, the nature of the social experience in different work situations, the nature and dynamics of cultural traditions at the local and regional level, and the like. The results of research in these areas will determine the soundness of decisions about educational futures.

Even at a rather technical level, there is substantial room for improvement in the data situation. Beyond that, however, each of the five issues discussed in the preceding section carries with it the need for an expanded knowledge base in higher education planning: for a better understanding of the various ways in which higher education in Africa is interlinked with international interests, values, and ideas; for an accurate assessment of the political forces competing with higher education for scarce resources; for a realistic projection of the advantages and disadvantages of different kinds of trade-offs between autonomy and accountability in higher education; for a more comprehensive understanding of the relationship between higher education and work under the specific conditions of African countries, etc.

This notion of planning as research, which has already led a number of countries to incorporate into their educational planning structures an important research element (e.g., Indonesia, Senegal, Tanzania), should have considerable significance for the research agenda of higher education itself. Here again, African universities so far do not seem to be involved in any major way in the kind of research agenda which their own development and that of the rest of the educational system would need—notable exceptions such as the work of the Institute for Development Studies at the University of Nairobi or CRIDE in Zaire notwithstanding.

Planning as Communication and Participation

As this chapter argued earlier, communication and participation seem to be the key to mediating between the potentially conflicting notions of autonomy and accountability in higher education. If this is so, then one would need a notion of planning in higher education which recognizes how dependent the success of the planning effort is on the clarity of the process and on the effective participation of those affected by its results. Given the hierarchical and closed tradition of planning in most countries, this would require a major reorientation of structures, processes, and attitudes.

Communication and participation depend upon one another in the sense that effective participation by the "consumers" of education—students, parents, local communities, etc.—requires an open and easy system of communication in both directions. At the same time, even the most ideal conditions for communication will not lead people to use them if the actual decision-making process, target setting, and resource allocation turn out to be a closed affair in which only the top of the hierarchy participates.

Introducing genuinely participatory elements into the planning process is not easy, as shown by the numerous attempts at more broadly based forms of university governance. As we have seen, there are some modest, but encouraging, beginnings in some African countries. There is still a major task ahead, however, both in fully understanding the dynamics of participatory processes in planning,[52] and in persuading established planning bureaucracies to recognize the political need for a greater voice by those who stand to gain or, perhaps more often, to lose from the results of educational planning.[53]

It is clear that the role of the planner must be reassessed. Since the major determinant of the role in the past was the design of the plan based on a set of broad instructions about overall targets and on information concerning present and future conditions, a planning process that emphasizes communication and participation would materially alter that role. It would become critically important for the planner to serve as a facilitator of communication and interaction, especially along vertical lines. Given the difficulty of sustaining the effective articulation of the needs of different groups at or near the base of the social system, a great deal of skill and commitment is required if the planner is to identify these needs and serve as an effective agent as decisions are discussed, prepared, made, diffused, interpreted, and corrected.

In terms of "organizational location," planners will be needed at various points between the center and the periphery of the political-administrative system. Indeed, from the point of view of facilitating the articulation of needs, there will be greater need near the periphery ("barefoot planners," as someone has suggested[54]), while those closer to the center will have the special task of trying to provide some coordination and reconciliation of the messages received—a task that requires a particularly highly developed understanding of the dynamics of different groups and institutions in the society.

In the specific situation of higher education, the facilitating and mediating function of the planner places him at the critical interface between higher education and the various societal groups that have an interest in the development of higher education. Here again, the task is twofold: to articulate society's needs and concerns in the process of preparing alternative designs for the future development of higher education, and to make the intellectual and institutional needs of institutions of higher education known and understandable to the general public. Only on the basis of such mutual recognition can higher education planning avoid the conflict between autonomy and accountability:

Higher education will be permitted the autonomy it needs only if it is viewed as concurring in the mission that those outside education set for it, and as maintaining the quality and integrity while it adjusts to changing conditions. The erosion of autonomy comes from lack of agreement on mission or from deterioration in performance relative to an agreed-upon mission.[55]

This conclusion, drawn from a review of the problem of autonomy and accountability in American higher education, would seem to have fairly general validity.

Planning as Advocacy

We have argued for opening up the notion and practice of planning beyond a relatively limited set of forecasting and projection techniques to a more realistic and encompassing concern with both understanding and creating the conditions under which educational development and reform are possible. This shift is likely to erode the consensual nature of the planning process as we know it and to introduce into it an element of substantial conflict over the kinds of social futures of which education is to be a part. If we replace the somewhat naive notion of education as an "independent variable" in the development process with the more realistic position that, in many respects, education both reflects and reproduces the political and economic conditions of a society, then the interpretation of both the present and the likely or desirable future of these conditions is subject to intense disagreement. Even if they have a much better, research-based understanding of their society and of the forces that sustain it, citizens of a given country are likely to disagree on the weight to be attached to specific findings, and even more on the direction that the future developments ought to move in.

It is hard to see how those responsible for planning education within the context of a more comprehensive notion of educational development would escape the crosscurrents of these kinds of disagreements. Nor is it clear why they should, unless one would once again argue for the notion of the planner as a technician so far removed from the political reality of educational development and reform that his efforts leave that reality largely unaffected. Since the agenda and direction of developments and reforms in education touch upon and in turn are touched by some of the most fundamental considerations about a country's future—the equality of its citizens, the values of its cultural traditions, its sense of independence of and interaction with other peoples, its priorities about what is worth knowing and what isn't—planning the future of education cannot but be an intensely political vocation. Those involved in the task, if they understand its full dimension, will be unable to refrain from taking sides, from bringing their own values and visions of their societies' future to bear upon their interpretation of the present state of education, and how they assess the relative importance and desirability of alternative educational futures.

The political neutrality of planning in education has been a myth. Given the inherent political dynamics of educational development and reform, it is inconceivable that the present state of educational systems can be understood, and their future planned, outside "the hot and cold winds of politics."

NOTES

1. An earlier draft of this chapter was prepared for a conference on "Higher Education and Political Change in Africa," organized for the Rockefeller Foundation by James S. Coleman and Joseph E. Black at Bellagio in August 1978. The author has benefited greatly from comments made on the draft by participants at the conference. Jefferson Ayo, Ramadhani Ntuah, Peter Odor, and Megh Thapa assisted in the preparation of the paper. For further information regarding the title of this chapter, see note 34.

2. See, for example, J. Fielden and G. Lockwood, *Planning and Management in Universities: A Study of British Universities* (London: Chatto and Windus for Sussex University Press, 1973); Victor G. Onushkin, ed., *Planning the Development*

of Universities, vols. 1–4 (Paris: International Institute for Educational Planning, 1971–1975).

3. For case studies that are typical of this approach, see David Court, "Higher Education in East Africa," in *Higher Education and Social Change*, vol. 2, ed. Kenneth W. Thompson et al. (New York: Praeger, 1977), pp. 460–93; Aklilu Habte, "Higher Education in Ethiopia in the 1970s and Beyond," in *Education and Development Reconsidered: The Bellagio Conference Papers*, ed. F. Champion Ward (New York: Praeger, 1974), pp. 214–40.

4. Many observations on which this chapter is based were made while the author was director of UNESCO's International Institute for Educational Planning (IIEP) in Paris. Neither the institute nor UNESCO is, of course, responsible for any of the points made in the chapter.

5. For this section, I draw heavily on some of my earlier criticisms of the state of the art in educational planning. See Hans N. Weiler, "New Tasks in Planning the Development and Reform of Education: Implications for Training, Administrative Organization and Research," in *Educational Planning and Social Change*, ed. Hans N. Weiler (Paris: UNESCO, 1980); "Towards a Political Economy of Educational Planning," *Prospects* 8 (1978):247–67; "The Fallacies and Prospects of Educational Planning: Reflection on a Shopworn Craft," in *Vergleichende Erziehungswissenschaft: Festschrift für Hermann Rohrs*, ed. Ulrich Baumann et al. (Wiesbaden: Akademische Verlagsgesellschaft, 1981), pp. 157–67; "Education and Development: From the Age of Innocence to the Age of Skepticism," *Comparative Education* 14 (October 1978):179–98.

6. Henry M. Levin, "Qualitative Planning: A Broad View," in *Educational Planning: Towards a Qualitative Perspective*, ed. Raymond S. Adams (Paris: International Institute for Educational Planning, 1978), p. 56.

7. See, among many other examples of this "conventional" notion of educational planning, International Institute for Educational Planning, *Educational Development in Africa*, 3 vols. (Paris: UNESCO-IIEP, 1969); UNESCO, *International Conference on Educational Planning: A Survey of Basic Problems and Prospects* (Paris: UNESCO, 1968).

8. See the material on Africa in Thompson et al., eds., *Higher Education and Social Change*, pp. 3–214.

9. Court, "Higher Education in East Africa," passim.

10. Thompson et al., eds., *Higher Education and Social Change*.

11. This was the first of its kind; the most recent conference of African ministers of education was held in Lagos in 1976.

12. Gabriel Carron and Ta Ngoc Chau, *Regional Disparities in Educational Development* (Paris: International Institute for Educational Planning, 1978); Stephen P. Heyneman, *Regional Disparity in Educational Development: What to Do about It, What Not to Do about It, and Why* (Paris: International Institute for Educational Planning, 1978).

13. For some of the principles and techniques of "school mapping" at the pre-university level, see Jacques Hallak, *Planning the Location of Schools: An Instrument of Educational Policy* (Paris: International Institute for Educational Planning, 1977).

14. Raymond S. Adams and Hans N. Weiler, "Towards a Qualitative Perspective," in *Educational Planning: Towards a Qualitative Perspective*, ed. Adams, pp. 85–100.

15. Joseph Ki-Zerbo, "Africanization of Higher Education Curriculum," in *Creating the African University: Emerging Issues of the 1970s*, ed. T. M. Yesufu (Ibadan: Oxford University Press, 1973), pp. 20–26.

16. Michael P. Todaro and colleagues, "Education for National Development: The University," in *Education and Development Reconsidered*, ed. Ward, pp. 204–213.

17. Aimé Damiba, *Education in Africa in the Light of the Lagos Conference (1976)* (Paris: UNESCO, 1977), p. 24.

18. See Weiler, "Towards a Political Economy of Educational Planning."

19. Kenneth W. Thompson and Barbara R. Fogel, eds., *Higher Education and Social Change: Promising Experiments in Developing Countries.* Vol. 1: *Reports* (New York: Praeger, 1976), p. 154.

20. Edmundo Fuenzalida, "The Problem of Technological Innovation in Latin America," in *Transnational Capitalism and National Development: New Perspectives on Dependence*, ed. Jose J. Villamil (Atlantic Highlands, N.J.: Humanities Press, 1979), pp. 115–27.

21. Damiba, *Education in Africa*, p. 6.

22. Thompson and Fogel, eds., *Higher Education and Social Change*, p. 150.

23. Carl K. Eicher, "Overcoming Intellectual Dependence," in *Creating the African University*, ed. Yesufu, pp. 27–34.

24. Babs Fafunwa, "The Role of African Universities in Overall Educational Development," in *Higher Education and Social Change*, vol. 2, eds. Thompson et al., p. 512.

25. UNESCO, *The Development of Higher Education in Africa: Report of the Conference on the Development of Higher Education in Africa, Tananarive, 3–12 September 1962* (Paris: UNESCO, 1963), pp. 78–80.

26. Thompson et al., eds., *Higher Education and Social Change*, vol. 2, p. 21.

27. André Salifou, "On Refusing the Balkanization of the African University," *Prospects* 4 (Winter 1974):471–79.

28. Damiba, *Education in Africa*, p. 26.

29. UNESCO, *Development of Higher Education in Africa*.

30. UNESCO, Conference of Ministers of Education of African Member States, Lagos, 27 January–4 February 1976, *Final Report* (Paris: UNESCO, 1976).

31. As quoted in Damiba, *Education in Africa*, pp. 48–49.

32. Yesufu, ed., *Creating the African University*, p. 45.

33. Hans N. Weiler, "Evaluation of Purpose in Emerging Universities," in *Higher Education in the World Community*, ed. Stephen K. Bailey (Washington, D.C.: American Council on Education, 1977), pp. 29–33.

34. Nigeria, Federal Ministry of Education, *Investment in Education: The Report of the Commission on Post-School Certificate and Higher Education in Nigeria* (Lagos: Federal Ministry of Education, 1960), p. 31. When the Ashby Commission in 1960 made its recommendations for the development of higher education in Nigeria, it argued for an autonomous university council on the grounds that a "university has to be insulated from the hot and cold wind of politics."

35. Alex Kwapong, "University Autonomy, Accountability and Planning," in *Higher Education: Crisis and Support*, ed. International Council for Education Development (New York: ICED, 1974), p. 62.

36. Thompson and Fogel, eds., *Higher Education and Social Change*, p. 151.

37. Kwapong, "University Autonomy, Accountability and Planning," p. 62.

38. A. M. Nhonoli, "The University of Dar es Salaam: Emerging Issues of the 1970s," in *Creating the African University*, ed. Yesufu, pp. 174–79.

39. Court, "Higher Education in East Africa," pp. 483–86.

40. Julius K. Nyerere, *Freedom and Socialism* (Nairobi: Oxford University Press, 1968), p. 182.

41. Weiler, "Education and Development."

42. Damiba, *Education in Africa*, p. 18.

43. Court, "Higher Education in East Africa," pp. 211–12.

44. International Labour Office, *Employment, Growth, and Basic Needs: A One-World Problem* (Geneva: ILO, 1976); *Bibliography of Published Research of the World Employment Programme*, 3d ed. (Geneva: ILO, 1980).

45. Jacques Hallak, "Employment, the World of Work, and the New Perspectives for Educational Planning," in *Educational Planning and Social Change*, ed. Weiler, pp. 79–103; Martin Carnoy, Henry M. Levin, and Kenneth King, *Education, Work and Employment II* (Paris: UNESCO-IIEP, 1980).

46. UNESCO, *Final Report*, p. 74.

47. Osman Jama Dahir and Muse Hussein Askar, "Introduction of the Written Somali Language," in *Conference of Ministers of Education of African Member States, Lagos, 27 January–4 February 1976, Innovations in African Education*, ED/76MINEDAF/REF.4 (Paris: UNESCO, 1976), pp. 42–45.

48. As quoted by Damiba, *Education in Africa*, p. 26.

49. Ibid., p. 24.

50. W. Arthur Lewis, "The University in Developing Countries: Modernization and Tradition," in *Higher Education and Social Change*, vol. 2, ed. Thompson et al., pp. 516–17.

51. Weiler, ed., *Educational Planning and Social Change*; Henry M. Levin, "The Identity Crisis of Educational Planning," *Harvard Educational Review* 51 (February 1981):85–93; see also the conclusion of my debate with Boris Kluchnikov in "The Uses of Educational Planning: Some Further Thoughts," *Prospects* 11 (1981):149–53.

52. David R. Evans, *Responsive Educational Planning: Myth or Reality?*, Occasional Papers No. 47 (Paris: International Institute for Educational Planning, 1977).

53. Dragoljub Najman, *L'enseignement supérieur, pour quoi faire?* (Paris: Fayard, 1974), pp. 172–74.

54. Weiler, "New Tasks in Planning," p. 163.

55. Melvin A. Eggers, "Autonomy and Accountability in a Shrinking Enterprise," in *Higher Education in the World Community*, ed. Bailey, p. 182.

14

Policy Controversies in Higher Education Finance: Comparative Perspectives on the U.S. Private-Public Debate

Daniel C. Levy

Among the controversies in contemporary U.S. higher education policy, those involving finance are some of the most significant and most heated.* And among these, many turn to one degree or another on private-public questions. Should public policy favor public institutions, which draw most of their income from government, or private institutions, which usually draw the bulk of their income from nongovernmental sources? Or should public policy aim to alter the private-public income profile of either or both sectors? In the terms of one of the most important books on public policies for higher education, should we make the private sector more like the public sector or the public sector more like the private one?[1] Such controversies involve fundamental questions concerning what is truly private and public and how much the distinction still matters in U.S. higher education policy.[2]

Unfortunately for those who hope to see such policy controversies handled in an environment of calm and mutual respect, the arguments are becoming more rancorous. Private and public higher education institutions generally

*This is a slightly revised version of "Private versus Public Financing of Higher Education: U.S. Policy in Comparative Perspective," *Higher Education* No. 11 (1982), which was then substantially revised for "Alternative Private-Public Blends in Higher Education Finance: International Patterns," in *Private Education: Studies in Choice and Public Policy,* ed. Daniel C. Levy (New York: Oxford University Press, 1986), pp. 195–213. The author wishes to thank members of Yale University's Institution for Social and Policy Studies for their comments and the Andrew W. Mellon Foundation for financial support.

decreasingly manage to minimize controversies between them and to form a united higher education interest group. Instead, controversies have become especially acute as enrollments decline, federal and state governments seek to cut costs, and concern spreads about higher education's equity effects. Overall, retrenchment imposes an urgency in many financial controversies that are basic, if not omnipresent.

Conflicting parties invoke different economic theories, social values, and political realities to sustain their positions. Yet there is almost no consideration of how policymakers outside the United States have dealt with these controversies. Of course, financial policy elsewhere is made within private-public contexts that differ from those confronting U.S. policymakers.[3] But the same point could be made about elementary and high school education, and yet several authors have drawn fruitful comparisons.[4] Such comparisons may help us step back from the passion generated in our own debates. They may help stimulate, or even orient, comparisons involving our fifty states. Most importantly, cross-national experience should at least help put our choices into perspective. For example, few in the United States support either 100 percent private or 100 percent public funding. An economic theory that tends to favor private over public funding may simply tell us to increase our present private share if that share is "low." But how do we decide whether it is low or high? One approach, among others, is to see how our formulas and rationales compare to those found in other systems.

Certain basic themes run through the international private-public debate. While we cannot analyze them in depth, we can briefly outline them here, indicating as we go along how they play themselves out in different contexts. Advocates of private financing often claim that education yields private, or individual, as well as social returns. This is especially true of higher education. Furthermore, higher education has a privileged clientele drawing on tax revenue paid by society at large. Consequently, public funds are more justly invested at the primary and secondary levels. Beyond these equity issues, plural income sources ensure university autonomy, efficiency, responsiveness, pluralism, diversity, client choice, and responsibility. At an extreme, followers of Milton Friedman regard public subsidies as another "indiscriminate extension of governmental responsibility."[5] Advocates of public funding, on the other hand, argue that all education is a state responsibility. Externalities, both economic and noneconomic, make higher education mostly a public good, and only public funding can guarantee equal access.

Principal sources of private income include student payments (through tuition and fees) and donations by foundations and individuals. Public income comes through either government subsidies to institutions or student grants, but also through low-interest loans and tax exemptions.[6]

Private-public blends involve a number of important questions:

1. Is a given system composed of just one sector or dual private-public sectors?

2. If it is dual, what is the size of each sector?

3. What is the contribution of private funds to each sector?

4. What is the contribution of public funds to each sector?

Questions 1 and 2 are dealt with only summarily here. The first question is a structural one. I refer to dual sectors only if there are "universities," not just "technical institutions," in both sectors. Obviously, it is possible to develop a more complicated structural schema in order to cover higher education more fully. The second question is a quantitative one. My analysis focuses on questions 3 and 4.

FIVE PATTERNS OF FINANCING

The most extreme possibilities would deal with one sector, financed fully by either public or private funds. Many nations come close to the public extreme, none to the private extreme. There is, however, no single continuum running between the two extremes, either empirical or ideal typic. A system with a big private sector that receives substantial public funding is not necessarily more private than one with a small but privately funded private sector. International analysis discloses various combinations. In an effort to achieve inclusiveness with parsimony, I consecutively consider five dominant patterns. This does not deny the possibility of creating other equally valid combinations. Nor does this schema assume that funding alone determines privateness and publicness. Nevertheless, for purposes of this chapter, the schema I have used analyzes only how sectors are financed, not the degree to which they are privately or publicly governed or functionally oriented.

Boundaries among the five categories prove to be a bit arbitrary. The center of gravity in category I is far removed from the center in category II, but there is ambiguity on the border; the same applies to categories II and III. Especially as cases evolve over time, questions may arise over which category is most appropriate. I am admittedly trying to order, even force, complex and far-flung data into simplifying categories. In any case, the main purpose is to provide the reader with an orienting guide to the major international practices and rationales, not to pinpoint each and every case within a finely tuned schema.

Table 14.1 provides a brief guide to the terminology and variables used in developing the five patterns that follow.

Table 14.1
Terminology and Variables Used to Define Patterns

"Sectors":

1. "Single or Dual"
        Refers simply to the structural question (independent of the mode of
        financing) of whether the system has one sector (generally considered
        public) or two sectors.

If single sector:

2. "Statist" or "Public-Autonomous"?
        Refers primarily to whether public funds are distributed by the state
        ("Statist"), specifically by its ministries, or more by university and
        buffer organizations ("Public-Autonomous").

If dual sectors:

3. "Homogenized" or "Distinctive"?
        Refers to whether private and public sectors are financed very similarly
        ("Homogenized") or very differently ("Distinctive").

If distinctive:

4. "Minority is Private" or "Majority is Private"?
        Refers to whether less than half ("Minority is Private") or more than
        half ("Majority is Private") of the total enrollments are in the private
        sector.

Note: Criteria elaborated in text at beginning of sections on each pattern.

I. Statist (Single Sector: Public Funding Controlled by the Ministry)

Probably most nations rely on a single university sector, overwhelmingly
financed by the state. We might think of a 90 percent–90 percent operational
definition, at least 90 percent public enrollments and financing. The Statist
orientation of many of these systems stems from both the 90 percent–90
percent factor and from a strong ministerial role in distributing funds. Education or higher education ministries generally allocate funds directly to
given universities and even to units within the universities. There is little
institutional autonomy in distribution, although nations such as Sweden and
France have recently tried to encourage some.

Communist systems offer the most obvious and extreme cases, allowing
for the expected Yugoslav deviations. So it is interesting to note that even
here some private components enter. Soviet economists have acknowledged
that higher education depends on private funds insofar as parents sustain
their children's student livelihood.[7] There are some individual and foundation contributions in various nations, though figures are scarce. China has

exhorted its institutions to "do it themselves" by raising some funds through production. And then there are exceptional cases, such as Poland's Catholic University of Lublin. Mostly, however, the state dominates. There are no tuition fees, and state support for student expenses is even greater than the generous support common in Western Europe.[8] Students are often considered to be as worthy of financial support as workers are of their wages. Obviously, the degree of direct government control over financial allocation is much greater in most Communist systems than in most other Statist systems.

Less obvious is the almost total public financing of most continental West European systems. Among scattered institutional exceptions within Statist systems are Sweden's Stockholm School of Economics and religiously affiliated institutions in Italy and France. Commercial schools, like those in Greece, may not be considered part of "higher education." But most Statist systems have no important private higher education institutions. Depending upon how figures are calculated, university income may come nearly or fully 100 percent from the state, though sometimes not exclusively from the education ministry. Figures drop substantially lower only when one considers university budgets without professors' salaries, since professors are usually civil servants paid directly by the government. Student fees may appear to cover 20 percent, when they really cover only a few percent of total recurrent costs. There may also be some very limited income from landholdings and endowments, and a few private or special institutions get donations from religious organizations, Chambers of Commerce, and business firms. Possibly the most important exception to public funding occurs where business firms contribute to particular research endeavors, not computed within the annual recurrent subsidies.[9]

Most nations in pattern I have no fees or almost no fees.[10] Furthermore, widespread government aid covers some student living expenses, often including room, board, and books; loans are also common, usually based largely on parental income.[11] France provides some family tax relief and even some "pre-employment contracts" to students pledging to enter government employment. What varies among the West European nations is the extent of student aid and also the balance among different aid mechanisms, not the basic disposition to make higher education truly freer than even the absence of tuition alone would suggest.

A private-public debate is heard, but it is centered very near the public pole. Students have frequently asked for more aid, so that they could cover opportunity costs and achieve the security and quasi-worker status more characteristic of their East European counterparts. But a number of governments now prefer increased tuition (albeit through repayable loans). In fact, recent information indicates that some may be prepared to risk the political opposition of students by actively and openly considering tuition plans.

Many of the less developed countries also fit the Statist funding pattern. This is generally true, for example, of those tied to France through colonial experience. Many French-African universities are still linked with French universities that underwrite their degrees. Algeria, Benin, Chad, Gabon, the Ivory Coast, Mali, and Niger finance their public universities usually without student fees, by relying on government funds, sometimes including French government funds. Similar patterns hold for Belgian-African universities. Statist examples from elsewhere would include Afghanistan (even before the Soviet takeover), Burma, Malaysia, and Sri Lanka.[12] A central rationale for Statism in these less developed nations, just as it was in much of Latin America until recently, is that fully public and centrally directed systems are necessary to bolster government authority, shape development, and build nations.

II. Public-Autonomous (Single Sector: Public Funding with Autonomy)

With only minor variations, a number of Public-Autonomous systems could fit the Statist pattern. Again, there is only one university sector. Again, funding for all but the very few privately funded institutions comes overwhelmingly, if not fully, from the state. Yet there are important differences between patterns I and II. While no one questions that universities in pattern I are public, public-private ambiguity has often surrounded legal and popular usage in pattern II. Of course, we want to avoid governance questions here, but even in finance alone, the term "public" must be qualified in pattern II. Nations in pattern I have long traditions of full public funding. By contrast, nations in pattern II have traditions of mixed public and private funding. Only recently have pattern II nations turned overwhelmingly to public finance, and private finance is still significant in some of these cases. More importantly, traditionally mixed private-public funding reflects the traditionally non-Statist norms of allocation that have characterized—and continue to characterize—Public-Autonomous systems.

Great Britain's universities were historically referred to as "private." They were created by private groups and operated under their own charters. They have generally not been "under" government ministries nearly so directly as have Statist universities. This certainly applies to finance. While most pattern I nations regarded higher education as basically a state responsibility, nineteenth-century British authorities still saw the proper state role as limited, a greater role as interference. As A. Halsey and M. Trow have written: "Higher education in Britain was largely a matter of private enterprise."[13] Until recently, student fees accounted for a considerable portion of university income, much more than in the Statist pattern. But steadily declining fees and rising public subsidies have changed this. In 1920 the government accounted directly for only 34 percent of the university's income with a like share coming from student fees, while a half century later the government figure soared to over 80 percent, and the fee figure declined to under 10 percent. Furthermore, the government figure would be higher if we included indirect subsidies, e.g., payments to students to cover their fees. By 1970 the British universities' income profile came to resemble those of many U.S. state universities (less than 10 percent from fees, more than 70 percent from government), except that British finance comes predominantly from the national government, whereas it had earlier more closely approximated those of U.S. private universities.[14] As the trend toward government finance has continued, however, covering most tuition costs, British university funding has become more decidedly public. No longer does the pattern so closely resemble that of U.S. state universities, especially if we were to exclude Oxbridge from the comparison.

Even as Great Britain's financial source became more public, however, the allocation process remained comparatively autonomous. Government funds were neither targeted to specific intra-university destinations, nor even given directly to the universities. Instead, a much heralded buffer organization—the University Grants Committee (UGC)—played a key role. The UGC was created in 1919 to channel government funds as they grew in significance. In theory, and usually in practice as well, universities directed their requests to the UGC, the UGC reviewed these and then itself requested a total sum from the government, which in turn funded the UGC; the UGC gave block grants to each university, which then distributed the funds with a degree of autonomy often envied outside Great Britain. The UGC itself has been composed principally of part-time members from the academic community. At least until the 1970s a typical characterization has been that the UGC is an organization that appears on paper "illogical, unworkable and theoretically indefensible but which in real life—like so many British institutions deserving the same adjectives—works."[15]

A number of nations historically linked to Great Britain also show a similar Public-Autonomous orientation. There are no private universities in Australia (only specialized institutions, such as seminaries); fees, diminishing in importance over time (13 percent, 1965), were abolished in 1974. Still, there is of course variation within pattern II. New Zealand, Ireland, and Israel have Public-Autonomous universities that do derive much of their income from tuition. Typically, though, the government share has grown even in these nations. In its early years of nationhood Israel regarded defense and primary and secondary education as priority items and did not publicly fund its universities. As recently as 1965 the government still covered only half the financial costs, though by 1975 the figure had reached roughly 80 percent, with 10 percent coming from tuition.[16] Furthermore, all these countries have some sort of UGC replica (e.g., a "Planning and Grants Committee" in Israel), underscoring a degree of autonomy in financial allocations.

Policy debate in Public-Autonomous systems centers around the role of

UGCs and around fees. Many argue that UGCs, as they have increasingly become funnels for national government monopoly finance, have become mere covers for ministerial direction. In Great Britain itself, economic inflation, educational retrenchment, and political conservatism have hurt the UGC image among many academics witnessing the UGC's role in imposing the Thatcher administration's severe cutbacks. As Graeme Moodie has summarized the disillusionment: "What good is the UGC if it can't save us?" But Moodie proceeds to answer by restating "the value of having a known and friendly intermediary. . . . The UGC assures the maximum degree of self-rule possible in a given time period. More cannot reasonably be expected."[17] Not all observers would agree with Moodie, but if there is a prevalent contemporary view, it is that a tougher UGC became inevitable as government funding increased markedly, small-group understandings between university and UGC officials gave way to bureaucratic guidelines, and gentlemen's agreements could no longer suffice. Nonetheless, according to this view, UGCs still offer the universities a degree of protection from the effects of direct and directed Statist allocations.[18]

Some believe that the only solution to increased government control would be decreased government finance. Part of Britain's Conservative party has challenged the basic principles of state funding. Fees have recently been greatly increased, although this mostly affects overseas students. Moreover, a rather private institution has been founded at Buckingham to break the public monopoly. And again, as in the Statist systems, an emerging debate turns on proposals to impose tuition. Unlike the Statist pattern, the Public-Autonomous pattern has historical precedent for such private funding.

As with pattern I, there are pattern II examples of less developed nations that trace back to colonial influences. British Africa has generally developed more Public-Autonomous universities (some beginning under direct British tutelage) than has French Africa.[19] Many former British colonies even have their own versions of a UGC, e.g., Nigeria's National Universities Commission. But here one must remember that similar structures need not carry out similar functions. UGCs do not guarantee university autonomy under authoritarian regimes or amid conditions of economic hardship, though they may ameliorate otherwise harsher results. And other variations exist within pattern II that also follow some developed country/less developed country lines. Foreign finance is an important source in Africa and elsewhere in the Third World. Student fees have been more common in the former British colonies than in Great Britain itself, though they are often paid indirectly by government.[20] So, for example, Nigeria's University of Ilosho drew 12 percent (in 1968) of its income from fees, along with 20 percent from outside grants (mostly from the Ford and Rockefeller foundations), and two-thirds from the federal government.[21] White-controlled South African universities fit the significant-but-diminishing tuition pattern. Before World War II fees provided roughly two-thirds of these universities' income; they now provide one-third.[22] A non-African Public-Autonomous example from the less developed world might be Pakistan, but, as with Nigeria and other former British colonies, this depends upon the degree to which structure and heritage provide for more than the mere facade of autonomy.

III. Homogenized (Dual Sectors: Similar Funding for Each Sector)

Some systems that have two university sectors finance each much the same way—principally through public funds. Generally, the two sectors were once financed very differently, but the private sector could no longer sustain itself on private funds, or it undertook sufficiently public purposes that it could reasonably claim public subsidies. The basic rationale for this pattern is clear: Existing institutions that happen to be private are performing useful functions, and it would be at best pointless, at worst wasteful, to see them perish due to insufficient funds. Increased public finance thus evolves in somewhat the same way as in pattern II, except that it now affects two sectors. While some inter-sectoral financial differences often remain, in the source or in the allocation process, similarities are much more salient. If governance continues to be distinct between private and public institutions, then we may have interesting cases of public subsidy without concomitant control. Most often, however, public subsidy means strong public regulation of private institutions.

Pattern III holds for fewer cases than any other. Yet some degree of homogenization occurs over time in many dual systems, private institutions relying increasingly on public funds even if not to the same degree that public institutions do. Also, similar trends characterize funding at the primary and secondary levels in many nations.

A nominally private sector holds about one-third of Chile's enrollments. By the 1960s it had achieved roughly equal financial footing with its public counterpart, as both sectors derived over 90 percent of their income from public funds. This development accompanied declining private-public differences in both governance and mission. With a dramatic regime change to military rule (1973) and free-market economics, there has been a strong move to make all universities more self-financing. This would make the whole system more private, but would not by itself reintroduce private-public sector differences. Such differences could emerge if the junta imposes the startling plans it announced in 1980 and 1981, according to which it would continue to limit the size of all existing universities, allowing other enrollments only in new institutions—that must be 100 percent privately financed.

Education Acts of 1961 and 1970 put the Netherlands' private institutions (holding nearly half the enrollments) on equal financial footing with its public institutions. Tuition is minimal, and there are loans and subsidies. The state therefore assumes nearly the full financial burden though it has tried, thus far thwarted by political opposition, to push a tuition-loan plan. In Belgium, too, a substantial private sector has come to be publicly financed.[23] Canada might also fit the Homogenization pattern if one identifies many of its privately funded institutions (e.g., McGill and Laval) as private. The government has assumed most of the financial responsibility for all institutions, though fees may still be on the higher (Ireland, South Africa) than lower (Great Britain) side. The Canadian case points up fundamental similarities between patterns II and III. In both, there has been a growing feeling in recent decades that nearly all universities should be publicly funded, regardless of previous practices and structures.

IV. Distinctive, Minority Is Private (Dual Sectors: Smaller Sector Funded Privately; Larger Sector Funded Publicly)

Next we come to systems with distinctive dualism: public sectors basically supported by public funds, private sectors by private funds. Pattern IV has private sectors with usually around 10 to 20 percent (but up to 50 percent) of total enrollments, drawing their funds fully or predominantly from non-government sources. At least some of what are now pattern III cases were once pattern IV cases—until the private sector began to rely overwhelmingly on public funds. Thus, time emerges as a key factor. Experience seems to show that it is difficult, though far from impossible, for private universities to sustain themselves over long periods on private funds.

Pattern IV characterizes Latin America, save Chile, Brazil, Cuba, and Uruguay (Colombia is a borderline case between patterns IV and V). Most private institutions have been created fairly recently, only a few existing before this century, only a few more by mid-century. By 1980, however, roughly 20 percent of enrollments in Latin America's pattern IV cases (roughly 35 percent for all Latin America) were in the private sector.[24]

This surge of private growth effectively broke the single-sector, public-finance tradition, often constitutionally consecrated, e.g., in Argentina. The public sector remains as publicly financed as ever, usually charging only token tuitions and drawing at least 95 percent of its income from government. New private institutions, however, typically draw almost all their income from private sources. Tuition is the biggest component, often covering costs completely. It is especially dominant at the lower quality institutions, though only in rare cases does it cover less than two-thirds of the ongoing costs even at the more elite institutions. In fact, the elite institutions charge the highest tuitions, but they also draw on other private sources. No longer is it true that private giving and corporate donations are uniquely U.S. (or Anglo-American) characteristics. Some institutions, like Mexico's 15,500-student (in 1981) Autonomous University of Guadalajara, run strong alumni fund-raising campaigns. Others, like Venezuela's Metropolitan University

(3,000 in 1981), rely heavily on business support. Such support is especially important in much of Latin America in building campuses and plant facilities, but it may also account for roughly a third of ongoing annual expenses. International finance has also helped with capital expenditures. In return for these domestic and international contributions, elite private institutions are expected to be free from radical political activism, of high quality, and oriented toward commercial or industrial fields of study. Some, but not all, Catholic universities similarly attract business contributions, though not as much as the secular elite universities do. Naturally, however, most Catholic universities also count on direct and indirect church financing.

A 1971 study estimated that Latin America's private institutions rely 28 percent on government sources versus 87 percent for public institutions.[25] Even this shows a clear private-public distinction, but it greatly overestimates the public contributions to private institutions by including a) non-pattern IV Latin American nations and b) a disproportionate sample of older and more prestigious private institutions—both types much more likely than other private institutions to get some public aid. The fact that older (generally Catholic) universities more frequently get such aid supports the hypothesis that, over time, private institutions may become less privately financed.

Three major debates about private-public financing often emerge in pattern IV. One concerns the very growth of private institutions. Many critics regard the private sector as detrimental to public control and coordination of a vital sociopolitical enterprise. Most troublesome, they argue, is the private sector's inegalitarian role: Only the privileged can afford to attend. High-quality private education robs the public sector of many of its best personnel and reinforces privilege for the privileged. One response is that dual sectors are more equitable: Nearly all university students are privileged, but at least in the private university they pay their own way. Of course, private universities rarely grow in order to promote equity. More explicit reasons for private-sector growth have included changes in the socioeconomic composition of the student body, declining quality, growing numbers, and growing politicization within the public sector. Well-to-do families have been willing to pay private tuitions, and some businesses help fund "responsible" institutions that, therefore, need not depend on public subsidization.

A second debate is whether these new private sectors should receive any public funds. The private sector itself may be split, some emphasizing the need, others the dangerous strings. The public sector is also split, though mostly opposed, some emphasizing the high educational benefits-to-costs ratio, others the inequitability. A third debate concerns tuition in the public sector. Most governments and many economists of education favor it, but fierce student opposition still prevails in almost all cases. Whatever the future of these debates, private and public finance has been, to date, more intersectorally distinct in pattern IV than in any other pattern.

V. Distinctive, Majority Is Private (Dual Sectors: Larger Sector Funded Privately; Smaller Sector Funded Publicly)

Our last pattern characterizes systems where the majority of enrollments are found in the private sector. Again, public institutions are funded almost exclusively by the government. Some, like the Japanese, follow the Statist pattern; others, like the Indian, may follow the Public-Autonomous pattern. By contrast, private institutions are funded mostly by private funds, but usually not to the extent found in pattern IV.

Pattern V systems typically evolve where the state either cannot or will not expand the public sector, even in the face of rapidly growing demand for higher education. India offers a clear case. British rulers were not inclined towards massive expenditures in order to educate their colonial subjects. Instead, they gladly aided privately run institutions. Independent India thus found itself with a huge private sector, which it was not about to disestablish. Further, it explicitly made the primary and secondary levels its first two public education priorities, leaving public higher education third. One result is that government has provided 45 percent of the private colleges' income, mostly through grants-in-aid, and an even higher proportion for the private universities. Significantly, the private colleges hold nearly three-fourths of Indian enrollments.[26] Still, as of 1965, although the government met more than half the cost of Indian higher education, fees covered 35 percent and endowments and "other sources" the rest.[27]

Brazil offers another good example. Economic growth unleashed unprecedented demand for higher education in the 1960s, but the conservative military government would not let public institutions expand as freely as they did in most of Latin America. It kept entrance exams relatively stiff at the public universities, while permitting private institutions to absorb excess demand. The private sector jumped from 42 percent of the enrollment in 1955 to 67 percent, and increasing, in 1977. The private sector, particularly the Catholic university subsector, has petitioned for public subsidies, so far unsuccessfully. But Catholic universities do receive substantial public funds for graduate studies and research on the same basis that public universities do.

The internationally best known case in which the private sector holds the majority of enrollments—roughly 80 percent—is Japan. The bulk of Japan's enrollment boom was pushed into the private sector by strict entrance examinations at the public universities. Yet the private sector was constitutionally barred from receiving public subsidies. Then, concerned over low quality and especially over potentially serious protests by families with students in the private sector, the government saw fit to grant low-interest loans and to finance part of the professors' salaries. By the mid–1970s, new legislation authorized the government to finance up to 50 percent of the private sector's ongoing costs. No longer does Japan have a dichotomous system with private funds for the private sector versus public funds for the public sector. Still, a substantial gap remains, and tuition is perhaps five times higher in the private sector.[28]

In much of pattern V, therefore, private enrollments capture nearly three-quarters or even more of total enrollments. The extreme may be found in the Philippines, with 93 percent private enrollments, basically financed through private sources, mostly tuition.[29] But similar reasons for private growth, i.e., absorbing excess demand, may operate even where the private sector does not capture the majority of higher education enrollments. This is the case in most Latin American nations, predominantly characterized by large public sectors and smaller elite private sectors, and in Turkey, which has no elite private sector but 25 percent of its enrollments (in 1970) in the private sector nonetheless. Compared to the nations which truly fit pattern V (with majority private enrollments), however, these cases generate less pressure for public funding of private sectors.

Let us look briefly at why pattern V maintains substantial financial distinctions between sectors, but also why that distinction generally does not approach the dichotomous extent found in pattern IV. It is easy to understand why private-public financial distinctions are found in pattern V. The public budget is comparatively less strained than in other patterns because it supports a public sector with a relatively small share of the nation's students; the government can afford to finance this sector. That the government is not inclined to finance the private sector was suggested by its disinclination to accept the brunt of enrollment expansion into the public sector. Furthermore, private sector tuition is feasible because demand for higher education is so great, and new institutions do not face entrenched student interests defending age-old expectations of free education. In fact, demand is so great that it presents special opportunities for profit-making institutions in pattern V. The Philippines, with overwhelmingly private enrollments, is an excellent example. India is another. And though Turkey's private sector captures only a minority of total enrollments, it does accommodate excess demand and therefore can operate on a for-profit basis. According to one study, "The best advice one could offer an investor interested in high profits over short-term periods would be to go into the college business."[30] Similar dynamics have operated in Brazil, even though all its private institutions are legally nonprofit.

Powerful factors may draw the state to subsidize private sectors, however. The biggest obstacle is sectoral size. To finance the private sector is to undertake financial responsibility for most of the higher education system. But size itself may invite subsidization. By meeting demand, the private sector is fulfilling rather public functions. Considerable political pressure for public subsidization may come from students at the private institutions. The government cannot afford to see those institutions fold, turning angry students into the streets—or, ultimately, into the public universities. Nor can it always stand idly by as these students, frustrated on the job market, claim that low-quality private institutions must be improved through public regulation and subsidization. Low quality is often reflected in the under-representation of private institutions among "universities," as opposed to "colleges" or single-subject "schools," as in India, Turkey, Brazil, and the Philippines. Of these four examples, the least private-public difference is found in the Philippines, and even there 81 percent of the universities are private, while 95 percent of all Philippine "institutions of higher education" are private.[31]

Socioeconomic factors intensify the pressure for public assistance. Whereas private sector students in pattern IV tend to be more privileged than their public counterparts, in pattern V the opposite holds, and private sector students are less able to afford tuition. And so there is special difficulty in the equity questions. In pattern IV the privileged students pay for their private higher education; here, they go into the public sector and it is the relatively less privileged students who must settle for and pay for the private sector. In any case, it is doubtful that equity or even political pressures are as important as cost factors in stimulating public funding of private sectors: Paying part of the cost of education in a private institution is far cheaper than paying the full cost if all students must be educated in the public sector.

On balance, factors favoring some public funding of pattern V private institutions have generally outweighed unfavorable factors. At least we have seen that the government has become a major financier in the three most important pattern V cases, traditionally in India, recently in Japan, and still limitedly in Brazil. But in no case does public funding of the private sector approach the scale of public funding for the public sector.

COMPARATIVE PERSPECTIVES ON THE UNITED STATES

To summarize the five patterns and to provide a simplified guide for the study of U.S. higher education finance, Table 14.2 compresses the preceding discussion into a one-page sketch.

How might U.S. policy be understood against the backdrop of these five patterns? The question is briefly addressed here with specific reference to private sector size and private-public financial blends in both private and public sectors.

The United States has an unusually large private sector among the more developed nations. Only Japan's is proportionally larger, and it is much larger. In fact, few other developed nations have any substantial private sector at all. Of course, the U.S. private share has declined from half to just over one-fifth (21 percent) of total enrollments since 1950, but that proportional decline resulted mostly because public growth was even more intense than private growth. The U.S. private sector, seen in comparative perspec-

Table 14.2
Summary of Five Patterns

Single sectors

I. Statist
- almost no privately funded universities
- funds traditionally received from the state
- strong role of ministries in distributing funds among and within universities
- Examples: Communist nations, most of Western Europe, much of formerly French Africa

II. Public-Autonomous
- almost no privately funded universities
- traditionally mixed private-public funding, but now predominantly public funding
- important role of university, or "buffer organization" between university and state, in distributing funds among and within universities
- Examples: Australia, Great Britain, Israel, New Zealand, Nigeria

Dual sectors

III. Homogenized
- traditionally two sectors, funded differently
- evolution toward mostly public funding for private as well as public sectors
- sectoral dualism and distinctiveness now depend less on finance than on tradition and possibly governance and function
- Examples: Belgium, Canada, Chile, Netherlands

IV. Distinctive, Minority is Private
- private sector has more than 10% but less than 50% of total enrollments
- private sector relies mostly on private finance
- public sector relies mostly on public finance
- Examples: most of Latin America

V. Distinctive, Majority is Private
- private sector has more than 50% but less than 100% of total enrollments
- private sector relies mostly on private finance
- public sector relies mostly on public finance
- Examples: Brazil, India, Japan, Philippines

Note: There are empirically empty cells. No nation has a single sector that is financed principally through private funds. And no nation has dual sectors that are both financed principally through private funds. As discussed in the text, there are two forms of overlap. One is boundary overlap, where a case lies only a little more comfortably in one category than another. The second form of overlap concerns public sectors within III, IV, and V that, by themselves, would be Statist or Public-Autonomous.

tive, remains large in proportional terms, and it remains the largest in absolute numbers, with roughly 2.5 million students.

Still, with nearly four of five enrollments, the U.S. public sector is also comparatively large in absolute terms because an unusually great proportion of the relevant cohort group enters U.S. higher education. Whatever the ramifications of dual sectors, the absolute size of the public sector is a vital factor in determining levels of government expenditures, and that is a major reason that U.S. government expenditures are comparatively high. Additionally, the U.S. private sector does not seem quite so proportionally large if the less developed world is included. Even if we exclude systems in which private enrollments form the majority, many less developed nations have private sectors with less than half but nonetheless important shares of the system's enrollments.

Naturally, sectoral size concerns us here only insofar as the two sectors are financed differently. As historians of U.S. higher education have reminded us, no neat distinction between private financing for one sector and public financing for the other characterized the colonial or early independence period. For example, Harvard went into "financial panic" when the Massachusetts legislature stopped its funding in 1824, just as Columbia was troubled by the loss of state funds after 1819.[32] To be sure, more financial distinctiveness between the two sectors emerged after the 1819 Dartmouth decision and more after the Civil War. Nonetheless, the U.S. private sector has not always been as privately financed as many (non-European) private sectors have been, and the U.S. public sector has rarely been as publicly financed as have public sectors in Europe and elsewhere. Thus, in the United States we must be particularly careful not to assume that the private-public nomenclature reveals a private-public financial source.

Omitting the private sector, the financing of U.S. higher education would not seem very atypical in comparative perspective.[33] The public sector is financed overwhelmingly, roughly 79 percent (1979), through public funds. Public-sector tuition is usually around one-fourth or one-fifth the amount charged in the private sector, leading to a private-public "tuition gap" typically greater than $2,000 within individual states.[34] Income source varies considerably according to institutional type within the public sector. Research universities, for example, do best in the competition for federal funds.

Thus, the U.S. public sector alone might fit the Public-Autonomous pattern II. Within that pattern, it would stand closest to those systems (like the Israeli and unlike the British) in which the share from private sources has decreased proportionally but still remains substantial, i.e., 21 percent. A few observers claim to perceive such a great rise in state and federal government regulation of public sector expenditures that they fear incipient U.S. movement toward a Statist public pattern I. But that seems to be an unwarranted fear.

The U.S. private sector, by contrast, draws perhaps 76 percent (1979) of its income from private sources, according to the National Center for Educational Statistics. Tuition is especially important. Almost two-thirds of the private institutions (1977) rely on it for more than 70 percent of their income, and the sector as a whole relies on it for roughly half its income (1976).[35]

Notwithstanding important variation within the U.S. public sector, variation is even greater within the U.S. private sector. U.S. private universities depend more heavily on donations by individuals and on endowments and foundation or corporate giving than do any other higher education institutions in the world. (Even the much smaller contributions to the public universities are rather extraordinary when seen against a fairly generalized absence of such giving elsewhere. I might add that, very recently, corporation giving to U.S. higher education has been proportionally increasing, foundation giving proportionally declining.) Nonelite liberal arts colleges rely more on the church and donated services than on foundations and corporations. Tax exemptions for institutions and write-offs for donors also encourage the United States's extraordinary private contributions, though one can consider these partly as indirect government assistance. Finally, there is a for-profit private subsector, more completely private in terms of income source. It is especially important in vocationally oriented postsecondary education, and does not match the proportional enrollment shares reached in some pattern V systems (Distinctive, Majority Is Private).

More public financing for private higher education exists than is generally found in pattern IV (Distinctive, Minority Is Private). Analysis of pattern IV's private institutions, however, indicates that there are special circumstances which make virtually total private financing feasible. These generally include very little latitude for graduate education, for research, for costly courses, or for equal opportunity. Many U.S. private nonelite liberal arts colleges in fact approximate many of these conditions and do live almost exclusively off private funding. U.S. elite private universities usually approximate most of these conditions less closely and cannot survive on private finance. If liberal arts colleges alone comprised the private sector, the United States would fall much closer to pattern IV (Distinctive, Minority Is Private). But if the elite universities alone comprised the private sector, the United States would fall somewhat closer to pattern III (Homogenized). While this is especially true of institutions such as the Massachusetts and California Institutes of Technology, even the more conventional leaders (such as the University of Chicago, Columbia, Harvard, and Yale) have relied on the federal government for between one-third and one-half of their income, mostly for research and graduate education. In fact, because of the private research universities, the federal government gives more money per full-time equivalent (FTE) student to the private than to the public sector. Furthermore, many expensive private institutions simply could not survive without federal (and state) aid to students.[36]

Such data should be treated tentatively, however, as the federal government's financial role is being curtailed by the Reagan administration. This development may well increase the already critical role of state (rather than federal) finance, and it is here that the big private-public gap has been striking. (Thus the conservative political push to cut the federal financial role may have the paradoxical effect of hurting the private sector in particular.) While roughly forty states provide funds for the private sector, much of this comes indirectly, through student loans. Consequently, data show the private sector getting only about one-ninth, per FTE, what the public sector gets in state funds.[37] Generalizations about the balance of private and public funding, therefore, run the danger of aggregating very dissimilar data about different institutional types within either sector.

Generalizations also depend on whether one focuses on longitudinal or cross-national comparisons. Most assessments by U.S. scholars do the former. They point to the diminished size and increased public financing of the private sector. This chapter, however, has had a cross-national focus. From this perspective, higher education finance in the United States still appears remarkably private.

Let us sum up our findings on the privateness of U.S. finance, in comparison to most other developed nations. The U.S. private sector is extraordinarily large, and most U.S. private institutions still draw overwhelmingly on private resources. Research universities rely heavily on public funds, but most also rely heavily on private funds, particularly for their undergraduate programs. From a cross-national perspective, even this mixed financing appears unusually private for research universities. Finally, the public sector itself draws a comparatively high share of its income from private sources. Granted, public financing has become increasingly important for the system overall, but the same could be said of higher education in many if not most other nations, even leaving aside those nations where public finance has traditionally dominated.

Increased public finance has not been a universal inevitability, however. This is especially clear when one analyzes the developing world. Private sectors have arisen, often basically privately funded, where none existed previously. Others have expanded and/or are proportionally much bigger than in the United States. While there are obviously limits to comparisons between the United States and less developed systems, there are also benefits in comparisons rooted in the dual sector configuration. Policy debate focuses not just on the private-public income balance for one sector, but also on inter-sectoral relationships. For example, policies to help the private sector may involve raising tuition in the public sector, or they may emphasize student aid, which can be used at private or public institutions, rather than institutional aid, which usually goes to public institutions. Supporters of the public sector must weigh the desirability of government aid to private institutions. Such aid might drain resources away from the public institutions; but it also might save public institutions from assuming financial responsibility for students exiting from unaided private institutions. The appropriate tuition gap between private and public institutions becomes a key issue. And analysis of systems with distinctive sectors also reminds us that our own private sector grew not just from a tendency to voluntarism but also from a bias against heavy public expenditures and for freedom to purchase special or privileged education in a differentiated system.

Analysis of dual sector systems also suggests certain hypotheses about the interaction between private-public finance and other private-public relationships. An example of such a relationship is private-public size. Dual systems with fully private financing of private sectors tend to occur in systems with fairly new and small private sectors. Over time private institutions may take on certain tasks deemed worthy of public subsidies, or they may simply expand in size or activities to the point where private funding is no longer viable. Especially if the private sector is very large, the government may have to choose between subsidizing it or paying much more by absorbing increased public sector enrollments.

Finally, discussions about U.S. higher education finance should really be pursued largely on a state-by-state basis. The fifty state systems, not to mention more local networks, put intra-nation comparative analysis at a premium. Variation is enormous. While most state systems might basically approximate patterns IV (Distinctive, Minority Is Private) or II (Public-Autonomous), there would be great differences within those patterns, and many would show certain tendencies toward other patterns. Focusing on four-year institutions as of 1975, there was one state with no private enrollments and one with a majority in the private sector; variation from 14 to 54 percent was found among nine regions delineated by the Carnegie Council, with equally great variation in terms of public subsidies for private sectors and with substantial subsidization tending to characterize systems with proportionally large private sectors.[38]

Of course, the analogy between U.S. state systems and independent nations has obvious limitations. There is the overarching U.S. national authority and role, which limits the independence (financial and otherwise) of the individual state systems—and federal policy and regulations expanded this authority considerably in the 1960s and 1970s. Specifically, the federal role became more prominent than before in the finance of higher education. Moreover, U.S. students often choose to "purchase" their higher education outside their home states, and the permeability of state boundaries is still more markedly shown by the mobility of other higher education actors (professors, administrators, financiers). Still—as a matter for future empirical study—it would seem that the analogy might hold especially well for those U.S. states that do finance the higher education of the great majority of their own students within state boundaries, for undergraduates more than graduate students, and for public sector students more than students academically and financially capable of attending elite private institutions. The analogy might also be reinforced by the Reagan push, not just generally but also in higher education particularly, to slash federal authority and financing, turning much responsibility back to the states. Furthermore, the analogy may hold insofar as higher education is truly international, not nation-bound, in much of the world. One thinks especially of students from less developed countries purchasing higher education in more developed countries nearby or abroad, of the "brain drain" of professors, and from the more developed to the less developed countries, of "international transfers" of funds as well as academic models.

Unfortunately, but predictably, while the uncertain future of private-public financing in the U.S. state systems depends partly on future policy decisions, cross-national analysis offers neither consensus solutions nor clear and attractive alternatives that could be neatly copied. On the contrary, many other nations are also groping for better solutions. Additionally, many important systems do not even have private sectors. But many of these single sector systems are nonetheless debating the advantages and disadvantages of different private-public financial blends.[39] Perhaps we can learn something from those debates. And the experience of many dual sector systems illustrates some major dilemmas in working with different mixtures in different sectors. A cross-national perspective should help sensitize us to the reality, possibly even helping us to analyze it, that the private-public controversy in U.S. higher education finance is in fact a multitude of controversies, with different patterns and problems dominating in different statewide systems.

NOTES

1. David W. Breneman and Chester E. Finn, Jr., *Public Policy and Private Higher Education* (Washington, D.C.: Brookings Institution, 1978).

2. Daniel C. Levy, " 'Private' and 'Public': Analysis Amid Ambiguity in Higher Education," in *Private Education: Studies in Choice and Public Policy*, ed. Daniel C. Levy (New York: Oxford University Press, 1986), pp. 170–92.

3. For the most geographically wide-ranging exception to this void, see Roger L. Geiger, *Private Sectors in Higher Education: Structure, Function and Change in Eight Countries* (Ann Arbor: University of Michigan Press, 1986). See also Daniel C. Levy, *Higher Education and the State in Latin America: Private Challenge to Public Dominance* (Chicago: University of Chicago Press, 1986). For probably the most profound analysis of higher education contexts worldwide, see Burton R. Clark, *The Higher Education System: Academic Organization in Cross-National Perspective* (Berkeley: University of California Press, 1983).

4. See, for example, Estelle James, "Public Subsidies for Private and Public Education," in *Private Education*, ed. Levy; and Joel Sherman, "Government Finance of Private Education in Australia," *Comparative Education Review* 26 (1982):391–405.

5. Milton Friedman, *Capitalism and Freedom* (Chicago: University of Chicago Press, 1962), p. 85.

6. Except where indicated, I focus mostly on recurrent expenditures for undergraduate education.

7. Harold J. Noah, *Financing Soviet Schools* (New York: Columbia University, Teachers College Press, 1966), p. 74.

8. Frederic Pryor, *Public Expenditures in Communist and Capitalist Nations* (Homewood, Ill.: Richard D. Irwin, 1968), p. 202.

9. Most comparative analyses of higher education finance are limited to the more developed world. Among the useful exceptions are Douglas Windham, "Social Benefits and Subsidization of Higher Education," *Higher Education* 5 (1976):237–52; and Jean-Pierre Jallade, "Financing Higher Education: The Equity Aspects," *Comparative Education Review* 22 (1978):309–25. The *International Encyclopedia of Higher Education* (San Francisco: Jossey-Bass, 1977) was consulted on all patterns.

10. Mark Blaug and Maureen Woodhall, "Patterns of Subsidies to Higher Education in Europe," *Higher Education* 7 (1978):331–61; M. Woodhall, *Student Loans* (London: George Harrap, 1970); Lyman Glenny, ed., *Funding Higher Education: A Six-Nation Analysis* (New York: Praeger, 1979).

11. Barbara Burn et al., *Higher Education in Nine Countries* (New York: McGraw-Hill, 1971).

12. The Middle East presents a varied picture. Some nations such as Iran, Iraq, and Syria probably come closest to pattern I. But others have autonomous public institutions, and some have important private institutions.

13. A. H. Halsey and M. A. Trow, *The British Academics* (Cambridge, Mass.: Harvard University Press, 1971), p. 60.

14. Ibid., p. 63; Eric Hutchinson, "The Origins of the University Grants Committee," *Minerva* 13 (1975):612–13; and Blaug and Woodhall, "Patterns of Subsidies," pp. 343–47.

15. Sir John Wolfenden, "The Economic and Academic Freedom of Universities," *Royal Society of Medicine*, No. 63 (August 1970):844.

16. Shmuel Bendor, "Israel," in *International Encyclopedia of Higher Education*, ed. Asa S. Knowles (San Francisco: Jossey-Bass, 1977), pp. 2335–36; Burn et al., *Higher Education in Nine Countries*, p. 147; and *Reviews of National Policies for Education: Ireland* (Paris: OECD, 1969), p. 25.

17. Graeme C. Moodie, "Los académicos y el gobierno universitaio: algunas reflexiones sobre la experiencia Británica," in *Universidad Contemporánea: Antecedentes y Experiencias Internacionales*, ed. Iván Lavados, (Santiago, Chile: Corporación Promoción Universitaria, 1980), pp. 251, 258.

18. Robert O. Berdahl, *British Universities and the State* (Berkeley: University of California, 1959), is the classic book-length study dealing with the UGC. He is now preparing an updated analysis.

19. Eric Asby, *Universities: British, Indian, African* (Cambridge, Mass.: Harvard University Press, 1966).

20. Yet Tanzania has a quite Statist profile. One important area that I admittedly

ignore in Africa (e.g., Kenya), as well as elsewhere, concerns commercial schools, offering subjects such as hotel management. These schools are often not included in definitions or data on "higher education."

21. Pierre L. van den Berghe, *Power and Privilege at an African University* (Cambridge, Mass.: Shenkman, 1973), p. 62; and A. Callaway and A. Musone, *Financing of Education in Nigeria* (Paris: UNESCO, 1968).

22. Q. P. F. Horwood, "The Financing of Higher Education in South Africa, with Special Reference to the Universities," *South African Journal of Economics* 32 (September 1964):166.

23. Blaug and Woodhall, "Patterns of Subsidies," p. 388; Geiger, *Private Sectors in Higher Education*, pp. 80–83.

24. Except where otherwise stated, all information on Latin America is drawn from my book, *Higher Education and the State*. While some of the public institutions enjoy little autonomy, others, not totally unlike counterparts in pattern II (Public-Autonomous), manage to combine comparatively substantial autonomy (e.g., in distributing funds within the university) with a near government monopoly in finance. Elsewhere I try to show how and why: Levy, *University and Government in Mexico: Autonomy in an Authoritarian System* (New York: Praeger, 1980), pp. 100–137. Another English-language source is Edgardo Boeninger Kausel, "Alternative Policies for Financing Higher Education," in *The Financing of Education in Latin America* (Washington, D.C.: Inter-American Development Bank, n.d.), pp. 321–57.

25. Juan F. Castellanos, *Examen de una década* (Mexico City: Unión de Universidades de América Latina, 1976), p. 216.

26. Susanne Hoeber Rudolph and Lloyd I. Rudolph, "The Political System and the Education System," in *Education and Politics in India*, ed. S. H. Rudolph and L. Rudolph (Cambridge, Mass.: Harvard University Press, 1972), p. 29; D. M. Desai, *Some Critical Issues of Higher Education in India* (Bombay: A. R. Sheth, 1970), pp. 376–77.

27. J. L. Azad, "Financing Institutions of Higher Education in India," *Higher Education* 5 (1976):1–7; G. D. Parikh, "Some Aspects of University Finance," *Quest* (Bombay) 64 (1970):34–40.

28. William Cummings, Ikuo Amano, and Kazuyuki Kitamura, *Changes in the Japanese University* (New York: Praeger, 1979); Cummings, "The Japanese Private University," *Minerva* 11 (1973):348–71.

29. Edith Danskin, "Quality and Quantity in Higher Education in Thailand and Philippines," *Comparative Education Review* 15 (1979):316–21.

30. Ayse Oncu, "Higher Education as a Business: Growth of a Private Sector in Turkey" (Unpublished Ph.D. dissertation, Yale University, 1971), pp. 75, 85–87. Oncu shows that these profits are achieved even though tuitions are low, by U.S. standards. In much of the Third World, "low" by U.S. standards may be medium to high by local standards, p. 75.

31. Narcisco Albarracin, "The Private University and National Purpose," *Far Eastern University Journal* (Manila) 14 (1970):282.

32. John Whitehead, *The Separation of College and State* (New Haven: Yale University Press, 1973), pp. 100–101.

33. Edward Shils, "The American Private University," *Minerva* 11 (1973):6–29, offers a rare view at the U.S. private sector (including financing) in comparative perspective.

34. R. Geiger, *Private Sectors in Higher Education*, p. 167; Carnegie Council, *The Federal Role in Postsecondary Education* (San Francisco: Jossey-Bass, 1975), p. 36.

35. Carnegie Council, *The States and Private Higher Education* (San Francisco: Jossey-Bass, 1977), p. 19; National Institute of Education, *Higher Education Financing in the Fifty States* (Washington, D.C., 1979), p. 23; William Jellema, *From Red to Black?* (San Francisco: Jossey-Bass, 1973), pp. 56–87.

36. Waldemar Nielson, *The Endangered Sector* (New York: Columbia University Press, 1969), p. 23.

37. Carnegie Council, *The States and Private Higher Education*, p. 1; National Institute of Education, *Higher Education Financing in the Fifty States*, pp. 22–23.

38. Carnegie Council, *The States and Private Higher Education*, pp. 118–19.

39. Since the core of this piece was written, signs of privatization have become more notable. On the one hand, attempts to found private sectors have taken variable strides in some pattern II (New Zealand, Nigeria) and even pattern I (Italy, West Germany) cases. On the other hand, partly because of world economic troubles, the decades-long trend of increasing government spending has been called into increasing doubt in all five patterns.

Bibliographical Essay

POLITICS OF HIGHER EDUCATION

The notion that politics plays any sort of role in the life of the academy has until very recently been anathema to both those who work within the academy and those who study it. This is in part due to the bad connotation of the word "politics." But if we define politics as the maneuvering for power, then there is no question that higher education has been involved in politics—both internally and externally—since at least the Land Grant College Act of 1862.

Fortunately, the reluctance to recognize the role of politics in higher education is changing, albeit slowly. An early review of the literature (Samuel K. Gove and Barbara Whiteside Solomon, "The Politics of Higher Education: A Bibliographic Essay," *Journal of Higher Education* 39, April 1968) turned up very little research on the relationship between higher education and the political world at the state level:

Those writers who deal primarily with university-state relations concentrate on the encroachments by state governments on the autonomy of institutions, the erosion of traditional faculty freedoms, and interference with internal administration, rather than the process of policy-making. They take the view that state governments at best do not understand the peculiar problems of higher education and at worst use higher education for partisan political purposes (p. 182).

At the end of their review the authors concluded that:

Much more than an examination of the budgeting, purchasing, and personnel controls over state universities is needed. There are no materials dealing with the political aspects of state financing of public higher education. The descriptions of existing coordinating bodies neglect their position in the executive branch, their relations with the legislature and often their relations with the coordinated institutions. The role of the governor in higher education policy-making is largely unexplored, and the relationships between the legislatures and individual institutions have only been alluded to in the past. What is known about these areas has not been systematically recorded, and often common-sense statements take the place of needed empirical studies. This is true of higher education planning efforts, where it is important to the success of the plans, and in political science, where it results in the neglect of an area of policy-making, with important consequences for the political system (p. 195).

A 1975 survey of research on the administration and politics of higher education found, not unexpectedly, that progress had been made and that some of the gaps in the literature had been filled (Samuel K. Gove and Carol Everly Floyd, "Research on Higher Education Administration and Policy: An Uneven Report," *Public Administration Review* 35, Jan./Feb. 1975). Nonetheless, much remained to be done.

Our assessment of the literature on the politics of higher education since 1968 is that many of the voids noted in the earlier essays have been partially filled. Unfortunately, much of the literature on higher education is still limited to what the state university has done and should do to make its contribution to the state. Too little attention is given the relationship of the higher education system and politics in the state (p. 112).

The same authors suggested that in the future "particular attention needs to be focused on the study of policy outcomes. The only aspect on which significant policy outcomes research has been done is higher education finance." Despite all of these deficiencies and problems, the authors concluded their essay on a high note.

The body of literature on the administration and politics of higher education has grown significantly since the 1967 and 1968 essays. Part of the increase is a result of higher education's difficulties in the past few years. Much more derives from the realization of political scientists and others in academia that their own surroundings are as worthy of study and analysis as other segments of society (p. 117).

A more recent review of the literature is the definitive work by Edward R. Hines and Leif S. Hartmark, *The Politics of Higher Education*, Higher Education Research Report No. 7 (Washington, D.C.: AAHE-ERIC, 1980), an ERIC monograph published by the American Association for Higher Education. At the very outset of their seventy-five page monograph, which has chapters on the politics of higher education at the federal, state, and local levels, the authors wrestle with the notion of "politics."

Politics occurs at various levels within higher education or between the academy and the political process or governmental institutions. In this sense, politics is concerned basically with patterns of interaction or conflict over values, interests, and goals relating to the perceived needs of higher education and public authority (p. 3).

Somewhat later in the piece they point out some of the progress that has been made in the field and the areas that still need attention.

The past two decades of scholarship involving the politics of higher education have demonstrated unequivocally that higher education exists in a political environment and is a direct participant in the political process. With the challenges of scarce resources, declining enrollments, institutional competition, erosion of institutional autonomy, and governmental intervention or even indifference to higher education, colleges and universities will become more directly engaged in the political process at all levels of government.
Scholars should pay greater attention to the politics of higher education as these developments unfold. The field of inquiry has advanced significantly during the past decade, and it exhibits a broadening base of empirical research informed by many theoretical perspectives and research designs (p. 50).

Much has happened since the three above-mentioned essays were written, and many of the gaps that were a source of concern have been filled, at least partially. One such gap was the relationship of the governor to higher education. A three-day conference at the Wingspread Conference Center near Racine, Wisconsin in 1985 was devoted entirely to that topic. Participants in the conference, who came from all parts of the country, agreed that the states will continue to play the major role in higher education policymaking, especially since the federal government has made clear that it intends to continue its efforts to cut back its funding and involvement. The proceedings of the conference were published in the summer 1985 issue of *State Government*, and the papers presented will be published by Duke University Press.

A panel at the 1985 American Political Science Association meeting was devoted to the policy implications of elected higher education boards. At present five states (Colorado, Illinois, Michigan, Nebraska and Nevada) have such boards. The panel discussion made clear that there are striking differences even among these five boards, and that more research needs to be done on them.

The controversial subject of higher education coordination at the state level is the topic of the monograph by Lyman A. Glenny, *State Coordination of Higher Education—The Modern Concept* (Denver: State Higher Education Executive Officers Association, 1985), which asserts that coordination is alive and well. He concludes that "however well coordination works, tensions between higher education and the state can never be entirely eliminated, and thoughtful people understand this" (p. 20).

An equally controversial subject, private-public university competition, is considered in another monograph: John W. Gardner, Robert M. Atwell, and Robert O. Berdahl, *Cooperation and Conflict—The Public and Private Sectors in Higher Education* (Washington, D.C.: Association of Governing Boards of Universities and Colleges, 1985). Robert Berdahl presents a series of state case studies. The refrain throughout is that there should be cooperation between the private and public sectors. On the same note, John Gardner expresses the hope that the larger purposes of education will bring the two sectors together:

The public-private differences and most of the other differences that characterize American higher education should be seen in the larger context of shared goals, interests and values. There is so much to be accomplished by all working together—to maintain a climate in which higher education can flourish, to advance the purposes that bind all of us, to guard standards, to ensure the continuous evolution of our institutions, to serve and illuminate our civilization (p. 14).

At the 1984 Southern Political Science Association meeting a panel discussion was held on "The Study of the Politics of Higher Education—The State of the Art." It was generally agreed that the time has come for researchers in this field to move away from case studies and to move toward a more systematic investigation of the policymaking process in higher education. One important aspect of that process is the relationship between the internal governance of a university and the decisions that are made by external forces; state collective bargaining laws are but one example of such decisions.

Clearly, research in this field of inquiry has arrived at an important juncture. It is to be hoped that the authors who have contributed to the present volume will also have contributed to a move in the direction suggested by the panelists at the 1984 meeting and thereby expand the horizons of knowledge in the area of higher education politics and policy.

Index

Academic freedom, 103
Accountability, 12; issue for African Universities, 224–26; and autonomy, 52; and evaluation, 111; fiduciary, 15; procedural, 14; programmatic, 14; substantive, 14; systemic, 13–14
Accreditation, 117–18; black colleges and, 137, 140–41; role of government agencies, 132–34; improvements resulting from, 148–50; limits to, 125–27; need for coordination, 132; regional, 127–29; self-review, 129–32; and state program reviews, 90. *See also* Middle States Association
Adams, Charles S., 4, 5, 15, 23
Addis Ababa Conference of African Ministers of Education, 218, 229–30
Affirmative action, cornerstones of, 158
Africa: Association of African Universities, 224; "decolonization" of education, 228; educational finance in, 244–45; higher vs. basic education, 223–24; Lagos Conference

of Ministers of Education, 223–24; national vs. regional universities, 222–23; Statist system of educational finance, 241–42; Tananarive Conference on Higher Education, 223; universities and traditional cultures, 229
Age Discrimination in Employment Act Amendments (1978), 154, 158–59
American Association of Colleges of Teacher Education, 118
American Education Research Association, 113
American Institute of Physics, 195
Andrews, Kenneth R., 56
Andringa, Robert C., 21
Ashby Commission, 225, 229
Association of African Universities, 224
Astin, Alexander W., 107
Australia, educational finance in, 243
Autonomy: and accountability, 52; issue for African universities, 224–26; tradition of in higher education, 103

About the Contributors

JERRY D. BAILEY is Associate Dean of the School of Education and Professor of Education and Policy Administration at the University of Kansas. His research interests include politics of education and federal policy implementation.

SHEILA KISHLER BENNETT is a Graduate Student at Emory University in Atlanta. In addition to research on patterns of entry and advancement among women in higher education administration, she is involved in a number of studies of institutional factors that affect educational and developmental outcomes for undergraduate women. She is also conducting a study of women's part-time employment in the health service industry.

RICHARD M. ENGLERT is currently Dean, College of Education at Temple University. He continues to teach courses in educational administration, the field in which he received his doctorate from UCLA. His research and publications have been in the areas of collective bargaining in education, the politics of education, and evaluation.

SAMUEL K. GOVE is Professor of Political Science at the Institute of Government and Public Affairs, University of Illinois. Between 1967 and 1985 he was also the director of the institute. Professor Gove is a member of the National Academy of Public Administration and serves on the government relations committee of the national AAUP. He is coeditor of the volume *After Daley: Chicago Politics in Transition*.

KENNETH C. GREEN is Associate Director of UCLA's Higher Education Research Institute. His research focuses on state and federal higher education policy, including an assessment of the "enrollment crisis" in higher education and the impact of recent federal and state funding cuts on expenditures in American colleges and universities.

DARRYL G. GREER is Executive Director, New Jersey State College Governing Boards Association. He was formerly Director for Government Relations, The College Board, Washington, D.C. From 1979 to 1981 he served as policy planning officer in the office of the president to the College Board in New York City. Dr. Greer has also worked in state government as assistant to the chancellor of the Ohio Board of Regents and as legislative research associate to the Ohio Legislative Service Commission.

LEIF S. HARTMARK is Assistant to the President for Planning and Information Systems at the State University of New York at Albany. He has had extensive experience as a policy analyst, including planning and institutional research responsibilities at two SUNY campuses, and professional staff positions with the Wisconsin and Minnesota legislatures. Dr. Hartmark has published and presented papers in the areas of campus planning, budgeting and evaluation systems, methods for identifying peer institutions, and statewide budgeting and accountability systems. He is coauthor of an AAHE/ERIC research report, *The Politics of Higher Education*.

EDWARD R. HINES is Professor of Educational Administration and Director of the Center for Higher Education at Illinois State University. In addition to administrative experience at two universities, Dr. Hines has also been assistant professor of educational administration at SUNY–Albany, and has served on a statewide higher education commission appointed by the governor of New York. He is the author of over thirty publications dealing with administrative and policy issues in higher education and, with Leif Hartmark, coauthored *Politics of Higher Education*, an AAHE/ERIC research monograph published in 1981.

ROBERT LAWLESS is Chief Financial Officer of an airline. He was formerly Senior Vice Chancellor and Chief Planning Officer for the University of Houston-University Park.

DANIEL C. LEVY is Associate Professor of Educational Administration and Policy Studies at SUNY–Albany and a Faculty Fellow of the Rockefeller Institute of Government. For several years he was a research associate with

Yale University's Institution for Social and Policy Studies. Professor Levy is the author or coauthor of three books, the latest of which is *Higher Education and the State in Latin America* (University of Chicago Press, 1986) and is editor of *Private Education* (Oxford University Press, 1986). Professor Levy has also published numerous journal articles on higher education policy.

S. V. MARTORANA is Professor of Education, College of Education, and Senior Research Associate, Center for the Study of Higher Education, at Pennsylvania State University. He was the first Assistant Commissioner for Higher Education Planning appointed by the New York State Board of Regents and earlier organized and directed the State and Regional Planning Unit of the United States Office of Education. He has directed statewide studies of higher education and has served as a consultant to state higher education agencies in over half the states. At Pennsylvania State University he directed the first comprehensive nationwide examination of regionalism in postsecondary education.

BARRY MUNITZ is President of a Houston-based holding company. He previously served as Chancellor of the University of Houston and Academic Vice President at the University of Illinois.

LAWRENCE A. NESPOLI is Director of Instructional Programs and Legislative Liaison with the Maryland State Board for Community Colleges. Prior to his current position, he served as Executive Assistant to the President at Howard Community College in Columbia, Maryland. Dr. Nespoli has published in the area of state legislative and finance trends in higher education, and has taught at both Catholic University and Pennsylvania State University. While at Pennsylvania State University, he collaborated with S. V. Martorana on two volumes: *Regionalism in American Postsecondary Education: Concepts and Practices* and *Study, Talk, and Action.*

SHERRY H. PENNEY is Vice Chancellor for Academic Programs, Policy and Planning for the sixty-four–campus State University of New York. Previously she was Associate Provost of Yale University and a member of the Commission on Institutions of Higher Education of the New England Association of Schools and Colleges. She has participated on accreditation teams for the Middle States Association, Western Association, Southern Association, United States Department of Education, and has served as a reviewer for the Council on Postsecondary Accreditation. She is a board member and chairman-elect of the National Center for Higher Education Management Systems.

MARTIN S. QUIGLEY is Professor of Education, teaching graduate and undergraduate courses at Baruch College, City University of New York.

Since 1964 he has been president of Quigley Publishing Company, Inc. From April 1980 to April 1984 he served as mayor of Larchmont, New York.

ROBERT E. RUCKER is Assistant Professor in the Department of Sociology at the University of Nevada, Las Vegas. His research interests include social inequality, dependency, and population.

HOWARD L. SIMMONS, currently Associate Director of the Middle States Commission on Higher Education, has a strong interest in the development of black higher education. He is a fluent speaker of Spanish and Russian, and has served as a faculty member, department chairperson, and instructional dean at several colleges.

LEWIS C. SOLMON is Dean of the Graduate School of Education at UCLA. He has been secretary-treasurer of the Higher Education Research Institute in Los Angeles and has published seventeen books and more than sixty articles on economics and education.

THOMAS M. STAUFFER is Chancellor at the University of Houston–Clear Lake. Prior to his move to Texas in 1982, he was Director of the Division of External Relations at the American Council on Education, and Director of the National Commission on Higher Education Issues.

HANS N. WEILER has been on the faculty of Stanford University since 1965 and is now Professor of Education and Political Science, as well as Associate Dean for Academic Affairs. He has been Director of the International Institute of Educational Planning (IIEP) in Paris. His publications include *Education and Politics in Nigeria, Educational Planning and Social Change*, and numerous articles and monographs.

WILLIAM ZUMETA is Assistant Professor in the Graduate School of Public Affairs at the University of Washington, and is affiliated with the Higher Education Research Institute, UCLA. He is author or coauthor of a number of articles and monographs on regulatory policy and public policy toward higher education and science. His book, *Extending the Educational Ladder: The Changing Quality and Value of Postdoctoral Study* was published by Lexington Books in 1985.

Policy Studies Organization Publications issued with Greenwood Press

Intergovernmental Relations and Public Policy
J. Edwin Benton and David R. Morgan, editors

Citizen Participation in Public Decision Making
Jack DeSario and Stuart Langton, editors